Palgrave Macmillan Studies in Banking and Financial Institutions

Series editor
Philip Molyneux
University of Sharjah
Sharjah, UAE

The Palgrave Macmillan Studies in Banking and Financial Institutions series is international in orientation and includes studies of banking systems in particular countries or regions as well as contemporary themes such as Islamic Banking, Financial Exclusion, Mergers and Acquisitions, Risk Management, and IT in Banking. The books focus on research and practice and include up to date and innovative studies that cover issues which impact banking systems globally.

More information about this series at
http://www.springer.com/series/14678

Giusy Chesini · Elisa Giaretta
Andrea Paltrinieri
Editors

The Business of Banking

Models, Risk and Regulation

palgrave
macmillan

Editors
Giusy Chesini
Department of Economics
University of Verona
Verona, Italy

Elisa Giaretta
Department of Business Administration
University of Verona
Verona, Italy

Andrea Paltrinieri
Department of Economic and Statistical Sciences
University of Udine
Udine, Italy

Palgrave Macmillan Studies in Banking and Financial Institutions
ISBN 978-3-319-54893-7 ISBN 978-3-319-54894-4 (eBook)
DOI 10.1007/978-3-319-54894-4

Library of Congress Control Number: 2017943467

Printed on acid-free paper

This Palgrave Macmillan imprint is published by Springer Nature
The registered company is Springer International Publishing AG
The registered company address is: Gewerbestrasse 11, 6330 Cham, Switzerland

Acknowledgements

First and foremost, we would like to thank all our contributors, whose biographies are provided in this volume, without which the edited book would not have been possible.

Also, we want to express our gratitude to all participants of the 2016 Wolpertinger Conference—organized by the European Association of University Teachers of Banking and Finance in September 2016 at the University of Verona—for their insightful comments about all the papers included in this volume.

We would also like to show our gratitude to Professor Philip Molyneux (Professor of Banking and Finance and Dean of the College of Business, Law, Education and Social Sciences), editor in chief of the Palgrave Macmillan Studies in Banking and Financial Institution Series, for approving our book proposal and for his support during the process.

Also, many thanks to the Palgrave Macmillan team, Aimee Dibbens and Natasha Denby, for their support during the publishing process.

Special thanks to the institutions which kindly supported the Wolpertinger Conference in Verona and so contributed to make it a pleasant and fruitful event: Banco Popolare, Unicredit (Verona), and S&P Global Market Intelligence.

Finally, as conference organizers, we would like to thank Steven Ongena, Professor at the University of Zurich, for giving a plenary speech at the conference on "Relationship Lending Reloaded" and the other speakers at the Jack Revell Session on "The Financial System in the Macroeconomy" (Cesare Bisoni, University of Modena; Maurizio Faroni, General Director at Banco Popolare; Phil Molyneux, Bangor Business School; and Greg Udell, Indiana University).

Contents

Notes on Contributors

Mauro Aliano is an Assistant Professor of Banking and Finance at the University of Cagliari, Faculty of Economics, Law and Political Sciences. He is a specialist in applying statistics techniques for analyzing financial markets, in methods for analyzing financial instruments and in portfolio models. In 2012, he was a research fellow at the University of Rome Tor Vergata.

Francesca Arnaboldi is Associate Professor of Banking and Finance at the University of Milan, Italy. She holds an MSc in Financial Management from the University of London, CeFIMS, and a Ph.D. in Finance from the University of Bologna. She has been a visiting scholar at Stern School of Business, New York University. She is a member of the CEFIN (Centre for Research in Banking and Finance), University of Modena and Reggio Emilia and of the Centre for Banking Research, Cass Business School, City University. Her main areas of interest are international banking, bank competition and performance, financial innovation, bank regulation, and supervision.

Giusy Chesini is Associate Professor in Banking and Finance at the University of Verona, Italy. She holds a Ph.D. in financial markets and intermediaries from the University of Bergamo, Italy. Giusy is also the author of several papers and books related to the evolution of financial intermediation. Her research topics include financial markets, stock exchanges, banking and corporate finance.

Stefano Cosma is Professor of Banking at the University di Modena and Reggio Emilia, Italy. He holds a Ph.D. in Business Administration from University Cà Foscari, and a Master's degree in Organization and Management of Human Resources. He is a member of CEFIN (Centre for Research in Banking and Finance).

Fabrizio Crespi is researcher of Banking and Finance at the University of Cagliari and Contract professor at ALTIS—Post Graduate School Business and Society—at the Catholic University of Milan. His main research fields are as follows: organizational models of credit institutions and other financial intermediaries, internationalization and financial intermediaries, asset allocation, and portfolios optimization.

Paula Cruz-García is a Ph.D. student in Economics and Quantitative Finance at the University of Valencia. She graduated in Economics at the University of Valencia, and she holds a Master's degree in Quantitative Banking and Finance from the University of Valencia, Complutense University of Madrid, University of Castilla La Mancha, and the University of the Basque Country. Her main research interests are banking economics, financial economics, and econometrics.

Viktor Elliot is Assistant Professor in Banking, Finance and Accounting at the School of Business, Economics & Law, University of Gothenburg. His interests include performance management, risk and regulatory implications in banking, funds transfer pricing, and savings banks. Current research is conducted within the areas of financial exclusion, supply chain finance, and regulatory implications in banking.

Riccardo Ferretti is Professor of Banking and Finance at the University di Modena and Reggio Emilia, Italy. He holds a Ph.D. in Financial Markets and Portfolio Management from University of Bergamo. He has been a visiting Ph.D. student at Graduate School of Business

Administration, New York University. He is a member of CEFIN (Centre for Research in Banking and Finance).

Giuseppe Galloppo is Assistant Professor of Financial Markets and Institutions at Tuscia University, Viterbo, and a research fellow at the School of Economics, Tor Vergata University of Rome. He teaches banking and finance, with a particular focus on financial markets and institutions and risk methods. He is a specialist in applying statistical techniques and methods for analyzing financial instruments and portfolio models and for assessing risk profiles of securities and financial assets portfolios.

Juan Fernández de Guevara is Assistant Professor of Economics at the University of Valencia, where he graduated and obtained his Ph.D. (with special honors) in Economics. Since 2011, he is associate researcher of the Ivie. His specialized fields are banking, productivity analysis, and social capital. At present, he is a researcher in the SPINTAN Project of the European Union's Seventh Framework Programme and has been a consultant for the United Nations and the European Investment Bank (EIB). He has published fifteen books and chapters and more than twenty articles in specialized journals such as Journal of Banking and Finance, The Manchester School, The European Journal of Finance, Journal of International Money and Finance, Revista de Economía Aplicada, Regional Studies, Applied Economics Letters, among others, and has taken part in more than twenty-five national and international congresses.

Elisa Giaretta is a Research Fellow at the University of Verona, Italy, where she received a Ph.D. in Business Administration and Management. She works in the 'Polo Scientifico e Didattico di Studi sull'Impresa', an academic centre focused on the analysis of Italian enterprises. Her research topics include private equity, companies' networks and bank risks.

Elisabetta Gualandri is Full Professor of Banking and Finance in the "Marco Biagi" Department of Economics of the University of Modena and Reggio Emilia. She is a director of the European Association of University Teachers in Banking and Finance. She served as an auditor of

Banca d'Italia from 2007 to 2012, when she was appointed to the Board of BPER banca. Her recent research topics include regulation and supervision of financial intermediaries and markets, financial crisis, the financing of innovative SMEs, and public intervention programs.

Krzysztof Kil is Assistant Professor of Banking and Finance at the Cracow University of Economics, Faculty of Finance and Law, Poland. His research concentrates on the issues of bank stability and bank efficiency in Central and Eastern Europe.

Andrea Landi is Full Professor of Banking and Finance in the "Marco Biagi" Department of Economics of the University of Modena and Reggio Emilia, and the President of Fondazione Cassa di Risparmio di Modena from 2005 to 2015. He served as an auditor of Cassa Depositi e Prestiti from 2014 to 2016. His recent research topics include bank strategies, efficiency and performance, financial crisis, financing of innovative SMEs and public intervention programs, asset management.

Ted Lindblom is Professor of Business Administration at the University of Gothenburg, Sweden. His current research interests mainly concern corporate finance and banking. In the corporate finance area, he particularly focuses on corporate governance, capital budgeting, and financial structure decisions. In the banking area, his emphasis is on banking strategies, pricing, profitability, and risk management under different market condition and regulatory frameworks. He has authored and co-authored several articles and books regarding these issues.

Joaquín Maudos is Professor of Economics at the University of Valencia, Research Deputy Director at the Ivie and collaborator at the CUNEF. He has been visiting researcher at the Florida State University Finance Department, at the College of Business at Bangor University, and at the School of Business of the University of Glasgow. He has also been a consultant to the European Commission, the European Investment Bank, and the United Nations. He has jointly published seventeen books and nearly ninety articles in specialized journals (European Journal of Finance, Journal of Banking and Finance, Journal of Comparative Economics, Journal of Financial Services Research,

Journal of International Financial Markets, Institutions and Money, Journal of International Money and Finance, Regional Studies, Review of Income and Wealth, Journal of Business Economics and Management, etc.). He is a member of the Editorial Board of the journal Inversión & Finanzas, as well as director of competitive projects.

Milena Migliavacca is a Ph.D. candidate and Contract Professor of Financial Intermediaries at Catholic University in Milan and visiting Ph. D. student at Essex Business School, University of Essex. Her current research interests concern financial literacy, social impact investment, and deposit insurance schemes design.

Ewa Miklaszewska is a Professor in Banking and Finance at the Cracow University of Economics (CUE), Poland, where she chairs the Banking Division. She is an Associate Professor of Economics at the Jagiellonian University in Cracow, Department of Management and Public Communication. She has held several visiting positions at both foreign universities and Polish financial regulatory institutions. Her research interests focus on bank regulation and bank strategies.

Andrea Paltrinieri is Assistant Professor in Banking and Finance at the University of Udine, Italy. He holds a Ph.D. in Business Administration from the University of Verona, Italy. Research topics include asset management and institutional investors, with a particular focus on sovereign wealth funds, Islamic finance and the relative financial instruments such as sukuk, commodity markets and exchange traded products.

Viktoriia Paimanova is a researcher of Financial Markets and Institutions, School of Economics and Management, at V.N.Karazin Kharkiv National University (Ukraine). She focuses her interests on statistics and analyzing of financial markets, assessment of risk profiles and financial assets. In 2014–2016, she was a research fellow at Tuscia University (Italy).

Daniele Angelo Previati is Full Professor of Financial Markets and Institutions in the Department of Management of the University of Rome III and Professor at the SDA Business School, Bocconi University, Milan. He has been teaching banking and finance for more than 30 years, with particular focus on bank management, strategy, and organization in the financial services industry and e-finance. His main research interests relate to various perspectives on bank management: human resources management, intellectual capital, organizational change, stakeholder management, and finance for SMEs. He has published widely in academic journals and books. He has also acted as a consultant for banks and the Italian Central Bank on organization design and human resources management.

Valeria Venturelli is Associate Professor in Banking and Finance at the "Marco Biagi" Department of Economics of the University of Modena and Reggio Emilia, where she teaches Financial Markets and Institutions at both undergraduate level and graduate level. She graduated in Economics from the University of Modena and Reggio Emilia and received a Ph.D. in Financial Markets and Institutions from the Catholic University of Milan. Her main research interests are the economics of banking and other financial institutions and valuation methods. She is the author of several articles in leading academic journals. She has acted as a consultant to various public institutions and consulting firms. She is a member of CEFIN—Center for Studies in Banking and Finance and Softech-ICT.

List of Figures

List of Tables

1

Introduction

Giusy Chesini, Elisa Giaretta and Andrea Paltrinieri

This text comprises a selection of papers that offers new insights into banking business models, risks and regulation proposals in the aftermath of European financial crises. It investigates the main issues affecting the business of banking nowadays such as low interest rates and non-performing loans. The combined effect of low to negative interest rates and weak economic growth has encouraged banks to shift their business towards new areas, less related to interest rates, that financial markets and institutional investors are evaluating. Contributions also

G. Chesini (✉) · E. Giaretta
Department of Business Administration,
University of Verona, Verona, Italy
e-mail: giusy.chesini@univr.it

E. Giaretta
e-mail: elisa.giaretta@univr.it

A. Paltrinieri
Department of Economic and Statistical Sciences,
University of Udine, Udine, Italy
e-mail: andrea.paltrinieri@univr.it

G. Chesini et al. (eds.), *The Business of Banking*, Palgrave Macmillan Studies in Banking and Financial Institutions, DOI 10.1007/978-3-319-54894-4_1

offer new insights into topics not yet fully investigated by the literature such as banks' short-selling bans after Brexit, the European Deposit Guarantee Scheme and banks' risk appetite framework.

These chapters were originally presented as papers at the annual conference of the European Association of University Teachers of Banking and Finance (otherwise known as the Wolpertinger Conference) which was held at the University of Verona, Italy, at the beginning of September 2016.

In particular, the second chapter, "Interest Rates and Net Interest Margins: The Impact of Monetary policy," by Paula Cruz-García, Juan Fernández de Guevara, and Joaquín Maudos, examines the determinants of bank's net interest margin, focusing on the effect of interest rates, and thus monetary policy decisions. The analysis is carried with a panel of banks from 32 OECD countries over the period 2003–2014. The results show a quadratic relationship between net interest margins and interest rates, implying that the variation of the latter (and therefore monetary policy) has a greater effect when interest rates are low. An important implication of economic policy regarding the results obtained is that there is a trade-off between economic growth and financial stability associated with the impact of expansionary monetary policy when the level of interest rates is very low. As a result, if the current scenario of low and even negative interest rates persists for much longer in certain countries (such as in the Eurozone), it will have a negative effect on bank profitability and consequently on financial stability.

Chapter 3, "The Swedish Mortgage Market—Bank Funding, Margins and Risk Shifting", by Viktor Elliot and Ted Lindblom analyzes the Swedish mortgage market, especially focusing on bank funding, margins, and risk shifting. It discusses the move from mortgage-backed bonds to covered bonds regime in Sweden and its implications for bank's profitability and risk-taking. This chapter concludes by offering a discussion about the risk of a new financial crisis in Sweden.

In Chap. 4, "Incapability or Bad Luck? Testing the "Bad Management" Hypothesis in the Italian Banking System" by Fabrizio Crespi and Mauro Aliano, by using specific evidences from the Italian banking sector and following a microeconomic approach, the authors test the "bad management" hypothesis first introduced by Berger and

Deyoung (1997), which suggests that poor managerial practice causes an increase in problem loans after a lag. This chapter gives a contribution to the existing literature in this field; in that, it investigates nonperforming loans (NPLs) and other soured loans jointly. Their results confirm the "bad management" hypothesis, in that they discover a positive (lagged) relation between the value of past due/overdrawn loans and NPLs which, in a management perspective, indicates the incapability of the credit manager to anticipate or to recover (at least partially) problematic credits.

The fifth chapter, "Why Do US Banks React Differently to Short Selling Bans?" by Daniele Angelo Previati, Giuseppe Galloppo, Mauro Aliano and Viktoriia Paimanova, is about short-selling ban which caught high attention of policy modeling in different countries. This work is one of the first to explain the evidence of different bank price reactions in terms of country and stock market conditions, and to consider both stock price reaction and risk side. All in all, their findings suggest that the impact of the ban on the overall market efficiency is heterogeneous and, in most cases, modest for the countries analyzed. Indeed, you either do not observe any improvements or they are only short-lived. This chapter checks the short selling response of US banks, listed in the SP500 in 2008. For the first time, we document that banks react to ban restrictions differently, mostly because of their variety in terms of fundamental factors (balance sheet indicators). Considering that, US banks show different reactions to the ban on short selling. Policy makers should decide which of firm characteristics are better to choose and whether interventions are effective on the market.

Chapter 6, "Reputational Risk in Banking: Important to Whom?" by Ewa Miklaszewska and Krzysztof Kil, aims to examine the relevance of reputational risk for banks and the incentives to manage it. The efforts to manage reputational risk as a self-standing type of risk, and not within an operational risk framework, are quite recent. Consequently, in the empirical part of this chapter, the authors propose a methodology to measure reputational risk, based on the bank stakeholders' perspective.

Chapter 7, "The Business Model of Banks: A Review of the Theoretical and Empirical Literature" by Stefano Cosma, Riccardo Ferretti, Elisabetta Gualandri, Andrea Landi, and Valeria Venturelli considers that the business model (BM) has become a key concept in banking literature. The topic's relevance is due to the impact of the crisis on bank profitability and risk levels, leading to new challenges for bank managers, analysts, and regulators. This chapter deals first of all with the definition of BM in the management literature; afterward the focus is on bank business model (BBM) and the business model analysis (BMA) literature, also considering the nexus with bank diversification. The point of view of supervisory authorities is critically analyzed with specific regard to BMA embedded in the Supervisory Review and Evaluation Process (SREP).

Chapter 8, "On European Deposit Guarantee Schemes" by Milena Migliavacca, aims to provide a dynamic overview of the Deposit Protection Schemes (DPSs) across the EU28. Using data gathered by the World Bank's Bank Regulation and Supervision Surveys, the analysis critically systematizes the different features that shape the national DPSs' design. Finally, this study highlights the area where legislative intervention is most needed in order to reach a full-fledged European Deposit Insurance Scheme (EDIS).

Finally, Chap. 9, "A Technical Approach to Deposit Guarantee Schemes" by Francesca Arnaboldi, fits within the debate on deposit guarantee schemes in the European Union, currently under revision, investigating the changes proposed by directive 2014/49/EU of the European Parliament and the Council and regulated by the European Banking Authority. For Italian banks, new rules introduce risk-based contributions to be paid ex ante to the national deposit guarantee scheme. The framework proposed by the European Banking Authority results in a better classification for Italian banks, which requires lower payments to the scheme. Concerns are raised about the effectiveness of the European Banking Authority guidelines.

2

Interest Rates and Net Interest Margins: The Impact of Monetary Policy

Paula Cruz-García, Juan Fernández de Guevara and Joaquín Maudos

2.1 Introduction

Several central banks have adopted an expansionary monetary policy in recent years so as to combat the impact of the last financial crisis on the economy. In addition to the low monetary policy interest rates (Fig. 2.1) resulting from the measures adopted (both conventional and unconventional), there is also a fall in the long-run natural rate of interest[1]: This derives from an excess of savings in relation to investment due to demographic factors (such as the ageing of the population and the

P. Cruz-García (✉) · J. Fernández de Guevara · J. Maudos
University of Valencia, Valencia, Spain
e-mail: paula.cruz@uv.es

J. Fernández de Guevara
e-mail: radoselo@uv.es

J. Maudos
e-mail: joaquin.maudos@uv.es

J. Fernández de Guevara · J. Maudos
Instituto Valenciano de Investigaciones Económicas, Valencia, Spain

G. Chesini et al. (eds.), *The Business of Banking*, Palgrave Macmillan Studies in Banking and Financial Institutions, DOI 10.1007/978-3-319-54894-4_2

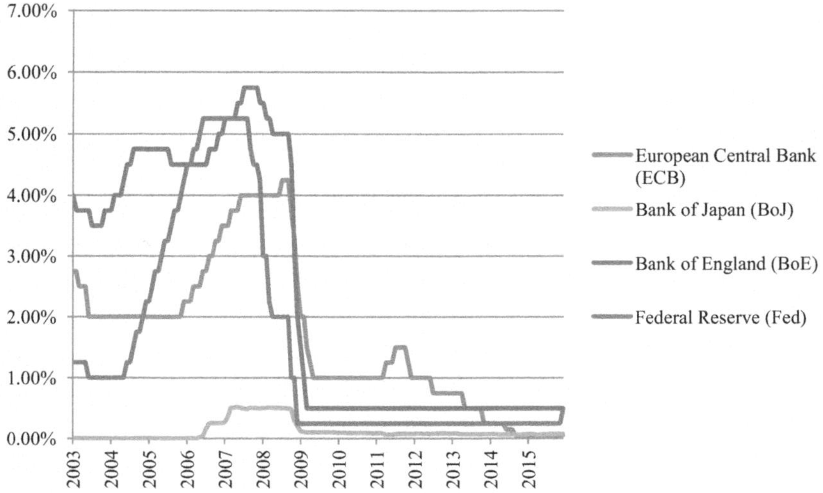

Fig. 2.1 Intervention interest rates by the main Central Banks. *Source: Bank of Spain.*

depression in consumption which this entails), a lower rate of technological progress (with the consequent secular stagnation of economies), low prices of raw materials, particularly oil, and increased demand for safe assets (pushing prices upward and decreasing yields), etc. What all of this leads to is a scenario of very low (or even negative) interest rates. In fact, a high percentage of debt in many countries has negative interest rates.

According to a recent analysis by the International Monetary Fund (2016), the expansionary monetary policies adopted by some central banks have eased the access to finance (by reducing the cost of funding and increasing the availability of credit), thus stimulating aggregate demand. However, a prolonged period of reduced interest rates can impair bank intermediation margins (and therefore profitability), given the existence of a floor in deposit interest rates, since it is difficult for banks to pass on the drop in interest rates to the deposits interest rates, at least in the case of households.[2] For this reason, the net interest margin is seen to be most affected in those banks with a greater proportion of financing via deposits. Likewise, the greater the proportion of variable interest rate loans in a bank, the greater the deterioration of its profitability, as a result of the fall in financial revenues due to the reduction of the money market interest rates.

The European Central Bank (2016), on the other hand, highlights in its Annual Report that the expansionary measures adopted have a positive impact. The positive impact is driven by the fact that the drop in interest rates has led to an improvement in the quality of bank assets (since less risky projects are financed), an increase in lending activity and a drop in non-performing loans as a result of economic recovery.

Other papers, such as Rostagno et al. (2016), also provide empirical evidence of the increase in credit growth due to the policy of negative rates, showing that loans to companies have increased in the Eurozone with the current expansionary policy.

Taking the above mentioned into account, it is important to differentiate between the impact that falling interest rates have had up until now and the impact of these extremely low, or even negative, rates persisting for a prolonged period. To date, the effect has not been negative, as stated by the IMF and the ECB. However, the IMF warns that if this scenario persists for much longer, it will have an adverse effect on the net interest margin and therefore on bank profitability, primarily due to the floor in interest rates on deposits, as well as a flattening of the yield curve which has taken place with the falling interest rates.

In this context, the objective of this study is to analyse the impact of the variation of interest rates on the net interest margin and the possible existence of a non-linear relationship which would explain why the impact of monetary policy differs depending on the level of interest rates. Thus, if the relationship is quadratic, a fall in interest rates could be harmful for bank margins if the level of rates is low, while the same drop in rates can have beneficial effects with high rates (as a result of the reactivation of the demand for credit, reducing non-performing loans, etc.).

Since there are very few works to date which have empirically analysed the effect of a prolonged period of low-interest rates on banking net interest margins (and therefore on profitability), further evidence is needed on this subject. But given the current context of such low rates, this issue has attracted attention as shown by the recent works by Borio et al. (2015) and by Claessens et al. (2016). Using samples of banks from various countries, both papers provide evidence demonstrating the existence of a non-linear relationship between interest rates and the net interest margin. In addition to these two works, are those by Genay and Podjasek (2014) which analyse the effects of expansionary monetary policy on the bank margin in the USA, and Busch and Memmel (2015) for German banks.

Our work provides further empirical evidence for a sample of 32 countries from around the world for the period 2003–2014, a period that includes years of expansion in which accommodative monetary policies were adopted and the subsequent years of crisis in which expansionary monetary policy measures were implemented, both conventional (such as a decrease in intervention rates), as well as unconventional (QE, negative rates which penalise excess bank reserves, etc.). The work is focused on quantifying the impact of short-term interest rates on bank interest margins, testing the hypothesis of whether the relationship between interest rates and the margin is indeed quadratic. However, we also consider the impact of other variables as determinants of net interest margins, which capture the characteristics of each bank (market power, credit risk, risk aversion, operating costs, etc.), along with other control variables (market risk, etc.). We have taken variables used as determinants in the model by Ho and Saunders (1981) and some of their additions together with the reference framework by Borio et al. (2015).

The results obtained indicate that the impact of interest rates on the intermediation margin is quadratic rather than linear. Accordingly, taking into account this concave relationship and the current low rates, a normalisation in monetary policy would have a significant effect on margin recovery. Similarly, this result also shows that if this situation persists for much longer (and even worse, if the negative rates which penalise excess bank reserves in some countries are increased), it could have a negative impact on financial stability as a result of the fall in bank profitability, which is already at an extremely low level (and below the cost of raising capital) at least in European banking.

In addition to this introduction, our paper is structured as follows. Section 2.2 examines the theoretical framework on the determinants of bank intermediation margins and presents the testable hypothesis. Section 2.3 describes the sample used, defines the variables of the model and the empirical approach, and explains the methodology used.

Section 2.4 shows the results obtained and Sect. 2.5 checks the robustness of the results. Finally, Sect. 2.6 presents the conclusions and the economic policy implications.

2.2 Theoretical Framework and Testable Hypothesis

2.2.1 Theoretical Framework

There are various theoretical frameworks in which the behaviour of net interest margins is modelled (see, for example, Zarruk 1989; or Wong 1997). However, most of the works in the literature take the model developed by Ho and Saunders (1981) as a starting point. Allen (1988) extended this model by incorporating different types of loans and deposits. In this extension, the author showed that the margins can be reduced when one considers the cross elasticity of demand between banking products. Angbazo (1997), on the other hand, expanded the original model by taking into account credit risk as well as interest rate risk. Maudos and Fernández de Guevara (2004) extended the model to include operating costs. In addition, their analysis of net interest margins in the main sectors of European banking uses a direct measure of the degree of market power, such as the Lerner index. Carbó and Rodríguez (2007) included non-interest income as a determinant of the margin.

In all these models, the bank is considered as an (risk averse) intermediary, maximising the expected utility of its wealth $EU(\bar{W})$, between suppliers and demanders of loans in a static framework over a single period. In the model, the banks set interest rates (r_L and r_D) on their loans (L) and deposits (D), setting markups a and b on the money market interest rate (r). Banking activity is subject to two types of risks: (1) the uncertain profitability of their loans associated with default risk; and (2) the risk that banks take because of their position in the money market to which they call on when they need to grant new loans or to place excess liquidity. Both risks are introduced by assuming that interest rates on loans and the money market have a probability function with variance

α_L^2 *y* α_C^2, respectively. In addition, both risks are related (with covariance σ_{LC}). For each additional loan or deposit, banks must assume operating costs $Exp(Q_L)$ or $Exp(Q_D)$, respectively. Finally, the loans and deposits reach banks according to Poisson processes which depend on the spreads that banks set on the interbank interest rate. These processes include the parameters that determine the market power (α/β) of banks in their markets.

In an application for the case of German banking, Entrop et al. (2015) include the cost of the maturity transformation, defining the equation that describes the determinants of the intermediation margin (*s*) in the following way:

$$s = \frac{1}{2}\frac{\alpha}{\beta} + \frac{1}{2}\left(\frac{Exp(Q_L)}{Q_L(1+r)} + \frac{Exp(Q_D)}{Q_D(1+r)}\right) - \frac{1}{2}\frac{r_L - r_D}{(1+r)}$$
$$+ \frac{1}{4}\frac{U''(\bar{W})}{U'(\bar{W})}\frac{((Q_L + 2L_0)(\sigma_L^2 + 2\sigma_{LC} + \sigma_C^2)) - 2(\sigma_{LD} + \sigma_{CD})(D_0 + L_0) + \sigma_D^2(2D_0 + Q_D)}{(1+r)}$$

With these additions to the original model by Ho and Saunders (1981), the determinants of the net interest margin are the level of interest rates (r, r_L *and* r_D), the degree of competition (α/β), risk (credit risk, as well as market risk, and their interaction- σ_L^2, σ_C^2 and σ_{LC}-), bank risk aversion, $-1/2U''(\bar{W})/U'(\bar{W})$, the overheads, the volume of the initial credit portfolio L_0 and of deposits D_0, and the average size of operations Q_L and Q_D.

Other group of papers (see Gerali et al. 2010) use a dynamic stochastic general equilibrium model with an imperfect competition. These authors postulate a linear relationship between bank margin and the level of interest rates. Alesandri and Nelson (2015) consider a simple version of former model in partial equilibrium with the same conclusion.

More recently, Borio et al. (2015) used the Monti-Klein model for the case where oligopolistic competition exists between N banks, incorporating the cost of maturity transformation, the capital requirements coefficient and an equation for provisions for possible loans losses. The determinants of the net interest margin included in the empirical application are the three-month interbank interest rate, the slope of the yield curve and the interest rate risk, in addition to macroeconomic indicators and variables that approximate the characteristics of each bank (bank size, risk aversion, liquidity and efficiency). This paper focuses on the influence of monetary policy on the intermediation margin both through the impact of the short-term interest rates and the slope of the yield curve. These authors find that the level of interest rates, which is the key variable in our work, has a positive non-linear relationship with the net interest margin, depending on the curvature of the value of elasticity of demand for loans and deposits and on capital requirements.

In the same vein, Claessens et al. (2016) provide empirical evidence on the negative effect of the drop in interest rates on net interest margin, with the impact being greater when interest rates started at a low level, obtaining a quadratic relationship between the money market interest rates and the net interest margin.

2.2.2 Testable Hypothesis

In this context, our work takes into account all previous contributions in so far as we analyse the determinants of the net interest margin by including the various explanatory variables put forward, but with emphasis on the effect of interest rates and hence the impact of monetary policy.

Our testable hypothesis is the following: controlling for bank characteristics and macroeconomic variables, an increase in interest rates has a positive effect on net interest margin, the impact being greater when interest rates are low. In other words, we expect a positive and concave relationship between net interest income and the level of interest rates.

2.3 Data, Definition of Variables and Methodology

2.3.1 Data

The data used for the empirical analysis come from the BankScope database (Bureau Van Dijk), which contains information on the balance and the income statement of a representative sample of banks from around the world. To control the influence of other macroeconomic variables which affect the intermediation margin, the World Bank database is used, while the money market interest rates come from the OECD database.

The sample used includes financial institutions (banks, savings banks, credit unions and other types of banks) from 32 OECD[3] countries.

The period examined is from 2003 to 2014. Excluded from the sample are those banks that do not provide the necessary data with which to calculate any of the variables required for econometric specification and those whose input prices, necessary for estimating the Lerner index of market power, are outside the range of the 2.5 standard deviations on either side of the mean calculated for each year. With these filters, the panel of data finally used is made up of 54,540 observations.

Variables

In order to carry out the empirical contrast, we used variables put forward by Ho and Saunders (1981) and their subsequent extensions, adding the level of interest rate and its square, as do Borio et al. (2015). Therefore, the following variables are needed for econometric specification: the level of short-term interest rates, market power, the degree of bank risk aversion, money market volatility (interest rate risk), credit risk, the interaction between both types of risk, the volume of credit, liquidity reserves and average production costs. Each of these variables is approximated as indicated below:

Level of Interest Rates

We use the three-month interbank market interest rate (*Short-term interest rate*) to approximate the level of short-term interest rates. The expected sign of this variable on the net interest margin is positive.

To capture a possible non-linear relationship between the level of interest rates and the intermediation margin, the square of the level of interest rates is included as an explanatory variable.

Market Power

As an approximation of market power, two alternative measures are used. The first is the *Lerner index* of market power, which is estimated at bank level using the approach commonly taken in other works, such as Berg and Kim (1994) or Maudos and Fernández de Guevara (2004).

The Lerner index measures the ability of companies to set a price above the marginal cost and is defined as the price-cost margin in relation to the price:

$$\text{Lerner index}_i = \frac{P_i - \text{MC}_i}{P_i}$$

where P_i is the average price of banking products, which is approximated by the total assets and is measured as a ratio between total income and total assets, and MC_i is the marginal cost of production, which is calculated based on the following translog cost function:

$$\ln C_i = \alpha_0 + \alpha_1 \ln \text{TA}_i + \frac{1}{2}\alpha_k(\ln \text{TA}_i)^2 + \sum_{j=1}^{3} \beta_j \ln w_{\text{ji}} + \frac{1}{2}\sum_{j=1}^{3}\sum_{k=1}^{3} \beta_{\text{jk}} \ln w_{\text{ji}} \ln w_{\text{ki}} + \frac{1}{2}\sum_{j=1}^{3} \gamma_j \ln \text{TA}_i \ln w_{\text{ji}} + \mu_1 \text{Trend} + \mu_2 \frac{1}{2}\text{Trend}^2 + \mu_3 \text{Trend} \ln\text{TA}_i + \sum_{j=1}^{3} \delta_j \text{Trend} \ln w_{\text{ji}} + \ln u_i$$

where C_i is the total costs of the bank (financial and operating costs) and TA_i is total assets. The definition of the price of production factors is the following:

w_1: Price of labour = Staff costs/total assets[4].

w_2: Price of capital = Operating costs (except staff costs)/fixed assets.

w_3: Price of deposits = Financial costs/deposits.

The cost function estimate is carried out by using a data panel consisting of all the banks in the analysis. So as to capture the influence of specific variables for each bank, fixed effects are introduced in the cost function estimate. Finally, a trend variable was also introduced (*Trend*) to show the effect of technological change, resulting in displacement of the cost function over time. As is a common practice, the estimate was made by imposing the restrictions of symmetry and grade one homogeneity in *input* prices.

The second indicator of market power is the Herfindahl index which approximates the structure or concentration of the market. Although it is common to use market concentration measures as indicators of competition, such measures have significant limitations for two reasons. Firstly, the theory shows that when judging competition, it is not always the number of competitors (or the concentration) that is relevant, but the rivalry that exists between them. And secondly, indicators of concentration do not show variations between banks in the same country.

Therefore, since the Lerner index is a measure of market power that is theoretically better grounded than the Herfindahl index, as well as presenting variations at bank level, it will be the preference in the estimate. However, the sensitivity of the results will be analysed using the Herfindahl index.

The expected sign of the variables (both the Lerner index and Herfindahl index) is positive, since banks with greater market power can set higher margins.

Bank Size

The logarithm of loan volumes (*log-loans*) is included as a proxy for bank size, since for a given credit risk, the potential losses will be proportional to the loan volume, and consequently the risk premium applicable to the margin. Alternatively, as in Borio et al. (2015), the logarithm for total assets (*log-assets*) is also included to verify the robustness of the estimate. In both cases, the expected sign is positive.

Risk Aversion

The degree of bank risk aversion (*Risk aversion*) follows the approach used by McShane and Sharpe (1985) and is approximated by the following ratio:

$$\text{RISKAVER} = \frac{\text{Equity}}{\text{Total Assets}}$$

The expected sign of this variable is positive, since banks with greater risk aversion will set a higher margin.[5]

Credit Risk

Given the possibility of non-payment or default on loans, banks include a risk premium, which is implicit in the interest rates charged on such transactions. Credit risk is approximated by the ratio between the provision for insolvencies and the volume of credit granted (*Prov/loans*), since the greater the likelihood of insolvency and non-performing loans, the more provisions banks will provide. The expected sign of this variable is positive.

Interest Rate Risk

Money market uncertainty is approximated by using the coefficient of variation calculated with monthly data on the three-month interbank interest rate (*Interest rate risk*). The expected sign is positive since, *ceteris paribus*, greater volatility means higher risk and thus a greater intermediation margin is needed to offset this risk.

Interaction Between Credit Risk and Market Risk (*Risk Covariance*)

Interaction between credit risk and market risk (*Risk covariance*) is proxied by the product of the measurement of credit risk and the interest rate risk. The expected sign of this variable is positive, since given a higher correlation between both types of risk, banks require a greater intermediation margin.

Average Cost of Transactions (*Average Cost*)

This is defined as the ratio between total operating costs divided by total assets. As demonstrated by Maudos and Fernández de Guevara (2004), the expected sign is positive, since the intermediation margin should cover at least the operating costs.

Liquid Reserves (*Reserves*)

A high volume of liquid reserves has a positive effect on the bank intermediation margin to the extent that they mean an opportunity cost by banks forgoing investment of these reserves in profitable assets. As a result, banks have to set a higher intermediation margin to offset lower interest income. This variable is approximated using the ratio between liquid reserves and total assets.

It is common practice in some studies to add other control variables. In particular, also included are implicit interest payments and an indicator of management quality. In addition, GDP growth is included to capture the possible influence of the economic cycle in determining the net interest margin.

Implicit Interest Payments

Following Ho and Saunders (1981), Angbazo (1997) and Saunders and Schumacher (2000), among others, an indicator of implicit interest payments is included. As an approximation to these payments, we use the variable operating expenses net of non-interest revenues as a percentage of total assets (*Implicit interest rates*). The expected sign of this variable is positive since higher implicit payments mean increased transaction costs which demand wider margins to compensate banks for the costs this entails (instead of fees being charged explicitly, they are implicit in the form of a greater margin).

Efficiency

Efficient management involves choosing the most profitable assets and the lowest cost deposits. Management quality is therefore approximated by the ratio between operating costs and the operating income (cost to income ratio, *Efficiency*). The expected sign of this variable is negative, since the higher the ratio, the greater the operating inefficiency and thus the smaller the margin.

GDP Growth

As is common practice in studies which analyse banking margins, the estimate of the annual GDP growth rate (*GDP growth*) is included to control for the possible influence of the economic cycle on the net interest margin.

Net Interest Margin

Finally, the dependent variable to account for, i.e. the net interest margin per unit of assets (NII), is defined as the difference between revenue and financial costs in relation to total assets.

Table 2.1 shows the weighted average of each of the variables concerned in our study for the countries analysed.

Table 2.1 Descriptive statistics (2003–2014 averages)

	Net interest margin/ total assets (%)	Short-term interest rate (%)	Implicit interest payments (%)	Efficiency	Lerner index	Herfindahl index	Volatility of market interest rates (%)	Credit risk (prov/loans) (%)
Australia	1.83	4.70	0.87	45.95	0.26	0.08	7.11	0.18
Austria	2.04	2.15	0.99	68.17	0.27	0.06	17.64	1.09
Belgium	1.63	2.01	0.70	69.40	0.27	0.11	17.85	0.09
Canada	1.88	2.52	0.91	73.06	0.28	0.15	8.31	0.22
Chile	3.67	4.33	1.28	58.55	0.36	0.07	20.52	1.01
Colombia	4.79	5.88	1.29	63.48	0.39	0.06	8.23	7.41
Czech Republic	1.88	1.87	1.12	72.94	0.33	0.10	11.37	0.46
Denmark	3.22	2.27	1.57	67.50	0.36	0.18	14.30	1.45
Finland	1.42	1.30	0.63	68.85	0.37	0.25	25.78	0.17
France	2.06	2.09	0.77	78.80	0.30	0.05	18.31	0.02
Germany	2.39	2.22	1.38	70.28	0.25	0.03	16.50	3.01
Greece	2.21	2.21	0.71	60.96	0.32	0.11	17.34	1.74
Hungary	3.70	6.36	2.18	97.47	0.31	0.09	14.68	2.72
Iceland	3.31	8.49	−0.01	39.08	0.30	0.92	10.10	2.23
Ireland	0.84	2.02	−0.22	31.56	0.38	0.26	18.38	0.27
Israel	2.14	3.07	1.23	73.30	0.27	0.20	19.10	0.49
Italy	2.58	2.52	1.38	71.71	0.30	0.06	15.82	0.79
Japan	1.69	0.30	1.18	100.02	0.29	0.18	15.21	0.64
Korea, Rep.	2.15	3.66	0.59	61.91	0.32	0.05	6.12	2.01
Latvia	2.22	4.53	0.63	71.66	0.40	0.07	26.43	1.73
Luxembourg	0.96	1.56	−0.22	58.39	0.38	0.04	18.48	−0.19
Mexico	8.31	4.91	4.91	67.89	0.34	47.10	5.31	4.71

(continued)

Table 2.1 (continued)

	Net interest margin/ total assets (%)	Short-term interest rate (%)	Implicit interest payments (%)	Efficiency	Lerner index	Herfindahl index	Volatility of market interest rates (%)	Credit risk (prov/loans) (%)
Netherlands	1.42	1.87	−0.08	48.78	0.39	0.23	20.06	0.64
New Zealand	2.01	4.68	0.73	54.10	0.31	0.12	6.22	0.22
Norway	2.13	3.00	1.01	61.76	0.32	0.13	11.30	0.22
Poland	3.04	4.53	1.13	63.23	0.34	0.06	8.22	1.11
Portugal	2.28	1.11	1.21	68.50	0.29	0.08	28.60	1.01
Russian Federati	5.31	7.71	2.66	80.44	0.37	0.06	20.57	−1.45
Slovak Republic	2.83	2.19	1.25	65.12	0.36	0.10	22.47	1.13
Slovenia	2.16	2.34	0.77	53.67	0.28	0.11	22.14	3.05
South Africa	3.82	7.00	1.19	68.57	0.36	0.08	5.91	1.60
Spain	1.87	2.30	0.75	67.58	0.30	0.07	16.74	2.61
Sweden	3.03	1.86	1.47	62.24	0.4	0.1344	27.15	0.3
Switzerland	1.38	0.78	0.48	67.97	0.32	0.1101	49.25	1.32
UK	1.61	2.79	0.85	65.41	0.72	0.0804	12.38	0.86
USA	3.12	2.01	1.59	69.87	0.35	0.0387	20.52	0.58

	Loans (log)	Total assets (log)	Risk aversion (%)	Operating costs (% total assets)	Reserves (% total assets)	GDP growth (%)	Number of obs.
Australia	14.98	15.53	7.27	1.83	4.12	2.86	322
Austria	12.48	13.17	8.36	2.58	1.55	1.68	1983
Belgium	13.23	14.74	9.04	2.06	1.19	1.63	449

(continued)

Table 2.1 (continued)

	Loans (log)	Total assets (log)	Risk aversion (%)	Operating costs (% total assets)	Reserves (% total assets)	GDP growth (%)	Number of obs.
Canada	14.29	14.91	8.46	2.14	2.37	2.41	490
Chile	13.99	14.56	14.35	3.02	6.53	4.77	79
Colombia	12.71	13.67	18.08	5.45	6.12	4.85	401
Czech Republic	13.76	14.53	10.02	3.21	2.75	2.76	232
Denmark	12.57	13.18	13.27	3.14	3.82	0.52	842
Finland	13.55	14.23	8.79	2.02	2.35	0.49	195
France	14.10	14.95	9.87	2.65	1.7	1.65	2474
Germany	12.99	13.63	7.05	2.49	2.24	1.34	12923
Greece	14.67	15.23	11.17	1.97	2.79	0.05	120
Hungary	12.97	13.89	10.88	4.72	6.15	2.16	70
Iceland	11.45	11.98	15.14	3.48	5.81	3.58	105
Ireland	14.13	15.76	14.12	1.62	2.08	3.18	129
Israel	15.38	15.86	6.41	2.45	11.32	3.36	80
Italy	13.05	13.61	11.05	2.55	1.24	0.81	2969
Japan	14.32	14.97	5.41	1.33	2.27	1.64	3265
Korea, Rep.	15.18	16.28	10.59	2.46	5.08	4.21	242
Latvia	12.02	13.24	10.35	2.64	7.59	3.54	202
Luxembourg	12.64	14.68	9.50	1.45	2.95	3.05	585
Mexico	13.87	14.89	14.03	7.70	4.96	3.24	27
Netherlands	13.80	15.17	11.20	1.35	7.26	1.48	167
New Zealand	14.52	14.91	8.98	1.42	4.3	2.65	95
Norway	12.83	13.04	9.86	1.54	2.66	1.7	1211

(continued)

Table 2.1 (continued)

	Loans (log)	Total assets (log)	Risk aversion (%)	Operating costs (% total assets)	Reserves (% total assets)	GDP growth (%)	Number of obs.
Poland	14.02	14.62	12.02	2.77	4.18	4.24	277
Portugal	12.32	13.06	11.22	2.13	1.34	−0.19	500
Russian Federati	10.51	11.25	20.43	19.40	6.4	3.62	7012
Slovak Republic	13.51	14.16	15.57	2.53	5.97	3.74	132
Slovenia	13.71	14.33	8.81	1.92	3.61	1.44	158
South Africa	13.50	14.52	11.64	4.90	15.26	3.2	166
Spain	14.29	15.02	8.58	1.60	1.39	2.03	778
Sweden	12.26	12.68	13.75	3.08	0.71	1.98	993
Switzerland	12.55	13.07	8.23	2.09	4.21	2.08	4473
UK	12.66	13.79	11.07	1.99	4.64	1.62	1369
USA	13.98	14.5	10.67	2.88	3.8	2.66	9786

Source: BankScope and authors' calculations

2.3.2 Methodology

With all the variables described, the following equation is estimated:

$$\begin{aligned}\mathrm{NII}_t = f(&\mathrm{NII}_{t-1}, \text{Short-term interest rate}_t, \text{Short-term interest rate}_t^2,\\ &\text{Implicit interest payments}_t, \text{Efficiency}_t, \text{Lerner index}_t, \text{Interest rate risk}_t,\\ &\text{Credit risk}_t, \text{Risk covariance}_t, \text{Size}_t, \text{Risk aversion}_t,\\ &\text{Average cost}_t, \text{Reserves}_t, \text{GDP growth}_t)\end{aligned}$$

The analysis of the net interest margin determinants is based on an estimation of a dynamic panel data model using the Generalized Method of Moments based on Arellano and Bond (1991) and Blundell and Bond (1998). In addition to including the net interest margin with its time lag as an explanatory variable to capture the inertia in its evolution, possible endogeneity problems are corrected by estimating the model in differences and using the lagged variables as instruments. Time effects are included in the estimation to show the impact of specific variables in each year.

2.4 Results

2.4.1 Base Scenario

Before commenting on the results obtained from the econometric estimation, it is important to analyse how the main variable in our study has evolved: short-term interest rates. As shown in Fig. 2.2, short-term interest rates (approximated by the three-month interbank interest rate) suffered a sharp increase during the years prior to the recent financial crisis, due to the accommodative monetary policy adopted by the main central banks. When the crisis hit in 2007, interest rates dropped sharply as a result of the expansionary monetary policies implemented to combat the effects of the crisis and have generally remained at levels close to zero since 2010.

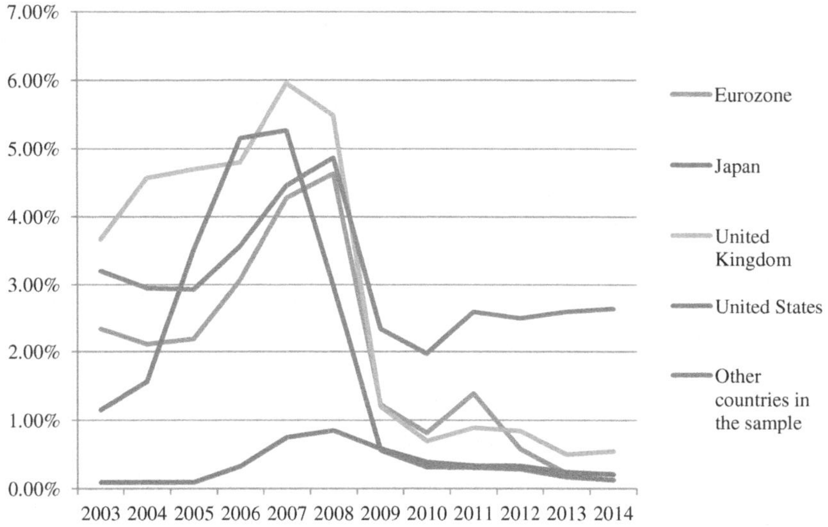

Fig. 2.2 Three-month interbank rates evolution. *Source* OECD and authors' calculations

Furthermore, it is also worth observing the evolution of the net interest margin, as it is the dependent variable in our study. As can be seen in Fig. 2.3, there are significant differences in the level of net interest margins between countries/geographical areas throughout the period analysed. The UK, Japan and the Eurozone have lower margins, while they are much higher in the USA and the group called "other countries".

We can also observe that the margin has fallen in the USA, the Eurozone and Japan, but increased in the group "other countries" and remained more or less stable in the UK.

Table 2.2 presents the results of the estimation of the equation which explains the net interest margin. The first column estimates the determinants of the intermediation margin, assuming a linear relationship between the margin and short-term interest rates. As can be seen, the effect of the level of interest rates is not statistically significant, thus discarding a linear relationship between the intermediation margin and the level of interest rates. The second column also includes the square of short-term interest rates, obtaining a positive and significant impact on

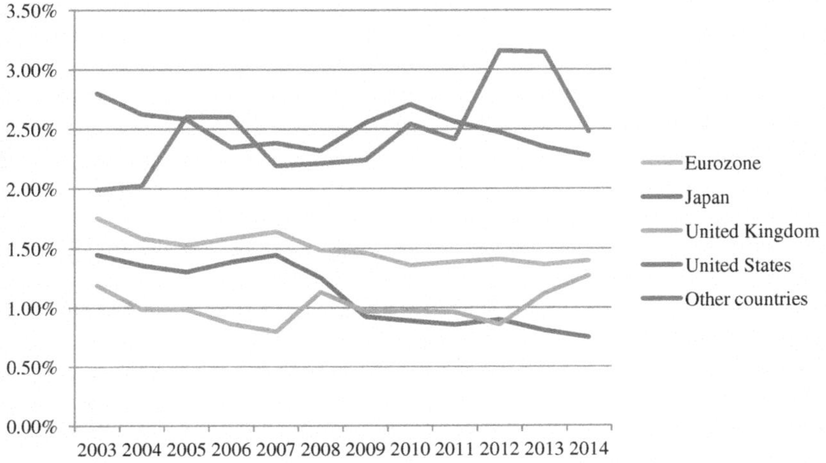

Fig. 2.3 Net interest income evolution (% total assets). *Source: BankScope and authors' calculations*

the level but negative for the square, which shows a quadratic rather than linear relationship. Consequently, a change in interest rates has a greater impact on the net interest margin the lower the level of interest rates. Table 2.2 also shows that the maximum in the relationship between interest rates and the margin is observed at 0.085 (8.5%).

Of the remaining variables, i.e. implicit interest payments, operating efficiency, bank size, risk aversion and GDP growth, they are significant and have the expected sign. Thus, higher implicit payments, lower efficiency, larger banks, greater risk aversion, and a positive GDP growth increase net interest margins.

Robustness of the Results

The third and fourth column analyses the robustness of the results to changes in the empirical approach to some of the determinants of the net interest margin. As shown in column 3, the results are maintained when the size is approximated by the total asset logarithm. Likewise, the results do not vary when market power is approximated by the Herfindahl index (column 4).

Table 2.2 Determinants of net interest income: 2003–2014

	[1]	[2]	[3]	[4]
NIM-1	0.278***	0.295***	0.281***	0.225***
	(0.056)	(0.052)	(0.052)	(0.081)
Short-term interest rate	0.090	0.451**	0.408**	1.350**
	(0.080)	(0.183)	(0.181)	(0.568)
Short-term interest rate^2		−2.663**	−2.510**	−9.775**
		(1.240)	(1.236)	(3.827)
Implicit interest payments	0.463***	0.426***	0.476***	0.501**
	(0.144)	(0.134)	(0.131)	(0.232)
Efficiency	−0.008**	−0.008**	−0.008**	0.006
	(0.004)	(0.004)	(0.004)	(0.010)
Lerner index	0.035	0.360	0.282	
	(0.746)	(0.704)	(0.702)	
Herfindahl index				0.042
				(0.038)
Interest rate risk	0.004	0.012	0.013	0.019
	(0.007)	(0.008)	(0.008)	(0.012)
Credit risk (provisions/loans)	0.000	0.005	0.001	0.051
	(0.010)	(0.009)	(0.009)	(0.045)
Risk covariance	−0.023	−0.020	−0.022	−0.063*
	(0.026)	(0.024)	(0.024)	(0.034)
Log (loans)	0.278***	0.313***		1.392**
	(0.099)	(0.093)		(0.567)
Log (total assets)			0.325***	
			(0.112)	
Risk aversión	0.092***	0.091***	0.096***	0.234**
	(0.031)	(0.029)	(0.030)	(0.108)
Average cost	−0.004	−0.022	−0.021	−0.064**
	(0.013)	(0.014)	(0.014)	(0.031)
Reserves	0.055	0.036	0.035	0.232**
	(0.041)	(0.038)	(0.038)	(0.096)
GDP growth	0.191***	0.204***	0.218***	0.445***
	(0.056)	(0.052)	(0.055)	(0.128)
Constant	−0.038**	−0.053***	−0.056***	−0.255**
	(0.016)	(0.016)	(0.020)	(0.109)
Max. short-term interest rate		0.085	0.081	0.069
Number observations	38,835	38,835	38,835	38,835
Arellano-Bond test for AR(1) in first differences [p-valour]	−2.37 [0.018]	−2.34 [0.019]	−2.35 [0.019]	−0.76 [0.450]

(continued)

Table 2.2 (continued)

	[1]	[2]	[3]	[4]
Arellano-Bond test for AR(2) in first differences [p-valour]	−0.32 [0.748]	−0.58 [0.559]	−0.64 [0.524]	−0.90 [0.370]
Sargan test of overid. Restrictions [p-valour]	23.26 [0.445]	22.77 [0.415]	25.84 [0.259]	4.09 [0.664]

* $p < 0.10$, ** $p < 0.05$, *** $p < 0.01$
Estimations are done using the generalised method of moments (GMM) based on Arellano and Bond (1991) and Blundell and Bond (1998), where Lerner index is instrumented with Herfindahl index, and NIM and other endogenous variables are instrumented with their own first and second differences. All estimations include fixed and time effects. Format of the data in the table: Coef. (Robust Std. Error)
Source: Authors' calculations

2.5 Economic Impact of the Determinants of Net Interest Margin

To be able to assess how the variation of each explanatory variable affects the net interest margin it is not enough to simply compare the magnitude of the estimated coefficient, but rather, the intra-sample variation of each variable must be taken into account in order to know the economic impact. Figure 2.4 therefore quantifies the impact of an interquartile variation in each of the explanatory variables (a change from percentile 25 to 75 of the distribution), taking the estimated parameters in column 2 as references. The variables are ordered from highest to lowest impact, and the bars in the figure in a more subdued colour represent variables which are not statistically significant.

As can be seen in the figure, the most important determinants of the net interest margin for the period analysed are the level of interest rates (due to the large increase caused by accommodative monetary policy during the years before the crisis, as well as the sharp fall in rates as a result of aggressive monetary policy followed by the major central banks to combat the financial crisis), bank size, the degree of risk aversion, the economic cycle and operating efficiency. Thus, a variation in short-term interest rates which means going from percentile 25 to 75 of the distribution entails an increase in the intermediation margin of 119 basis points. In the case of bank size, growth in net interest income would be

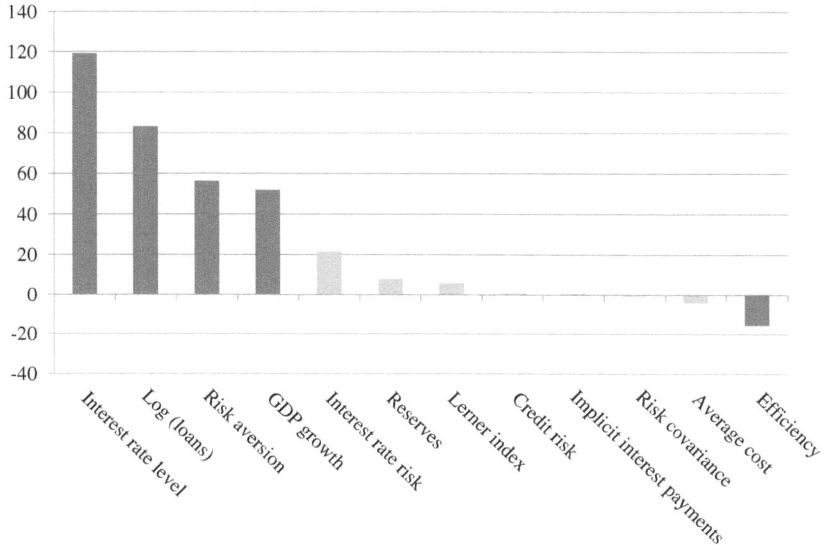

Fig. 2.4 Economic impact of the net interest margin determinants (bp). The graph shows the effect on net interest income of a variation of 25–75 percentile of the distribution in each of the explanatory variables. The bars that have a more subdued colour correspond to variables whose effect is not statistically significant. The variables are sorted from highest to lowest impact on net interest income. The equation [2] of the Table 2.2 was used for the analysis. *Source: Authors' calculations*

83 pb to an equivalent variation of the variable. This variation in the case of banks' risk aversion implies an increase in the intermediation margin of 56 pb; being 51 pb in the case of GDP growth. Finally, a variation in the operating efficiency of percentile 25 and 75 entails a drop of 15 pb in the intermediation margin.

Focusing on the impact of interest rates, if instead of using the interquartile variation range we use the variation which has taken place in the period analysed, as seen in Table 2.3 and Fig. 2.5 from 2003 to 2007 (subperiod of expansion), the increase in the intermediation margin explained by the increase in interest rates is 98 bp in the Eurozone, 231 bp in the USA, 117 bp in the UK, 31 bp in Japan and 61 bp in the group "other countries". During the subperiod of the crisis 2008–2014, interest rates fell primarily as a result of the expansionary monetary policy

Table 2.3 Observed changes in interest rate and yield slope curve and predicted changes in net interest margin (bp)

	Change in three-month interest rate 2003–2007	Predicted change in net interest margin 2003–2007	Change in three-month interest rate 2008–2014	Predicted change in net interest margin 2008–2014	Change in three-month interest rate 2003–2014	Predicted change in net interest margin 2003–2014
Eurozone	194	98	−442	−147	−212	−84
USA	412	231	−284	−107	−103	−43
UK	229	117	−495	−158	−313	−115
Japan	66	31	−64	−28	12	5
Other countries in the sample	126	61	−222	−87	−56	−24

Source: Authors' calculation

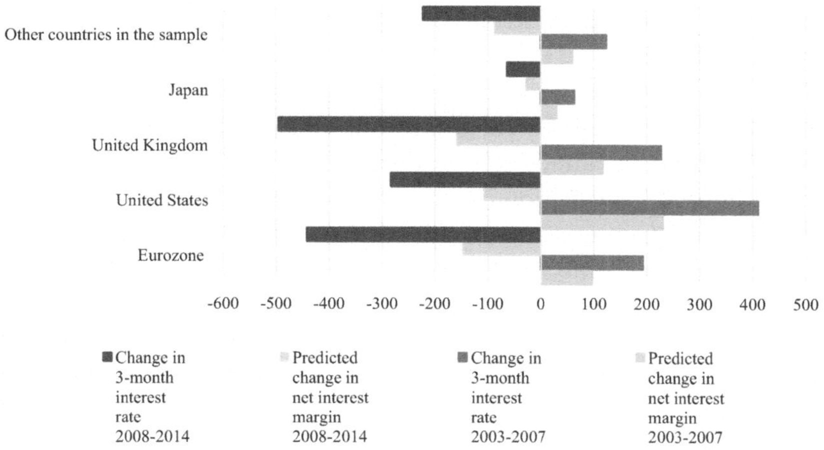

Fig. 2.5 Observed changes in interest rates and predicted changes in the net interest margin (bp). *Source: Authors' calculations*

measures taken, which led to a fall in the net interest margin of 147 bp in the Eurozone, 107 bp in the USA, 158 bp in the UK, 28 bp in Japan and 87 bp in the group "other countries". For the entire period analysed, the total effect of the variation in interest rates on the intermediation margin was a fall of 84 bp in the Eurozone, 43 bp in the USA, 115 bp in the UK, 24 bp in the group "other countries", and an increase of 5 bp in Japan.

2.6 Conclusions

A cause for concern today is the impact that unconventional monetary policy measures adopted by several central banks to combat the crisis could have on bank interest margins and thus on the profitability. Although the effect has been positive so far, the prolonged low level of interest rates in some countries (as is the case with those belonging to the Eurozone) might end up negatively affecting the intermediation margin, given the existence of a floor in the level of interest rates on bank deposits. The quadratic, rather than linear, relationship between net interest margin and interest rates mean that a further drop in rates will damage profitability.

In this context, the results obtained in this study for a large sample of banks in OECD countries for the period 2003–2014 confirm that the above-mentioned quadratic relationship does indeed exist. This indicates that the impact of a variation in interest rates is higher for low levels than for high values. Consequently, if this current scenario of very low-interest rates persists over time (and even worse, if there is a further drop), banking margins could be adversely affected and therefore, profitability.

This result is in line with the evidence obtained recently by Borio et al. (2015) and Claessens et al. (2016), who also obtained a positive quadratic relationship between net interest margin and the level of short-term interest rates.

An important implication of economic policy regarding the results obtained is that there is a trade-off between economic growth and financial stability associated with the impact of expansionary monetary policy when the level of interest rates is very low. Thus, while on the one hand expansionary measures are adopted to combat the crisis (increasing the rate of inflation and encouraging economic growth), the negative impact on the net interest margin also negatively affects the profitability of banks, thus increasing the likelihood of a systemic crisis.

In this context, of particular concern is the case of the banks in the Eurozone, which currently have a problem with low profitability as a consequence of the regulatory pressure and the high amount of non-performing assets. The fact that the inflation rate is well below the ECB target of 2% justifies the expansionary measures taken (such as the expanded asset purchase programme (APP) and the penalty of up to −0.4% of excess of reserve requirements and deposit facility). But taking into account the results obtained in this paper, these same measures can have a negative impact on bank profitability. This explains the IMF's recent warning (2016) not to further increase the negative interest rates on marginal deposit facility and excess reserves. Until now the expansionary monetary policy has stimulated the volume and quality of bank lending and, by this way, profitability. But now that interest rates are so low (even negative), monetary policy is holding back banks' profitability.

Notes

1. See Laubach and Williams (2015).
2. In the same vein, the recent study by Borio and Zabbai (2016) analyses both the negative and the positive effects of unconventional monetary policy measures that are being adopted. The authors conclude that although there is evidence that these measures are successful in improving financial conditions, over time they could have a negative impact on bank profitability.
3. Australia, Austria, Belgium, Canada, Colombia, Czech Republic, Denmark, Finland, France, Germany, Greece, Iceland, Ireland, Israel, Italy, Japan, Rep. Korea, Latvia, Netherlands, New Zealand, Norway, Poland, Portugal, Russian Federation, Slovak Republic, Slovenia, South Africa, Spain, Sweden, Switzerland, UK and USA.
4. The price of labour is approximated by the ratio of Staff costs/total assets.
5. The ratio own resources/assets is a capitalisation measurement with limitations, due to the influence of regulation on own resources, as a measure of risk aversion. Therefore, the results should be interpreted with caution.

Acknowledgments Authors gratefully acknowledge comments of an anonymous referee, the useful comments of Alin Marius Andrieş (discussant of the paper in the Wolpertinger Conference 2016) and the financial support of the Spanish Ministry of Science and Innovation (research project ECO2013-43959-R). Joaquin Maudos also acknowledges financial support of Generalitat Valenciana (research project PROMETEOII/2014/046). Paula Cruz-García also acknowledges financial support of Spanish Ministry of Education (FPU2014/00936).

References

Alessandri, P., and B. Nelson. 2015. Simple banking: Profitability and the yield curve. *Journal of Money, Credit and Banking* 47 (1): 143–175.

Allen, L. 1988. The determinants of bank interest margins: A note. *Journal of Financial and Quantitative Analysis* 23 (2): 231–235.

Angbazo, L. 1997. Commercial bank net interest margins, default risk, interest-rate risk and off-balance sheet banking. *Journal of Banking & Finance* 21: 55–87.

Arellano, M., and S. Bond. 1991. Some tests of specification for panel data: Monte Carlo evidence and an application to employment equations. *Review of Economic Studies* 58: 277–297.
Berg, S.A., and M. Kim. 1994. Oligopolistic Interdependence and the Structure of Production in Banking: An Empirical Evaluation. *Journal of Money, Credit and Banking,* 26 (2): 309–322.
Blundell, R., and S. Bond. 1998. Initial conditions and moment restrictions in dynamic panel data models. *Journal of Econometrics* 87 (1): 115–143.
Borio, C. E. and A. Zabai. 2016. Unconventional monetary policies: A re-appraisal. *BIS Working Papers*, 570.
Borio, C. E., L. Gambacorta, and B. Hofmann. 2015. The influence of monetary policy on bank profitability. *BIS Working Papers*, 514.
Busch, R. and C. Memmel. 2015. Banks' net interest margin and the level of interest rates, Discussion Papers 16/2015, *Deutsche Bundesbank, Research Centre.*
Carbó, S., and F. Rodriguez. 2007. The determinants of banks' margins in European banking. *Journal of Banking & Finance* 31: 2043–2063.
Claessens, S., N. Coleman, and M. Donnelly. 2016. Low-for-long interest rates and net interest margins of banks in advanced foreign economies. *IFDP Notes.*
Entrop, O., C. Memmel, B. Ruprecht, and M. Wilkens. 2015. Determinants of bank interest margins: Impact of maturity transformation. *Journal of Banking & Finance* 54: 1–19.
European Central Bank. 2016. *Annual Report.*
Genay, H., and R. Podjasek. 2014. What is the impact of a low interest rate environment on bank profitability? *Chicago Fed Letter*, (Jul).
Gerali, A., S. Neri, L. Sessa, and F. Signoretti. 2010. Credit and banking in a DSGE model of the euro area. *Journal of Money, Credit and Banking* 42: 107–141.
Ho, T., and A. Saunders. 1981. The determinants of banks interest margins: Theory and empirical evidence. *Journal of Financial and Quantitative Analysis* 16 (4): 581–600.
International Money Fund. 2016. Negative interest rate policy (NIRP): Implications for monetary transmission and bank profitability in the Euro Area. In *Euro Area Policies Selected Issues*, IMF Country Report No. 16/220.
Laubach T. and J. Williams. 2015. Measuring the natural rate of interest redux, Federal Reserve Bank of San Francisco. Working Paper, No. 2015–16, October.

Maudos, J., and J. Fernández de Guevara. 2004. Factors explaining the interest margin in the banking sectors of the European Union. *Journal of Banking & Finance* 28 (9): 2259–2281.

McShane and Sharpe. 1985. A time series/cross section analysis of the determinants of Australian Trading bank loan/deposit interest margins: 1962–1981. *Journal of Banking & Finance,* 9: 115–136.

Rostagno, M., U. Bindseil, A. Kamps, W. Lemke, T. Sugo, and T. Vlassopoulos. 2016. Breaking through the zero line: The ECB's negative interest rate policy. Presentation at Brookings Institution seminar negative interest rates: Lessons learned... so far, Washington D.C., June 6, 2016.

Saunders, A., and L. Schumacher. 2000. The determinants of bank interest rate margins: An international study. *Journal of International Money and Finance* 19: 813–832.

Wong, K.P. 1997. On the determinants of bank interest margins under credit and interest rate risk. *Journal of Banking & Finance* 21: 251–271.

Zarruk, E.R. 1989. Bank margins with uncertain deposit level and risk aversion. *Journal of Banking & Finance* 13: 797–810.

3

The Swedish Mortgage Market: Bank Funding, Margins, and Risk Shifting

Viktor Elliot and Ted Lindblom

3.1 Introduction

The Swedish household indebtedness is among the highest in the world (BCBS 2016), and the vast majority of this debt is mortgages.[1] The Swedish Bankers' Association (SBA 2015) reports that almost nine out of ten homeowner households are indebted, and the debt ratio of these households, measured as loans in relation to disposable income, has on average increased steadily since the mid-1990s. According to the Swedish Financial Supervisory Authority (SFSA 2016), in the first half of this decade, the share of households with a greater debt ratio than 450% has almost doubled (from ~35% in 2011 to ~60% in 2015). This is explained partly by the conversion of rental apartments, primarily in urban locations, into condominiums and, partly, as a result of rocketing property prices. Residential construction in urban areas has not been in pace with the growth of citizens in these areas, while the interest rate

V. Elliot (✉) · T. Lindblom
University of Gothenburg, Gothenburg, Sweden
e-mail: viktor.elliot@gu.se

G. Chesini et al. (eds.), *The Business of Banking*, Palgrave Macmillan Studies in Banking and Financial Institutions, DOI 10.1007/978-3-319-54894-4_3

environment has been and still is historically low. In the past 2 years, the repurchasing rate (repo rate) of the Swedish Central bank has been continuously cut and is, since February 1, 2015, below zero. In addition, the average monthly interest rates of treasury bills, 2-year government bonds, and, lately, 5-year government bonds are negative.

The extremely low interest rate environment has put pressure on mortgage interest rates offered by Swedish banks. At present, both the short- and the medium-term mortgage rates are down to the crisis and post-crisis levels in 2009–2010. The long-term rates are at an all-time low (in modern time) and substantially lower (150–200 basis points) than they were 6 years ago. Mortgage-lending accounts for approximately 30% of total lending provided by the major Swedish banks, and the banks have readily accommodated the growing demand for debt on the household market. In order to meet the increasing demand for household debt, the banks have gradually increased their reliance on market funding, a strategy that *ceteris paribus* implies higher funding costs and potentially lower margins. Considering the great importance of mortgage lending in the balance sheets of the major Swedish banks, it may appear as a paradox that these banks on average show high profitability in accounting as well as in market value terms. This suggests that the banks have been able to secure lower funding costs in some other way. As will be shown in this chapter, the implementation of the covered bonds legislation [see *"the Covered Bond (Issuance) Act (2003:1223*")], on the Swedish mortgage market in 2004, seems to be one major explanation for their profitability.

In 2006–2008, Swedish banks gradually replaced residential mortgage-backed bonds (MBS) with covered bonds (CB). The market for CBs has thereafter grown large in Sweden, making CBs one of the most important sources of funding for Swedish banks (Sandström et al. 2013).[2] Today, about a quarter of the banks' average total lending is financed by CBs. Certain properties (these are discussed in greater detail below) of the CBs make them *"often seen as close substitutes for high-quality government bonds"* (Prokopczuk et al. 2012: 1), suggesting lower risk for investors and lower risk premiums to be paid by the issuing bank. Hence, the bank can offer homeowners lower interest rates on granted mortgage loans and still make a "good" profit. This may seem as a "win-win-win" situation, but it is questionable whether it is sustainable in the long run. As noted by (Carbó-Valverde et al. 2012: 2) "*...banks might not view MBS and CB as substitutes since there are some real and regulatory differences between issuing MBS and issuing CB.*" We will argue throughout this chapter that these differences are fundamental to understand the risk shifting on the Swedish mortgage market and why Swedish banks have been able to maintain, or even increase, their margins on mortgages over the past decade.

More specifically, we aim to compare Swedish banks' mortgage lending and funding rates over a period of 15 years in order to illustrate changes in risk and bank mortgage margins stemming from the financial crisis and the move from the MBS regime to the CB regime. The study seeks to contribute to the ongoing debate of whether Sweden is heading for another real estate-related financial crisis. In Sect. 2, we outline the key characteristics of the MBS and the CB as well as discuss briefly the Swedish context and the increasing use of CBs on the Swedish market. Section 3 describes our method, and the results of our analysis are reported and discussed in Sect. 4. Section 5 concludes the chapter.

3.2 Covered Bonds—Essential Features

To understand the effects on risk shifting and profitability for banks when moving from the MBS to the CB as one of the key mortgage funding sources,[3] the first part of this section briefly compares the two securities. In many respects, CBs are similar to MBSs (Carbó-Valverde et al. 2012). Both have fixed maturities, their principal amount (face value) is repaid at maturity, and they are collateralized by a pool of underlying assets primarily in the form of residential mortgages. The most distinguishing feature differentiating the CB from the MBS is that the former is held on the balance sheet, whereas the latter is not (Larsson 2013). This means that the holder of a CB retains a dual recourse, i.e., a high-priority claim on the assets that serves as collateral in the cover pool *and* an unsecured claim on the assets of the issuing institution (the originator) in case of default (Schwarcz 2011, 2013; Martín et al. 2014). In addition, different from the MBS, the CB cover pool is dynamic

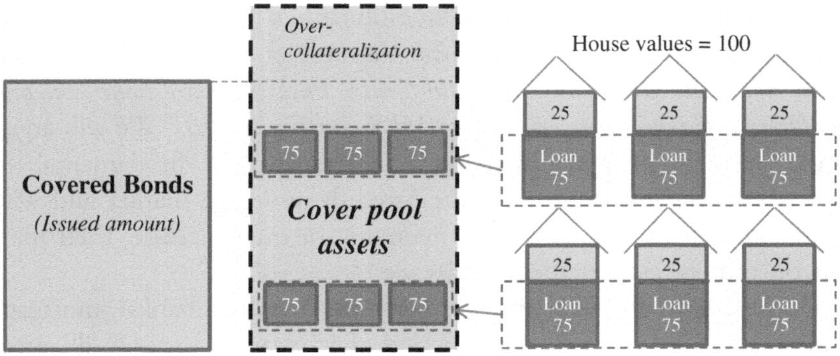

Fig. 3.1 Illustration of overcapitalization of CB issues

(Martín et al. 2014), requiring the issuer to continuously replace insufficient (low-quality) assets in the cover pool by assets of adequate quality over its full lifetime. The implied *"overcollateralization"* in terms of *"a surplus of collateral over indebtedness"* (Schwarcz 2013: 143) of the CB is illustrated in Fig. 3.1. As banks are also substituting prepaid and/or defaulted mortgages with new loans, it *"keeps the size of the pool predictable"* (Carbó-Valverde et al. 2012: 7).

Finally, CBs require frequent arm's-length assessments of the issuing banks' management of the cover pool by a third party. This party is either appointed by the issuer for approval by the regulator (i.e., under a special law-based framework, which is also referred to as a "legislative" CB regime) or stipulated by a contractual agreement (i.e., under a general law-based framework or a "structured" CB regime).

Over the past decade, the CB market has grown tremendously (at least until 2013 from when it has decreased somewhat). At the end of 2015, the global CB market included 30 countries with aggregate outstanding volumes of approximately EUR 2500 bn. The vast majority of the CB market is located in Europe, but in recent years countries such as Canada, Australia, New Zealand and Singapore have implemented regulatory frameworks allowing for CB issuance (ECBC 2016).

3.2.1 The Swedish Market for CBs

The debate about whether to allow CB issuance in Sweden was initiated in 1993 when the Swedish Bankers Association (SBA) submitted a white-collar paper to the Treasury Department in Sweden. It was argued that "Golden Bonds," as they were commonly called during that time, could mitigate a shortage of funding vehicles for large investors (primarily insurance firms) that was expected to rise when new legislation was introduced in 1994. The SBA suggested that Sweden would follow the Danish (and German) example and allow single investors an exception to the EU regulations for large exposures specifically for these golden bonds. In 1996, a government inquire was issued to shed further light on whether new legislation related to golden bonds was to be introduced. The report that followed the inquiry (SOU 1997) concluded that there were no major reasons to allow golden bonds issuance, and the introduction was put on hold. The SBA continued to argue for CBs, and in 2003, the legislation was changed to allow CB issuance in Sweden.

Like in many other countries in the EU, CBs are issued under a legislative regime in Sweden. This suggests that there is *"a high degree of certainty regarding the investors' legal rights and responsibilities in the event of issuer insolvency, and lower transaction costs in structuring a covered bond transaction"* (Schwarcz 2011: 569). It also means that issues of CBs, as well as measures that might have to be taken during their lifetime, are more rigid than under the alternative structured CB regime.[4] At the beginning of 2006, there were three issuing financial institutions on the Swedish CB market (SBA 2015). The following year three additional institutions joined, and at present, there are eight issuing financial institutions on the Swedish CB market. As shown in Fig. 3.2, the outstanding stock of CBs has more than quadruplet since 2006, making Sweden the fifth largest CB market in the world in terms of volumes.

In 2014, the four largest banks in Sweden accounted for 83% of the total stock. Three of these banks issue CBs through their own "building societies," which are sanctioned by the SFSA to act as issuers of CBs. As illustrated in Fig. 3.3, in this model, the funds obtained by the issuing

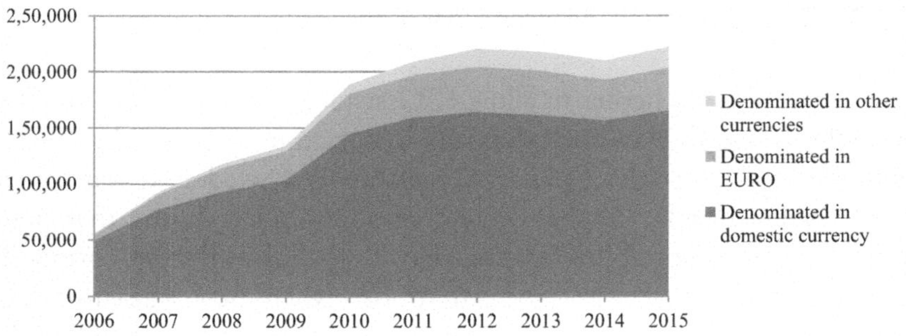

Fig. 3.2 Growth (in mEuro) of outstanding CBs on the Swedish market since 2006. *Source* Data from the Association of Swedish Covered Bond issuers

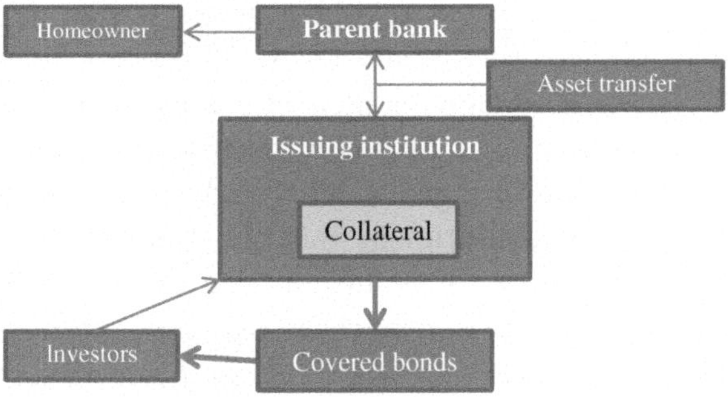

Fig. 3.3 Indirect issuing of CBs through a bank-owned "building society"

institution are transferred to the parent bank for financing its mortgage lending to primarily homeowners.

The remaining large bank and some of the other institutions are issuing CBs directly by themselves. Their model is illustrated in Fig. 3.4.

Financial institutions that issue CBs on the Swedish market are legally required to act as market makers on the secondary market for outstanding CBs. In order to reduce the risk of not being able to refinancing maturing CBs, it is common that issuing institutions repurchase a large share of the CBs about 9–12 months before the maturity date. This is commonly done by offering investors to exchange maturing bonds for bonds with a longer maturity and (likely) another interest rate

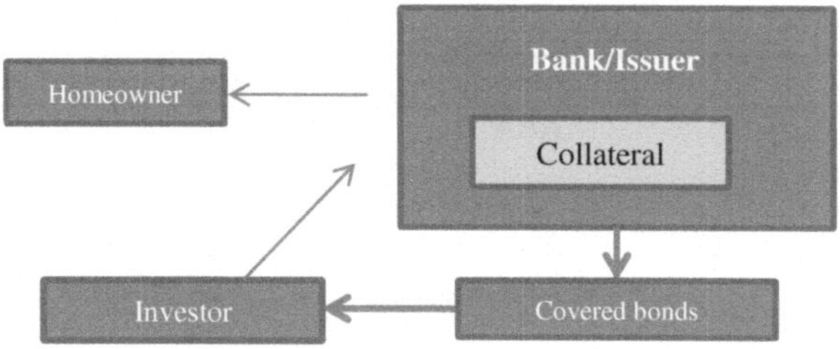

Fig. 3.4 Direct issuing of CBs through a bank-owned "building society"

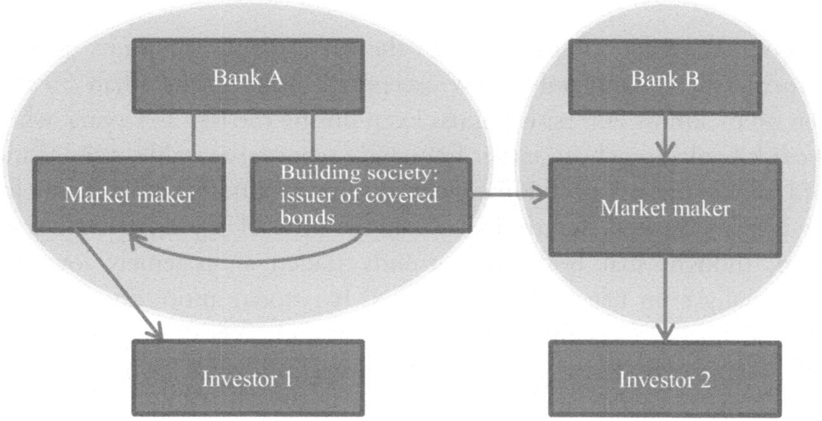

Fig. 3.5 Illustration of the roles of actors involved in CB issues. *Source* Based on Sandström et al. (2013: 8)

(Sandström et al. 2013). The roles of the different actors on the secondary market are illustrated in Fig. 3.5.

As shown in Table 3.1, the Swedish CBs are highly rated by international rating agencies. Due to the high credit ratings, the CBs are expected to be traded at prices (interest rates) at par with or close to government bonds (cf. Prokopczuk et al. 2012). The diagram in Fig. 3.9 (see Appendix) reveals that this has been only partly true since these bonds were introduced on the Swedish market. From 2004 to mid-2007, the spreads between 2- and 5-year CBs and government bonds were very small. At some occasions, the risk premium of the 2-year CBs was even

Table 3.1 Credit ratings of CBs issued by Swedish institutions

	Moody's	Standard and Poor's
Swedbank	AAA	Aaa
Handelsbanken	–	Aaa
Landshypotek	AAA/Stable	–
Länsförsäkringar Bank	AAA/Stable	Aaa/Stable
Nordea	AAA/Stable	Aaa/Stable
SBAB/SCBC	–	Aaa
SEB	–	Aaa
Skandiabanken	–	Aaa

Source Collected from the webpage of each institution, 2016-09-28

negative. However, after mid-2007, the average risk premiums of both maturities have, with only a few exceptions, been greater than 50 and even up to almost 200 basis points. Even during the last 2–3 years, when Swedish banks have been rather frequently reported as stable, strong, and solid banks, the risk premiums seem to settle around 50 basis points for the 2-year CBs and slightly higher for the ones of 5-year. It should be noted, though, that both are currently traded at extremely low and occasionally even negative interest rates. It is today more expensive for banks to finance their mortgage lending through deposits and savings—even *before* considering operational transaction costs. How this has affected the mortgage rates offered by the banks is examined in Sect. 4.

3.3 Sources of Data and Selection of Banks

There is no comprehensive database covering the Swedish mortgage market, the CB market and the banks mortgage rates together. Accordingly, we have relied on several different sources to collect the data for our analysis including the Swedish Bankers' Association (SBA), the Swedish Central bank (Riksbanken), the Swedish Financial Supervisory Authority (SFSA), Statistics Sweden (SCB), and the Swedish banks.

While volumes and bond rates are actual, it should be noted that there is no publically available data on actual mortgage interest rates.[5] To mitigate this problem, we have relied on the officially offered interest rates by the banks as a proxy for actual rates paid. However, since mid-2015, Swedish banks are by law required to reveal their actual average mortgage rates on a monthly basis providing some indication of the rates that consumers of mortgages actually pay (this is further discussed in the next section).

We have selected five banks [Swedbank, Svenska Handelsbanken (including Stadshypotek), Skandinaviska Enskilda Banken (SEB), Nordea and SBAB (including Swedish Covered Bond Corporation)] which together dominate the Swedish markets for residential mortgages and CBs. The combined market shares of these five banks summed up to approximately 90% on both markets in 2014, and their market shares have remained stable over the time period studied, i.e., 2000–2016 (SBA 2015). These five banks also offer publicly available data about their officially offered mortgage rates over the full period (except Svenska Handelsbanken from which data are available between 2005[6] and 2016).

Table 3.2 offers an overview of importance of mortgage lending (between 30 and 70% of total lending to the public are residential mortgages) and CB funding in the selected banks.

In the next section, we analyze the interest-rate environment on the Swedish mortgage market focusing on bank margins and risk shifting. Because of the dispersion of data sources that our analysis is based on we try to, as far as possible, clarify the limitations of the data in connection to each of the figures presented.

Table 3.2 Key figures (in SEKm) of selected banks as of December 31, 2015

	Lending to the public	Deposits from the public	Outstanding CBs	Equity	Total assets
Nordea	3,132,884	1,776,716	1,024,762	285,169	5,944,393
Handelsbanken	1,866,467	753,855	603,952	128,268	2,522,133
SEB	1,353,386	883,785	310,178	142,798	2,495,964
Swedbank	1,413,955	748,271	531,219	123,342	2,148,855
SBAB	296,981	76,639	187,280	11,848	374,552
Total	**8,063,673**	**4,239,266**	**2,657,391**	**691,425**	**13,485,897**

Note that these are group level figures and include the banks' foreign operations
Source Data from the Swedish Bankers Association and the Annual Reports of individual banks

3.4 Mortgage Rates of Swedish Banks

In the new Millennium, banks operating on the Swedish market have increased their lending to households, non-financial business firms and other organizations in each year but 2009. In total, the banks' lending has more than tripled between 2000 and 2015. This corresponds to an average annual increase by almost 8%. Approximately, half of the lending is used to finance private homes through mortgages. This lending has in fact increased annually without any interruption during the specified period of study. Residential mortgages are offered to variable (3 months) as well as fixed interest rates over various maturities (1–10 years).[7] In the Appendix, Fig. 3.10 displays how the interest rates, officially offered by the five major Swedish banks that grant residential mortgages, on average have developed until today for 3-month, 2, 5, and 10-year fixed mortgage rates, respectively.

The diagram in Fig. 3.10 exhibits a clear tendency of decreasing official interest rates on both short- and long-term residential mortgages. On average, the offered interest rates by the five banks did increase between mid-2005 and the financial crisis, but since mid-2011, their average interest rates have declined steadily. A more detailed analysis, which is displayed in Fig. 3.11, reveals that the offered interest rates by the individual banks deviated relatively more at the beginning of the period. The diagrams in the figure show that this has been the case for the offered short-term rates, in particular. The officially offered 3-month rates of the banks differed markedly (up to 85 basis points between the lowest and highest offered average monthly rate) until October 2007. Subsequently, these rates have barely deviated at all until April 2015. Except for a few single months, the standard deviation did on a monthly basis vary between 1 and 10 basis points only. The fixed 2-year and 5-year interest rates offered by the banks display a similar pattern—albeit not as pronounced and to the end of 2004 only. After the introduction of CBs, these rates have converged and with a few exceptions barely differed until April 2015. The fixed 10-year mortgage rates have been less differentiated during the lion part of the period. On average, the 10-year mortgage rates show the largest deviation in 2000 and in the aftermath of the financial crisis from 2009 to 2011. Like the other officially offered mortgage rates, from April 2015 and onward the banks' highest and lowest offered 10-year mortgage rates have differed more extensively.

3.4.1 Residential Mortgage Rates and Bank Margins

Figure 3.7 displays the average discount given by the banks from May 2015 to May 2016. We have no information of the average discounts on the banks' mortgage rates prior to 2015, let alone to the actual interest rates paid by their customers. It seems reasonable to assume that discounts have been given in a similar range as displayed in Fig. 3.6, but it is less likely to assume that the largest discounts are given on shorter-term lending rates. In a less low rate environment, the opposite may very well be the case.

Assuming that Figs. 3.10 and 3.11 reflect the interest rates charged by the banks on their mortgage lending accurately in relative terms; competition in banks' mortgage lending at the beginning and toward the very end of the period seems rather week. This observation is in accordance with the SBA (2011) report in which it is concluded that the banks' mortgage lending increased markedly from 2000 to 2007. Under this period, the market shares of the five banks have remained intact.

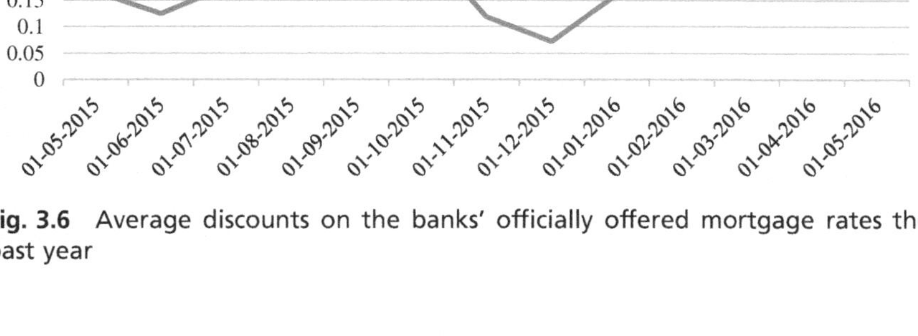

Fig. 3.6 Average discounts on the banks' officially offered mortgage rates the past year

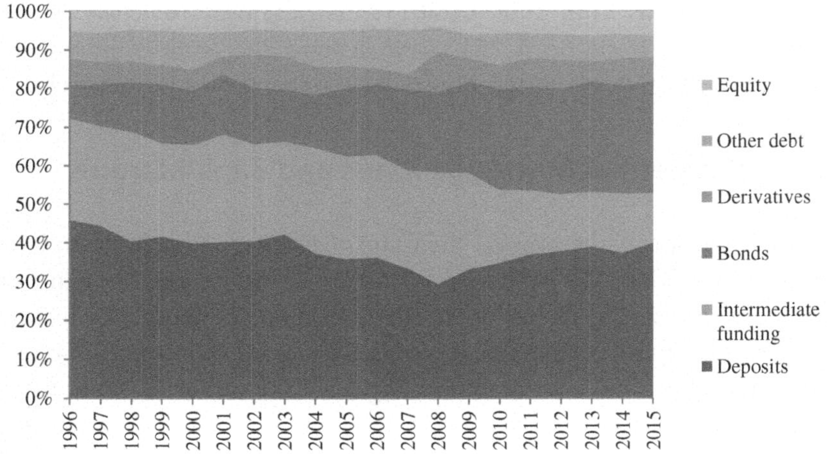

Fig. 3.7 Aggregate bank funding 1996–2015. *Source* Data from the Swedish Bankers Association

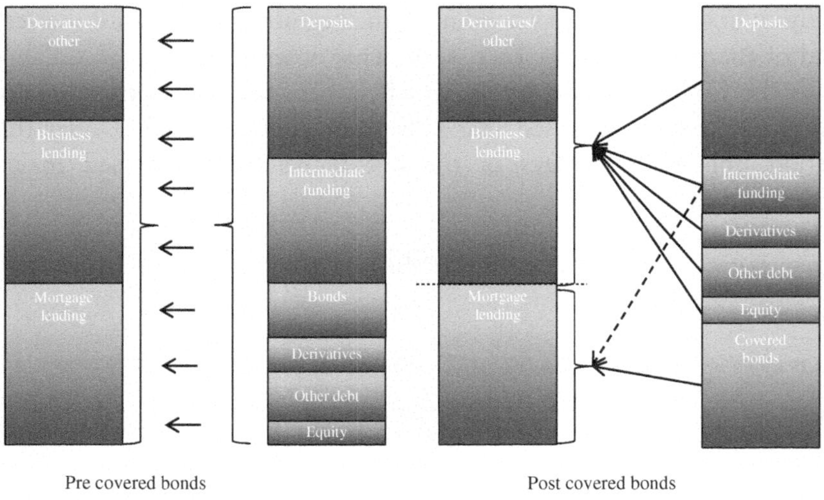

Fig. 3.8 Pre- and post-CB claims by different bank funds providers on bank assets in case of bankruptcy

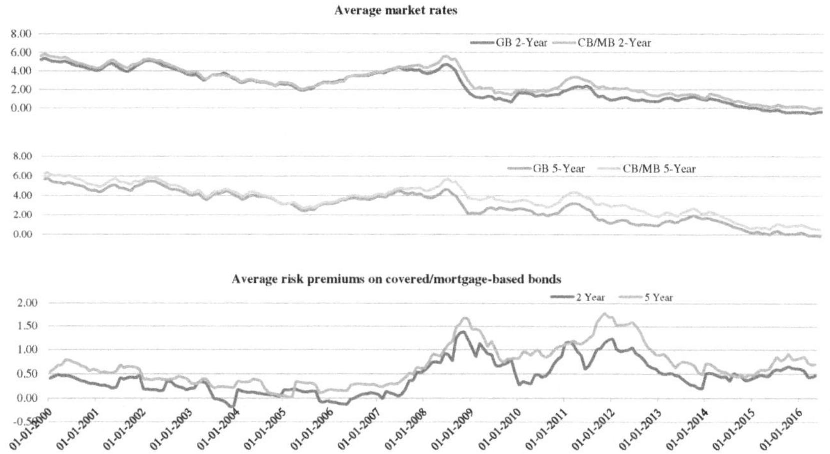

Fig. 3.9 Average market rates and risk premiums on 2- and 5-year covered bonds (CB/MB) relative government bonds (GB) for 2000–2016

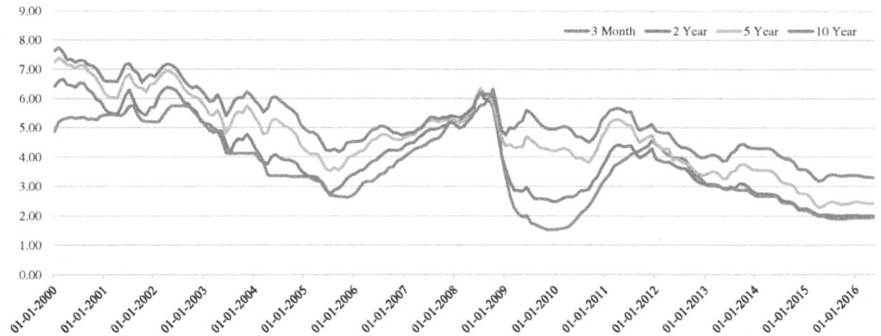

Fig. 3.10 Average official mortgage rates of the five Swedish "mortgage" banks from 2000 to 2016

However, on average, their lending portfolio changed dramatically. First, the share of renewed mortgage loans with variable rates declined to around 50% or less. This share increased again during 2008 and, particularly 2009, in which year the proportion of new mortgage loans with a variable (3-month) interest rate peaked at 85%. Second, mortgage loans with fixed medium-term interest rates over one to 5 years gained popularity from 2000 to 2007. In contrast to this development, Fig. 3.12

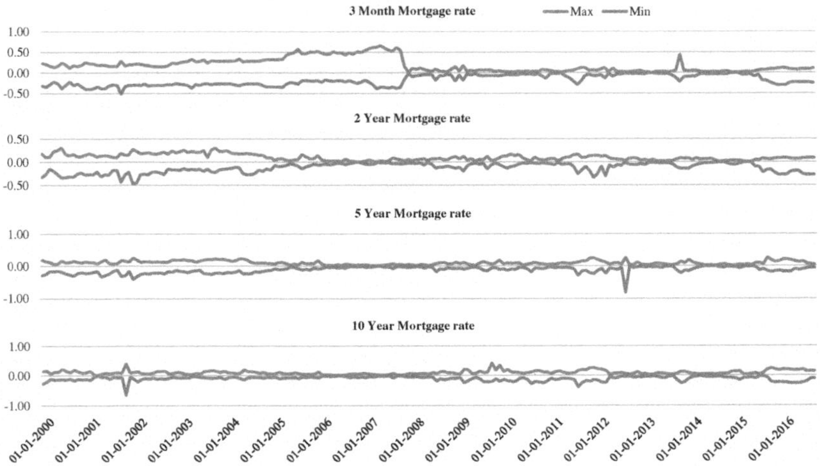

Fig. 3.11 Deviations of the banks' officially offered mortgage rates from 2000 to 2016

suggests that the average bank earned more on loans with a "variable" interest rate during this period. From early 2001 to the end of 2007, the average margin on 3-month mortgage loans was equal to or greater than the corresponding margins on medium- and long-term fixed rate loans. Irrespective of the interest rate maturities, the average mortgage margins have increased significantly from the end of 2011. To what extent this is the case does of course depends on the actual interest rates charged by the banks. Considering their average discounts, all mortgage rate margins become lower. At the end of the period, the average interest rate margins on the banks' mortgage loans with long-term fixed rates became more attractive for the banks in relative terms. On average, their greatest margins were still on the 3-month and 2-year interest rate maturities.

Our comparative analysis hitherto rests on the assumption that the average bank continuously matches the interest rate maturities on its borrowing and lending. However, the financial crisis clearly showed that Swedish banks were in general borrowing short and lending long (cf. Lindblom et al. 2011). In Fig. 3.13, the average interest rate margins for mortgage loans are computed as the difference between the offered mortgage rates on the loans of the average bank and the 3-month

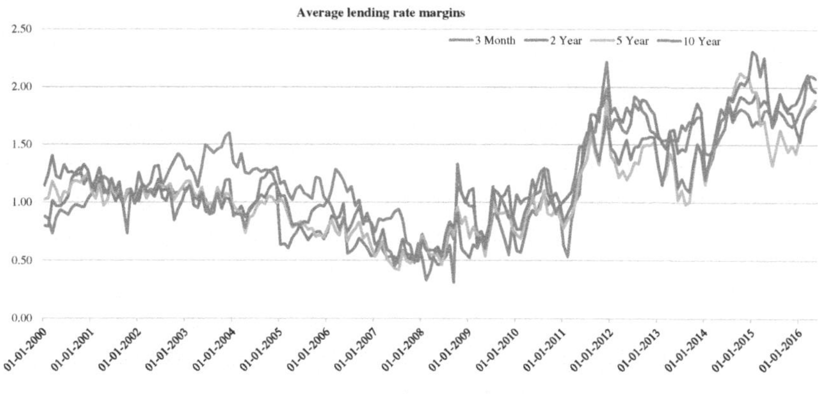

Fig. 3.12 Marginal mortgage lending margins of the average bank from 2000 to 2016

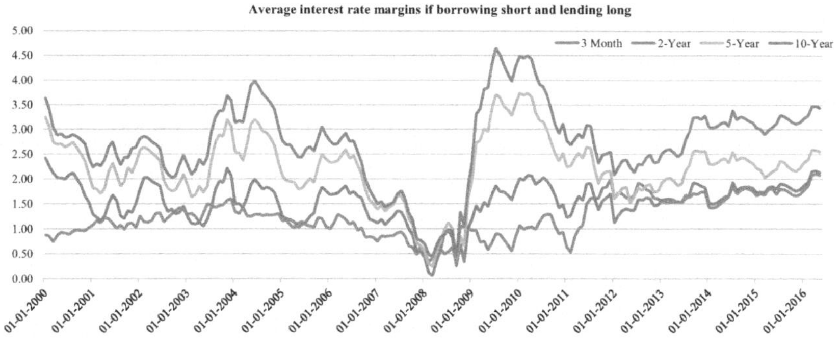

Fig. 3.13 Illustration of average interest rate margins if borrowing short and lending long

funding rate. Figure 3.13 demonstrates what can be interpreted as a temptation for borrowing short and lending long. Instead of interest rate margins around 1%, the banks would get considerably greater margins by financing medium- and long-term fixed rate mortgages with short-term funds. These funds include ordinary savings and deposits, which constitute important sources of funds for Swedish banks.

The diagram in Fig. 3.13 suggests that it would be profitable for the average bank to borrow short and lend long during the first years after the outbreak of the financial crisis, too. However, the banks almost lent to the 3-month rate only in 2009, and thereafter, they seem to have adapted to the gradually implemented new regulatory regime, which is focused on both sustainable capital adequacy and liquidity reserve requirements for banks. Figure 3.12 shows that the lending margins of the average bank have in general been around 1.5–2% from early 2012 and onward. In pace with the increasingly lower interest rates on government securities and outstanding CBs, the banks seem to have been able to increase their average margins steadily on mortgage loans with different interest rate maturities.

3.4.2 Risk Shifting and CB Funding on the Swedish Mortgage Market

In some countries, like Canada and Australia, the local regulators impose a cap on CB issuance in order to limit the subordination of depositors to CB investors. As exemplified by Fig. 3.7, Sweden has followed the Danish and German tradition without any caps. The figure shows that starting in 2006, CBs have gradually replaced intermediate funding among the Swedish banks. The figure clearly shows that this trend started prior to the financial crisis (2008–2009) and the introduction of new liquidity regulations (2013) in Sweden.

To illustrate the risk shifting that this change in funding imposes, Fig. 3.8 compares the pre- and post-CB claims by different bank funds providers on bank assets in case of bankruptcy. As shown in the figure, the non-CB funds providers are made substantially worse off in a bank insolvency situation and as will be further discussed in our concluding remarks, and this should be reflected in the price that banks have to pay for non-CB funds.

3.5 Concluding Remarks

This paper set out compare Swedish banks' mortgage lending and funding rates over a period of 15 years. By illustrating changes in risk and bank mortgage margins stemming from the financial crisis and the move from the MBS regime to the CB regime, we seek to contribute to the ongoing debate on whether Sweden is heading for another real estate-related financial crisis. Our instruments are the lending and funding rates, and our analysis points to at least three key insights.

Firstly, the move from MBS to CBs means that the funding costs should, all else equal, go down for the Swedish banks. While there may exist systemic uncertainties related to the shifting of risk (through seniority), the banks seem to have been able to translate the reduced funding costs into higher margins on mortgages. From a crisis perspective, this may be seen as a good thing as the banks are able to charge higher premiums, which will work as an extra cushion during a crisis.

Secondly, prior to the crisis banks relied heavily on short-term funding to finance mortgages. The lessons from the 2007/2009 financial crisis, in combination with a stricter regulatory framework, have led to a better matching between the asset and liability side of their balance sheets. This process should be costly, both in terms of funding and administrative costs. However, the banks have been able to internalize these costs and still remain highly profitable, and we show that this seems to work through two interrelated channels—the move to a CBs regime as discussed above and through limited competition. The latter is also supported by our previous work (see Elliot 2015; Elliot and Lindblom 2015, 2016).

Thirdly, some propagators of a soon to strike financial crisis in Sweden have compared the current situation to the period leading up to the Swedish financial crisis in the early 1990s. However, several important differences have been discussed that may have implications for whether this claim is true or not: (i) the indebtedness growth is much larger this time, (ii) the currency is no longer fixed, (iii) the inflation is close to zero and interest rates are either close to or even below zero, and (iv) the financial service sector is currently moving toward a much stricter regulatory regime, whereas the late 1980s was marked by deregulation. We add to these differences by providing evidence that the banks, in contrast to the period prior to crisis in the 1990s, have been able to maintain high margins while also reducing their risk (through higher capital ratios, more liquid assets and better matching between assets and liabilities). Thus, even though we do not wish to make a claim as to whether a new crisis is on the horizon, this paper indicates that the Swedish banks are at least better prepared this time.

We strongly suggest that future research extends the analysis related to the risk shifting outlined in this chapter. It seems particularly relevant to analyze whether non-CB providers of bank funds charge a higher price when banks replace MBS funding with CB funding. Such analysis will need to account for the fact that depositors may be insensitive to bank credit risk because of deposit insurance schemes. Accordingly, we suggest the analysis to focus on subordinated bank debt (such as contingent convertibles and bank equity).

Notes

1. There exists no systematic data on the composition of household debt but Statistics Sweden estimates that approximately 80% of total household indebtedness is mortgages.
2. According to ECBC (2014), the Swedish CB market belongs to the five largest in the world and in 2013; Sweden was the second largest issuer of new covered bonds.
3. A mortgage loan in Sweden typically consists of four key components: CBs (both in SEK and Euro), other bonds, deposits and equity, and the vast majority of bank funding consist of CBs and deposits.
4. As is described and thoroughly explained by, e.g., Schwarcz (2011), both the legislative and the structured covered bond regimes are each subject to pros and cons. The structured covered bond regime may be less certain regarding legal aspects (which are to be contractually specified) and give rise to higher transaction costs, but this regime tends to offer greater flexibility for the parties to, for example, adjust to changing market conditions.
5. Private as well as business customers commonly negotiate discounts in the range of 10–100 basis points.
6. From 2005, the 3-month rates are available, whereas the other maturities are made available from 2008.
7. After the financial crisis, banks no longer offer mortgage rates on a daily basis. In our analysis, the 3-month rate is regarded as a variable rate.

References

BCBS. 2016. BIS Statistical Bulletin, available at https://www.bis.org/statistics/bulletin1612.htm.

Carbó-Valverde, Santiago, Richard J. Rosen, and Francisco Rodríguez-Fernández. 2012. Are covered bonds a substitute for mortgage-backed securities? *Federal Reserve Bank of Chicago,* WP 2011–2014.

ECBC. 2014. ECBC Publication—September—9th edition.

ECBC. 2016. ECBC Publication—August—11th edition.

ECBC. http://ecbc.hypo.org/Content/Default.asp?PageID=503.

Elliot, V. 2015. *Performance management systems, regulation and change in Swedish Banks*. Dissertation. BAS Publisher: Gothenburg.

Elliot, V. and Lindblom, T. 2015. Funds transfer pricing in banks: Implications of Basel III. In *Performance Management Systems, Regulation and Change in Swedish Banks,* ed. V. Elliot. Dissertation, BAS Publisher: Gothenburg.

Elliot, V. and Lindblom, T. 2016. Funds transfer pricing in banks under different market structures. Working paper.

Larsson, C.F. 2013. What did Frederick the great know about financial engineering? A survey of recent covered bond market developments and research. *The North American Journal of Economics and Finance* 25: 22–39.

Lindblom, T., M. Olsson, and M. Willesson. 2011. Financial Crisis and Bank Profitability. In *Bank Performance,* ed. P. Molyneux, 83–105. Risk and Firm Financing, Basingstoke, UK: Palgrave Macmillan.

Martín, Rebeca A., José M. Marqués Sevillano, and Luna R. González. 2014. Covered bonds: The Renaissance of an old acquaintance, *Banks and Bank Systems* 9 (1): 46–60.

Prokopczuk, Marcel, Jan B. Siewert, and Volker Vonhoff. 2012. Credit Risk in Covered Bonds (working paper, September 20).

Sandström, Maria, David Forsman, Johanna Stenkula von Rosen, and Johanna Fager Wettergren. 2013. Marknaden för svenska säkerställda obligationer och kopplingar till den finansiella stabiliteten, *Penning- och valutapolitik,* vol. 2.

Schwarcz, Steven L. 2011. The Conundrum of Covered Bonds, *The Business Lawyer* 66: 56.

Schwarcz, Steven L. 2013. Securitization, Structured Finance, and Covered Bonds. *The Journal of Corporation Law* 39 (1): 129–154.

SBA. 2011. *Bank- och finansstatistik.* Swedish Bankers' Association: Stockholm.

SBA. 2015. *Bank och Finansstatistik.* Bankföreningen: Stockholm.

SFSA. 2016. Tillsynen över bankerna och kreditmarknadsföretagen, Dnr 15-15698.

SOU. 1997. *Säkrare obligationer? Statens offentliga utredningar 1997:110.* Finansdepartementet: Stockholm.

4

Incapability or Bad Luck? Testing the "Bad Management" Hypothesis in the Italian Banking System

Fabrizio Crespi and Mauro Aliano

4.1 Introduction

The pattern of growth of nonperforming loans (NPLs) in the banking sector of a country has always been considered an important issue in determining the onset of a banking crisis and the consequent instruments that should be used by authorities to prevent bank failures.

In this chapter, we add a contribution to the strand of literature starting with Berger and DeYoung (1997), by testing the "bad management hypothesis" in the Italian banking sector using a more detailed dataset about the composition of NPLs: That means that we can distinguish between substandard/past due loans and restructured exposures, on the one hand, and bad loans on the other. This possibility allows us to investigate if and how much the substandard/past due loans and restructured exposures translate into bad loans over time or, put in a

F. Crespi (✉) · M. Aliano
University of Cagliari, Cagliari, Italy
e-mail: Fabrizio.crespi@unicatt.it

G. Chesini et al. (eds.), *The Business of Banking*, Palgrave Macmillan Studies in Banking and Financial Institutions, DOI 10.1007/978-3-319-54894-4_4

different way, we can prove if credit managers are able to recover, at least partially, problematic credits. This part of the analysis is a novel in literature: Preceding studies have not investigated in this specific way the worsening in credit quality, which may indeed suggest the management incapability, *ceteris paribus,* to manage bad loans. In this regard, starting from our proprietary database, we insert a measure of bank credit health among the determinants of NPLs which acts as proxy of a worsening in the quality of credit.

We created a dataset composed of 48 banks of a single country (Italy) which cover about 82% of the market (measured as total assets in 2013), and we investigate a critical period for the Italian banking sector lasting four years (2010–2013): This stretch of time covers in fact the preceding period and the aftermath of the government debt crisis in Italy (2011–2012) and corresponds with a strong increase in NPLs for the entire banking system.

Considering that all banks in our sample operate mainly in Italy and are subject to the same economic conditions, we exclude macroeconomic explanatory variables from our analysis. We also prefer to investigate a group of banks of one single country, avoiding a comparison with other banking systems in which different economic conditions and accounting rules could alter the significance of results (see Barisitz, 2011). The choice of Italy as a laboratory for our analysis is due to the better information about NPLs that we could get from bank balance sheets and to the critical importance and enormous volume of NPLs in the Italian banking sector: just to have an idea, the ratio of NPLs on loans was about 18% at the end of 2015, compared with a 3% in France and a 2% in the USA.

The results of our study confirm the "bad management hypothesis" first introduced by Berger and DeYoung (1997). Indeed, we find that more specialized banks and more efficient banks tend to have a better quality of credit. More interesting, from our point of view, is the general relationship between substandard/past due loans, restructured exposures, and bad loans. Our results indicate that problematic loans tend to transform into bad loans, demonstrating that credit managers were not able to implement recovery strategies for these critical positions during the investigated period. We think our results can be considered an interesting contribution to the strand of the literature regarding NPLs and bad management.

The rest of the chapter is organized as follows. Section 4.2 presents an overview of the main strands of literature about the determinants of NPLs. Section 4.3 briefly presents the characteristics of our dataset. Section 4.4 describes the model and the variable used to investigate the relationships between bank-specific determinants and NPLs. Section 4.5 presents the results of our analysis, and finally, Sect. 4.6 summarizes our findings.

4.2 Determinants of NPLs: Main Strands of Literature

The literature on NPLs is extensive and covers different topics regarding the causes and effects of deterioration of credit quality. However, in the majority of studies that investigate the determinants of NPLs, three topics can be considered fundamentals. The first is related to a strand of literature that investigates macroeconomic explanatory variables. A second group of studies emphasize the effect of bank-specific characteristics on problem loans; in particular, researchers have long since investigated the relationship between NPLs and bank efficiency (usually measured through a cost frontier approach). A third strand of literature combines macroeconomic (country-specific factors) and microeconomic variables (bank-specific factors) to explain aggregate NPLs.

4.2.1 Macroeconomic Factors

Various papers about NPLs start from the evidence that behind every financial crisis there are macroeconomic factors (or systematic factors) which influence the creditworthiness of borrowers. These studies commonly compare data from different countries (see Beck et al. 2013; Klein 2013) over a long period of time with the aim to evaluate the impact of different phases of the economic cycle on the appearing of NPLs.

The main results of this part of literature can be summarized as follows. First of all, there is significant empirical evidence regarding the anti-cyclical behavior of the NPLs, where real GDP growth can be considered the main driver of NPLs, i.e., higher real GDP growth translates into more income which improves the debt-servicing capacity of borrowers. Conversely, when there is a slowdown in the economy, the level of NPLs is likely to increase as unemployment rises and borrowers face greater difficulties to repay their debt.

Beck et al. (2013), in a comprehensive study of 75 countries over a ten-year period, confirm that real GDP growth has a negative impact on NPLs when considered through a fixed effects model, but, using dynamic Arellano-Bond estimations, also appears that lagged GDP growth significantly affects NPLs with a positive sign; this finding suggests that bank asset quality deteriorates with a lag in response to positive growth due to loose credit standards applied during the boom period. In any case, the authors affirm that economic activity is not able to fully explain the evolution of nonperforming loans across countries and over time; additional factors may negatively affect asset quality in countries with specific vulnerabilities. For example, exchange rate depreciations lead to an increase of nonperforming loans in countries with a high degree of lending in foreign currencies to unhedged borrowers; further, an increase in lending interest rates tend to increase NPLs.

Other macroeconomic variables, which were found to affect bank's asset quality, include disposable income (Rinaldi and Sanchis-Arellano 2006), lending interest rate and unemployment (Berge and Boye 2007), and inflation (Klein 2013).

Rinaldi and Sanchis-Arellano (2006) try to understand what explains household NPLs in seven euro area countries; their results suggest that, in the long run, an increase in the ratio of indebtedness to income is associated with higher levels of arrears. However, if the rise in the debt ratio is accompanied by a rise in disposable income, the negative effect is more than offset.

Similarly, Berge and Boye (2007) indicate that households' debt-servicing capacity generally depends on developments in their income, debt, borrowing rate, and collateral values. Higher incomes are expected to contribute to reducing the volume of problem loans.

However, incomes may be unevenly distributed across households. When unemployment is rising, many households may experience a substantial reduction in income. Using an equilibrium correction model of the logarithm of the share of problem loans (to total loans) in the household sector in Norway, during the period 1993–2005, the authors find that the share of problem loans could be reduced by 1.2% in the long run if real disposable income increases by 1%. On the other hand, a rise in the unemployment rate from 3 to 4% could increase the share of problem loans by just over 11%.

4.2.2 Bank-Specific Factors

Even if macroeconomic factors are rightly considerable the main cause of the increase of NPLs during time, they are not able to explain everything. In the same country, and in the same phase of the economic cycle, banks do normally register different amounts of NPLs in their balance sheets: It should then be obvious to think that also bank-specific factors influence bad loans. And in fact, various researchers have tried to discover significant relationships between NPLs and endogenous variables. The starting point of this strand of literature (or at least one of the most important contributions in this regard) can be considered the paper of Berger and Deyoung (1997).

The authors draw attention to the links between bank-specific characteristics and NPLs; using a Granger-causality analysis, they test a set of hypotheses that describe the intertemporal relationship among problem loans, cost efficiency, and financial capital. Specifically, they indicate four possible mechanisms, namely "bad luck," "bad management," "skimping," and "moral hazard," to formulate predictions of the link between credit quality and efficiency.

Under the "bad luck" hypothesis, external events precipitate an increase in problem loans for the bank. The bank is then forced to increase managerial effort and expenses dealing with the increase in problem loans.[1] Thus, under the bad luck hypothesis, we should expect increases in NPLs to Granger-cause (i.e., temporally precede) decreases in measured cost efficiency. Conversely, under the "bad management" hypothesis, low cost efficiency Granger-causes larger amounts of problem loans (a deterioration in asset quality) because management's failure to control operating costs immediately produces low cost efficiency, suggesting that poor managerial practice causes an increase in problem loans after a lag. The basic idea is that bad managers do not sufficiently monitor and control their operating expense, which is reflected in low measured cost efficiency. Specifically, so-called bad managers exhibit the following tendencies. They are not adept at credit scoring and select a relatively high proportion of investments with low or negative net present values; collateral against loans is improperly valued; and customers are not sufficiently monitored in order to ensure compliance with the loan contract. It is important to note that "bad luck" hypothesis and "bad management" hypothesis have an opposite temporal order, but both predict that NPLs will be negatively associated with cost efficiency.[2]

Under the "skimping" hypothesis, it is implied that resources allocated to underwriting and monitoring of loans affect both loan quality and measured cost efficiency. Banks face a trade-off between short-term operating costs and future loan quality. Management may choose to minimize short-term operating costs by reducing expenditure on monitoring borrowers in an attempt to enhance long-term profitability. Therefore, management delays having to deal with deterioration in asset quality until an unspecified future date. Thus, under the skimping hypothesis, we should expect a positive Granger-causation from measured efficiency to problem loans (i.e., an opposite sign in comparison with the bad management hypothesis). Finally, the "moral hazard" hypothesis implies that low financial capital Granger-cause high NPLs; the idea behind this hypothesis is that banks' managers have moral hazard incentives to increase the riskiness of their loan portfolios when their banks are thinly capitalized. The "moral hazard" hypothesis is then based on the classical problem of excessive risk-taking when another party is bearing part of the risk and cannot easily charge for or prevent that risk-taking.

The results of the study of Berger and DeYoung suggest that the intertemporal relationships between loan quality and cost efficiency run in both directions. However, the data favor the bad management hypothesis over the bad luck hypothesis and the skimping hypothesis. Finally, decreases in bank capital ratios generally precede increases in NPLs for banks with low capital ratios (moral hazard hypothesis).

Following the methodology of Berger and DeYoung, Williams (2004) investigates management behavior in European saving banks from six European countries (Denmark, France, Germany, Italy, Spain, and the UK), between 1990 and 1998.[3] The results of Williams are mixed: Managers in German banks exhibit strong statistical evidence of bad management, while there is weaker statistical evidence of bad management in Danish and Italian banks.

Podpiera and Weill (2008) continue along this line of research and examine the relationship between efficiency and bad loans in the Czech banking industry from 1994 to 2005. They extend the Granger-causality model developed by Berger and DeYoung by applying GMM dynamic panel estimators. Their findings provide empirical evidence in favor of a negative relationship between decreased cost efficiency and future NPLs (i.e., the bad management hypothesis). Interestingly, Podpiera and Weil use two different measures to assess credit quality: the conventional ratio of NPLs on total loans and a so-called compensated risk taking measure, which account for the fact that a certain amount of NPLs is normally expected and accounted for in the interest required on such more risky loans. Thus, the actual (uncompensated) risk-taking measure of a particular bank (associated with unexpected events) might be smaller if the bank gets sufficiently compensated on interest revenues from the entire loan portfolio. Therefore, a second measure is introduced and formulated as the share of NPLs in total loans minus the share of interest revenues in total loans. Indeed, if bank managers choose consciously to increase the risk of the loans portfolio, we should expect immediately an increase in interest revenue, and later an increase in NPLs. In this case, the risk of NPLs could be considered well priced in the conditions of loans, and the management behavior riskier but justified.

Other studies in the same stream include Karim et al. (2010) and Louzis et al. (2012); the former investigates bank efficiency and NPLs in Malaysia and Singapore and reaches conclusions similar to those of Berger and DeYoung; the latter is a more complex analysis, in which both macroeconomic and bank-specific determinants are taken into account (see Sect. 4.2.3).

In most cases, these kinds of studies are run using data from single countries and not considering macroeconomic factors in connection with bank-specific determinants.

4.2.3 Micro and Macro Approach

As indicated above, explanations of the size and growth of NPLs can be traced back to macroeconomic factors or to bank internal characteristics; *ça va sans dire* that these two set of causes could be analyzed jointly.

There are indeed few studies which follow this approach; they include, for example, Salas and Saurina (2002) which compare determinants of problem loans of Spanish commercial and saving banks using both macroeconomic and individual bank-level variables; Williams (2004) which investigates management behavior at European saving banks located in six different countries; and Klein (2013) which uses four explanatory bank-level variables, three country (macroeconomic) specific variables, and two global (macroeconomic) variables. Interestingly, the results of this last study broadly confirm that both bank-level and macroeconomic factors play a role in affecting banks' asset quality, although the contribution of bank-level factors is relatively small.

Louzis et al. (2012) analyze macroeconomic and bank-specific determinants of NPLs in Greece, in a comparative study of mortgage, business, and consumer loans portfolios, using a panel of data spanning from 2003 to 2009[4]. In this study, nine different hypotheses are tested using dynamic panel estimators, and two of them regard bad management. Specifically, bad management hypothesis (I) refers to the link between cost efficiency and future NPLs as in the preceding papers (even if inefficiency is simply measured using the ratio between operating expenses and operating income), while bad management hypothesis (II) investigates the relationship between performance and future NPLs, following the idea that past performance (ROE) could be interpreted as a proxy for the quality of management, and should be negatively correlated with a later deterioration of asset quality.

For all macroeconomic variables, the results of this study are compatible with the theoretical arguments, even if their impact is different depending on the type of loans analyzed.[5] Bad management hypothesis (I) is confirmed by a positive and statistically significant coefficient of the inefficiency index for all NPLs categories; the ROE indicator is statistically significant and negatively related to the mortgage and consumer NPLs, supporting the bad management hypothesis (II) for these types of loans.[6] Moral hazard and diversification hypotheses are rejected.

Finally, Chiorazzo et al. (2016) analyze country-specific determinants of NPLs jointly to banking-industry-specific determinants for 124 large European banks located in 21 European countries: Their results highlight the strong influence of country-specific variables on NPLs, while the influence of bank-specific variables is rather limited.

The review of the literature reported above indicates, ultimately, that both macroeconomic and microeconomic factors influence NPLs increases in the course of time, with the first playing the most important role. In this chapter, we will focus on bank-specific determinants, following the strand of literature starting with the study of Berger and DeYoung (1997); the difference of our study relative to preceding analyses lies in the fact that we can better discern the development of NPLs during time using a unique dataset; in particular, our aim is to understand whether bank management is able to recover impaired loans before they become definitively bad loans or, put in a different way, whether the bad management hypothesis is demonstrated by the incapability of the bank management in doing that.

4.3 Data Description and Variables

In order to investigate the "bad management hypothesis" in the Italian banking sector, we created a dataset composed of 48 banks including data and variables in the period 2010–2013. Data about NPLs were manually extracted from the unconsolidated balance sheet of single banks and were then integrated with other data taken from Bankscope (Bureau Van Dijk) and ABI Banking data (a specific database for Italian banks created by the category Association). It is important to note that (in the period investigated) NPLs were accounted in banks' balance sheet following the accounting rules imposed by Bank of Italy (Rule 272/2008), which considered four different categories of bad loans/impaired loans, namely:

(i) substandard loans (loans to customers in temporary difficulties that can be expected to be cleared up in a reasonable time)
(ii) past due/overdrawn more than 90 days
(iii) bad loans (loans to insolvent customers, even when insolvency is not ascertained by court)
(iv) restructured exposures (loan for which a bank, upon granting a moratorium on repayment, renegotiates the loan at lower than market interest rates).

Information about bad loans and other impaired loans is manually collected from the notes to the accounts of balance sheets. In particular, we calculated the ratio between each different form of gross bad/impaired loans and the total amount of credit to clients.

The classification reported above permits a better understanding of the credit exposure of banks and give us the possibility to investigate the bad management hypothesis (also) by looking at if and how much the substandard/past due loans translate into bad loans over time. It is indeed reasonable to think that good managers should be able to recover (at least partially) these kinds of loans before they became definitively bad loans; on the other hand, if a great amount of substandard/past due loans became bad loans, we can assert that a poor management is positively correlated with an increase in NPLs. It is important to stress that the preceding literature (probably due to lack of data) normally considers the total amount of NPLs, that is bad loans, substandard or "weak" loans, and past due loans all together, making it impossible to discern the internal dynamics and relations among these different categories of impaired loans.

The selection of banks in our dataset started from the analysis of the entire banking system that is all the banks surveyed in the ABI Banking database (558 banks). We then considered independent and holding banks for which an unconsolidated balance sheet was available, while banks controlled by foreign companies were discarded. We then selected the largest 48 banks in terms of total assets (2013) for two reasons: (i) Our dataset represents numerically about 9% of the banks operating in 2013, but about 82% of the total assets of the sector, 65% of loans to domestic clients, and 66% of NPLs of the system; (ii) The detailed data for the smaller bank unfortunately do not always exist. Table 4.1 reports a first description of our dataset.

Table 4.1 shows that the majority of banks are located in the north of Italy (the most industrialized zone of the country) and are commercial banks operating as limited companies. Only seven banks operate as cooperative banks (the classification presented in Table 4.1 follows the classification used in ABI Banking database). To better investigate bad loans, two other banks were finally excluded because they specifically engaged in activities (such as private banking and asset management) which do not produce significant amounts of NPLs.

As indicated above, we choose a specific period of time to investigate NPLs in the Italian banking sector: Indeed, even if a deterioration of economic conditions in Italy can be traced back to the outburst of the financial crisis at the end of 2008, different studies (see Chiorazzo et al. 2016) indicate that a strong increase of NPLs in banks' balance sheet is temporarily linked to the government debt crisis (2011–2012). With respect to the banks in our dataset, Table 4.2 shows how the mean ratio of impaired loans (i.e., the four categories of bad loans described above) on credit to clients changed during the investigated period.

The increase of NPLs actually went on also in 2014 and 2015, reaching an astronomic value of over 300 billion euro for the entire system. However, we decided to limit our analysis to the period 2010–2013 because, from 2014, some banks in our dataset started to implement securitization processes which altered the accounting amounts of NPLs and, from 2015, the introduction of different accounting rules makes new data not comparable to the past ones.

Table 4.1 Dataset description

Geographical area	Dimension	Commercial banks (ltd.)		Cooperative banks		Total	
		Obs.	Total assets 2013 (EUR billion)	Obs.	Total assets 2013 (EUR billion)	Obs.	Total assets 2013 (EUR billion)
Center		**9**	**442.10**	**1**	**14.99**	**10**	**457.09**
	Large	1	36.34		–	1	**36.34**
	Major	2	275.21		–	2	275.21
	Medium-sized	5	87.56		–	5	87.56
	Small	1	42.99	1	14.99	2	57.99
Northeast		**11**	**558.79**	**3**	**90.90**	**14**	**649.68**
	Large		–	1	42.68	1	42.68
	Major	1	398.31		–	1	398.31
	Medium-sized	4	94.52	1	42.11	5	136.64
	Small	6	65.95	1	6.10	7	72.06
Northwest		**20**	**895.75**	**2**	**75.82**	**22**	**971.57**
	Large	4	297.62	1	45.36	5	342.98
	Major	1	393.16		–	1	393.16
	Medium-sized	8	130.68	1	30.46	9	161.15
	Small	7	74.29		–	7	74.29
South		**3**	**45.87**	**1**	**9.34**	**4**	**55.20**
	Medium-sized	3	45.87		–	3	45.87
	Small		–	1	9.34	1	9.34
Total		**43**	**1942.51**	**7**	**191.05**	**50**	**2133.55**
All commercial, cooperative and mutual banks in ABI banking database						*558*	*2610.71*
% of our dataset						*9%*	*82%*

Source ABI banking Data and BvD data provider

Table 4.2 Mean ratio of impaired loans on credit to clients for the banks in our dataset

Year	Mean 2010 (%)	Mean 2011 (%)	Mean 2012 (%)	Mean 2013 (%)
Commercial banks (ltd.)	*8.37*	*9.86*	*11.68*	*14.88*
Center	11.34	13.98	17.62	22.17
Northeast	10.69	12.33	14.50	17.40
Northwest	5.31	6.20	6.88	9.44
South	12.12	13.69	16.47	20.87
Cooperative banks	*9.20*	*10.73*	*14.67*	*18.96*
Center	14.71	20.29	30.02	37.45
Northeast	8.02	8.82	12.28	15.64
Northwest	6.43	7.34	9.87	15.02
South	12.73	13.72	16.09	18.34
Total	8.49	9.99	12.11	15.46

4.4 Model and Variables

In the first draft of our model, we employ a simple panel regression in order to examine the bank-specific determinants of the credit quality (cq). As indicator of credit quality (or ex post risk), we utilize the ratio between bad loans and accounts receivable (credit to clients). A higher (lower) value denotes a deteriorating (better) quality of credit quality ceteris paribus.

$$cq_{i,t} = \frac{Bad_{i,t}}{ARc_{i,t}} \tag{4.1}$$

where $cq_{i,t}$ is a measure of the credit quality for the i-th bank in the year t, while $Bad_{i,t}$ is the amount of bad loans for the i-th bank in the year t, and $ARc_{i,t}$ is the amount of accounts receivable from clients for the i-th bank in the year t.

It is important to note that our dependent variable does not consist of the total amount of NPLs, but only of loans to insolvent customers (even when insolvency is not ascertained by court) that can be considered no more restorable. The aim of our analysis is indeed to investigate whether other forms of impaired loans (still restorable) turn into bad loans after a lag or, put in a different way, whether credit managers are able to restore these kinds of impaired loans before they turn into bad loans.

As independent variables, we insert a set of indicators which describe the economic and financial structure of banks in our sample, the weight of loans in the balance sheet, the weight of other problematic loans (not again bad loans), and the operational area. The objective is to catch bank-specific determinants of bad loans. The specification of our model is contained in the following formula:

$$cq_t = \alpha + \sum_{j}^{n} \beta_j X_{j_{t-1}} \quad (4.2)$$

where β_j is the coefficient associated with the independent variables j-th (X_j) at the time t-1. Through a Pool Least Square Method each coefficient is estimated, without compute in fixed[7] and random effects.

In Table 4.3, descriptive statistics of variables used are reported.

Our results show that the mean value of the credit quality (cq) variable gets worse over the time, increasing from 4.5 to 8.5% in the period. That is in line with the persistence of negative real economic conditions in Italy, and this evidence justifies a high standard deviation value. For the Arc variable, *viceversa,* a negative trend is recorded, that is there was a decrease of loans to clients with respect to the total volume of business (and this aspect may partly capture the so-called credit crunch phenomenon).

The increasingly positive value for Exp and Ris variables suggests a possible transformation degree of exposure delayed in bad loans, meaning that over time critical exposures have become bad loans, both for the continuation of the economic crisis and for the failure to select (screening activities) and manage (controlling activities) credit.

The net interest income on total asset (Netinc) presents very low values that, on average, become negative in 2013 due to losses on credit and receivables. The ratio between total asset and equity (inversely captured by the variable Equity) decreases progressively, denoting an increase of capitalization requirement; however, this measure fails to take

Table 4.3 Descriptive statistics of variables used

	cq	Arc	Exp	Ris	Netinc	Equity	Efficiency	Struct
Mean	0.0626	0.0006	0.0088	0.0065	0.0009	7.5414	2.0403	0.5392
Median	0.0529	0.0007	0.0056	0.0050	0.0017	7.7205	1.8095	0.6720
Std. Dev.	0.0480	0.0003	0.0106	0.0060	0.0093	3.5147	1.7523	1.2925
Skewness	1.2851	−0.7712	2.7909	0.9364	−2.4219	0.5115	−1.3287	-10.7091
Kurtosis	5.4342	2.5418	13.5879	3.3610	17.3394	3.2971	24.5107	130.1650
Jarque-Bera	100.2458	20.7131	1146.0720	29.0992	1832.6470	9.0789	3758.1650	133,037.4000

The table shows the descriptive statistics of the variables used in the Panel Regression (OLS) for the period 2010–2013. Credit quality (cq) is the ratio between bad loans and accounts receivable to clients, Arc is the ratio between accounts receivable to client (ARC) and total asset, Exp is the ratio between exposure delayed and ARC, Ris represents the coefficient associated with restructured exposure to ARC, Netinc is the coefficient of the ratio between net interest income and total assets, Equity is the coefficient associated with the ratio between equity and total assets, Efficiency is the ratio between operating income and operating expenses, Struct is given by the ratio total noninterest expenses/ (net interest income + net fees and commissions) account of risk-weighted asset (RWA). For the Efficiency and Struct variables, an erratic pattern seems to emerge.

As indicated, one of the variables used in our model is given by the ratio between accounts receivable to clients and total asset. This variable (named Arc) refers to the percentage of asset invested in loans to clients and provides a proxy of credit specialization for the banks investigated. A positive relation between credit quality and Arc (i.e., when the β_j associated is positive) indicates that when the relative (to total assets) amount of receivables raises the quality of credit falls (or a positive movement for cq is showed). Vice versa, if β_j is negative, the rise in percentage of credit improves the quality of credit (i.e., cq ratio falls).

Another variable used to define the determinants of bad loans is the ratio between exposure delayed (Past due) and account receivable to clients. Following the classification of impaired loans reported above, the numerator of this ratio refers to a kind of problematic credit which is not yet a bad loan, but the credit presents a significant delay in payment. A positive coefficient indicates the attitude of problematic credit to transform itself into bad loans, or the (in) ability of credit manager to manage difficulty positions. A negative coefficient, on the other hand, suggests a positive skill of credit management to recover problematic receivables. This coefficient indicates the relation between the exposures delayed at time t-1 and bad debts at time t; if this relation is positive, it means that during the year the exposures delayed (less severe and precedent condition) have been transformed in bad debt (most serious and next condition). Since the macroeconomic and financial scenario is the same for the banks in the sample, one possible explanation may be provided by the (in) ability of management to manage exposures delayed.

Another type of impaired loans is restructured exposures, i.e., a problematic credit for which the bank and client make a deal in order to define a new payments program. This variable is also measured as a percentage of accounts receivable to clients, and the interpretation of the sign of the β_j is the same as for exposure delayed.

An indicator of economic structure is specified by the ratio between net interest income and total assets. A positive value of β_j indicates that the banks with high interest income (scaled on total assets) present a low quality of credit, and vice versa. This indicator could be then interpreted in two different and opposite ways. On the one hand, if β_j is negative, the relative rise in net interest income improves the quality of credit, and this result could be interpreted as a sort of specialization efficiency; on the other hand, if β_j is positive, the net interest income and the quality of credit are negatively correlated, and this result could suggest that conscious managers impose higher interest rate on more risky clients (as in Podpiera and Weill 2008, that could be interpreted as a right behavior, because the risk of bad loans could be considered well priced in the conditions of loans).

The role of capital is studied by the ratio between equity and total asset; this indicator highlights the effect of the capitalization on bad loans ratio. If the coefficient is positive, more capital means more troubles in loans. If the coefficient is negative, better capitalized banks show a low bad loans to credit ratio.

The bank's operative framework is captured by a dummy variable that displayed 1 if the bank has a regional operating zone, 0 elsewhere. Through this variable, we testify whether, for the Italian banks, the environment impacts on credit quality.

Finally, we use two variables to investigate operating efficiency/inefficiency. The operating efficiency is analyzed trough the ratio between operating income and operating expenses; a negative coefficient for this variable indicates the management's attitude to generate profit from business activity and can be used as a proxy of good/bad management.

The impact of the costs structure is captured by the following ratio: total noninterest expenses/ (net interest income + net fees and commissions). This ratio quantifies the impact of the costs structure on gross revenues and may be interpreted as an inefficiency indicator. A positive value (what we expect) suggests a positive relation between operative inefficiency and bad loans, an inefficiency that goes behind (deepening) bad management.

In a further version of the model, we inserted a dummy variable associated with the use of advanced IRB at the beginning of period (2010); our aim was to investigate whether the use of more sophisticated models to value the credit risk of a loan could reduce the following appearing of bad loans.

4.5 Results

In this section, we show the estimations of the model presented above using OLS panel regression without fixed and random effect. The results are presented in Table 4.4.

The negative value of the coefficient *Arc* means that banks with a high value of ARC on total assets present a better credit quality than the other banks (i.e., the ratio of bad loans on credit to clients decrease). This result suggests that a progressive specialization in credit can improve the quality of credit.

The positive value of *Exp* (Exposure delayed) indicates a vicious circle in which past due loans became nonperforming loans or, from a management perspective, the incapability of credit managers to recover problematic credit (a different proof of the bad management hypothesis). A similar interpretation is provided by the variable *Ris*; also in this case, the positive coefficient shows that restructured exposures usually translate in bad loans, demonstrating a failure in credit management.

The negative value for net interest income (*Netinc*) suggests that the banks in our panel which are overspecialized in credit are better positioned in the management of the credit quality, and this result is in line with that showed for *Arc* variable. Summarizing, banks with a greater

Table 4.4 Panel regression. Bank-specific determinants on credit quality

	Model A	Model B	Model C
α	0.003986	0.00672[c]	
Arc	−12.18002[b]	−11.67315[b]	−10.74555[b]
Exp	0.752817[a]	0.766854[a]	0.760051[a]
Ris	0.419537[c]	0.499378[b]	0.507247[b]
Netinc	−0.388602[b]	−0.354188[c]	−0.340694[c]
Bad loans (−1)	1.118938[a]	1.127141[a]	1.127228[a]
Equity	0.0000594		
Regional	0.007892[b]	0.007343[b]	0.00696[b]
Efficiency		−0.001806[c]	−0.002132[c]
Size			0.0191[c]
Struct			0.000872
R-square	0.907171	0.909137	0.909137

[a] significative at 99%
[b] significative at 95%
[c] significative at 90%. R-square: 0.91. Total panel (balanced) observations: 138

ratio of credit to total assets and a greater ratio of net interest income to total assets seem more capable to manage credit risk, imposing higher interest rates on clients.

The variable equity on total asset is not significant, and similarly the capitalization level seems not to impact on quality of credit. The dummy variable, positive and significant, indicates that the regional banks are more exposed to bad loans. With regard to efficiency, the negative value indicates a negative relation, as expected, between efficiency and bad loans; and this indication is partially confirmed by the value showed by the variable *Struct*.

Similarly to Chiorazzo et al. (2016), we also find a significant autocorrelation for the bad loans ratio, suggesting that an increase in bad loans in one year creates more bad loans in the next year. Finally, the control variable size (log total assets) has a negative and statistically significant impact on credit quality.

To what concern the use of IRB models to asses credit risk, contrary to other studies, we discovered that the coefficient related to this dummy is not significant, and also trying with a detailed analysis that considers only the credit quality and the use of Advanced IRB, give us back a negative relation, that is Advanced IRB determines falls in credit quality.

Considering that our model could be affected by multicollinearity, we use variance inflation factor[8] (VIF) to check whether there is correlation between independent variables employed in the models presented. Logically, we expect a certain degree of correlation, especially among loan quality variables, but this correlation should result in a lagged relation, and not in a cross-sectional relation (i.e., intuitively the exposures delayed at time t are not correlated with exposures restructured at time t, but eventually with the exposures restructured at time t + 1), and then could be considered a conversion factor of the progressive credit worsening.

As can be seen in Table 4.5, all the variables employed in the model are less than 4[9] showing no problematic with VIF values.

Moreover, to better explain the relations between dependent variable and independent variables, we run a simple redundant period fixed effects tests. The F-Statistics, and the relative Prob. values, contained in Table 4.6, lead us to reject the hypothesis that period fixed effects are significant (at least at the 95% level).

Table 4.5 VIF test results

	Model A	Model B	Model C
Arc	1.065	1.235	1.316
Exp	1.370	1.261	1.266
Ris	1.282	1.199	1.199
Netinc	1.114	1.131	1.136
Bad loans (−1)	1.565	1.435	1.449
Equity	1.282		
Regional	0.132	1.136	1.149
Efficency		1.111	1.366
Size			1.064
Struct			1.266

The table shows the VIF's values for the models displayed in the Table 4.4

Table 4.6 Redundant Fixed Effects Tests

	Model A	Model B	Model C
Period F	2.35	1.38	2.42
Period Chi-square	5.07*	2.91	5.18*

The table shows the F-Statistics (F) and Chi-square values for the redundant fixed effects tests. *** significative at 99%, ** significative at 95%, * significative at 90%

Table 4.7 Panel regression. Bank-specific determinants on credit quality. GMM

	Model A	Model B	Model C
Arc	−9.617761[c]	−5.63208[c]	−5.558272[c]
Exp	0.770208[a]	0.782203[a]	0.784275[a]
Ris	0.405222[c]	0.501241[c]	0.492964[c]
Netinc	−0.336999[b]	−0.263731	−0.259638
Bad loans (−1)	1.128687[a]	1.137686[a]	1.139673[a]
Equity	0.000238		
Regional	0.007417[a]	0.007325[a]	0.007224[b]
Efficency		−0.001189	−0.001423
Size			0.010226
Struct			0.000526

The table shows the estimations of the coefficients for the models given by a panel generalized method of moments (GMM); we added constant to instrument list.
[a] significative at 99%
[b] significative at 95%, [c] significative at 90%. R-square: 0.91

Further analyses are developed to check the persistence of the data; in order to do that, we used dynamic panel data (system GMM) technique proposed by Arellano and Bond (1991). Results displayed in Table 4.7

confirm the intensity and direction of the relationships identified in Table 4.4, for the variables Exp and Ris.

4.6 Conclusion

The results of our analysis, as reported in Sect. 4.5, confirm the "bad management hypothesis" first introduced by Berger and DeYoung (1997). Indeed, we discovered that more specialized banks (higher ratio of loans to clients on total assets and higher ratio of net interest income on total assets) and more efficient banks (higher ratio of operating income on operating expenses and lower ratio of total noninterest expenses on net interest income + net fees and commissions) tend to have a better quality of credit. Nevertheless, is rather surprising that the use of IRB models is not significant in reducing NPLs during time.

More interesting, from our point of view, is the general relationship between past due loans, restructured exposures, and bad loans. As our results indicate, problematic loans (past due and restructured) tend to transform into bad loans, demonstrating that credit managers were not able to implement recovery strategies for these critical positions during the investigated period. And even if part of these results could be attributed to the stressed macroeconomic conditions of the time, it is licit to affirm that bad management plays a part.

These last results are useful to better understand the present situation of the Italian banking system: Indeed, the total amount of impaired loans in the balance sheets of Italian banks is often much greater than bad loans alone, also nowadays. Just to have an idea, gross bad loans at the end of 2015 for the whole banking system amounted to about 200 billions (see Bank of Italy, Statistic Bulletin, I 2016), but the total amount of gross NPLs (bad loans and other impaired loans) was 338 billions.

If the same process of transformation of impaired loans into bad loans registered in the period investigated in our analysis should persist also in the future, it is then easy to forecast that the level of bad loans in the system will remain very high, preventing banks to increase significantly the amount of credit notwithstanding the nonconventional impulses of monetary policy that we have seen in the last years. Moreover, the solution to the problem of NPLs in Italy, through securitization and/or government guarantees, could take much more time than that requested by ECB to banks in problematic situations (such as Monte Paschi di Siena).

Finally, it is not inappropriate to suggest that better models to investigate the dynamics of credit quality during time (probably, the current IRB models used by banks are not able to forecast the deterioration of credit quality in a period of stress economic condition), and more efficient procedures to manage problematic credits (from the first moments of their appearance in the balance sheet) should be implemented.

Notes

1. Extra operating costs include, for example, additional monitoring of borrowers, the expense of analyzing and negotiating possible workouts arrangements, and the cost of disposing of collateral if default later occurs.
2. It must be stressed that these two assumptions are not mutually exclusive, as the relationship may be bidirectional.
3. Actually, Williams (2004) estimates two different measures of bank efficiency to test the hypotheses of Berger and Deyoung, namely operating cost efficiency and profit efficiency. Moreover, problem loans are measured using the ratio of loan loss provision-to-loans instead of other typical balance sheet measure such as the ratio NPLs/total loans or NPLs/total assets.
4. The dataset is created using supervisory data for only nine largest Greek banks, even if they accounted for 87.68% of the Greek banking system.
5. For example, the quantitative impact of GDP growth on mortgage NPLs is attenuated compared to the NPLs of other loan types. Moreover, for all NPLs categories, the estimation results indicate that the coefficients of the macroeconomic variables are fairly stable across different models with different bank-specific variables.
6. On the other hand, the ROE indicator for the business NPLs is insignificant. The authors suggest that this may signify that the effect of management quality is mainly reflected on the efficiency of households'

credit granting procedures, which are primarily based on the development of quantitative modeling techniques, while the quality of case-by-case assignment procedures, which characterize business loans granting, does not differ substantially among banks.

7. The redundant fixed effects tests present a Prob. a value higher than 0.10 for the three following models.
8. VIF is expressed as followed:

$$\mathrm{VIF}_{i,j} = \frac{1}{1 - R_{i,j}^2}$$

where, $R_{i,j}^2$ represents the R squared when the i-th explanatory variables is regressed to the j-th explanatory variable.

9. For the VIF's measure thresholds, see also O'Brien (2007): "We demonstrate that the rules of thumb associated with VIF (and tolerance) need to be interpreted in the context of other factors that influence the stability of the estimates of the i-th regression."

References

Arellano, M., and S.R. Bond. 1991. Some tests of specification for panel data: Monte Carlo evidence and an application to employment equations. *Review of Economic Studies* 58 (2): 277–297. doi:10.2307/2297968.

Bank of Italy (2016), Statistic Bulletin I (2016).

Barisitz S. 2011. Nonperforming loans in western Europe—A selective comparison of countries and national definitions, Oesterreichische Nationalbank. *Focus on European Economic Integration* Q1/13.

Beck R., P. Jakubic, and A. Piloiu. 2013. Non performing loans. What matters in addition to the economic cycle, European Central Bank, Working paper series, No 1515.

Berger, A., and R. Deyoung. 1997. Problem loans and cost efficiency in commercial banks. *Journal of Banking & Finance* 21: 849–870.

Chiorazzo, V., V. D'Apice, F. Masala, and P. Morelli. 2016. *Non-performing loans in the wake of crises: What matters for large European banks?*. ABI, Temi di economia e finanza: Country vs. Bank Determinants.

Karim, M.Z.A., S. Chan, and S. Hassan. 2010. Bank efficiency and non-performing loans: Evidence from Malaysia and Singapore. *Prague Economic Papers* 2: 2010.

Klein, N. 2013. Non performing loans in CESEE: Determinants and impact on macroeconomic performance, IMF Working Paper, WP/13/72.

Louzis, D.P., A.T. Vouldis, and V.L., Metaxas. 2012. Macroeconomic and bank-specific determinants of non-performing loans in Greece: A comparative study of mortgage, business and consumer loan portfolios. *Journal of Banking & Finance* 36 (4) 1012–1027, ISSN 0378-4266, http://dx.doi.org/10.1016/j.jbankfin.2011.10.012.

O'Brien R. 2007. A caution regarding rules of thumb for variance inflation factors. Quality & Quantity: International Journal of Methodology, 41 (5): 673–690.

Podpiera, J., and L. Weill. 2008. Bad luck or bad management? Emerging banking market experience. *Journal of Financial Stability* 4: 135–148.

Rinaldi, L., and A. Sanchis-Arellano. 2006. Household debt sustainability: What explains household non-performing loans? An empirical analysis, ECB Working Paper.

Salas, V., and J. Saurina. 2002. Credit risk in two institutional regimes: Spanish commercial and savings banks. *Journal of Financial Services Research* 22: 203–224.

Williams, J. 2004. Determining management behavior in European banking. *Journal of Banking & Finance.* 28 (10): 2427–2460.

5

Why Do US Banks React Differently to Short Selling Bans?

Daniele Angelo Previati, Giuseppe Galloppo, Mauro Aliano and Viktoriia Paimanova

5.1 Introduction and Motivations of the Study

Financial crisis brought significant decreases in market indices, led to active selling of stocks, and raised the possibility of a total collapse. Short selling ban was expected to bring lower stock price volatility and raise investor's confidence. In this context, a policy intervention can change the net expected present value of an individual bank, basically because such kind of interventions aims to reduce the speculative selling pressure on a single title stock, according to policy regulators. Consequently, it should calm down the price reduction and net expected present value of

D.A. Previati (✉)
Bocconi University, Milan, Italy
e-mail: daniele.previati@uniroma3.it

G. Galloppo · V. Paimanova
University of Tuscia, Viterbo, Italy

M. Aliano
University of Cagliari, Cagliari, Italy

G. Chesini et al. (eds.), *The Business of Banking*, Palgrave Macmillan Studies in Banking and Financial Institutions, DOI 10.1007/978-3-319-54894-4_5

every single stock. Second, the intervention may reduce both volatility and probability of default of financial companies.

Previous studies showed a rather controversial role of selling bans on stock price reaction, because it could even result in crashing of stock market liquidity and increase of bid-ask spreads.

The main research hypothesis, investigated in our paper, relates to the effect on stock prices in terms of financial returns and risks, caused by short selling restrictions during the financial crisis in the US banking sector. To be specific, we deal with two research questions. The first research hypothesis, which corresponds to the title of the paper, aims to verify, whether there are different reactions of banks in accordance with their structural characteristics. In this sense, we operate in two ways: On the one hand (Sect. 5.4.1), we perform an analysis of the temporal dynamics of firms' fundamentals; on the other, we check the action of the short selling ban on bank value, so as proxied by its stock price (we discuss it in Sect. 5.4.2). The second research hypothesis is to verify the effect of short selling ban on the systematic risk component of the intervention, and whether the structural characteristics of the bank cause reduction of this component (please, see Sect. 5.4.3).

There are three main findings in this research. The first one shows how short ban restrictions affected firm fundamentals in the USA. In reality, it did not cause any big improvements in profitability of firms, leverage, and liquidity. So, short selling ban did not bring the results that might have been expected by official bodies, when implementing it in the short-time period and did not make lots of changes in the long-time period. Second finding relates to our observation about the stock price. One year after the ban period for US banks, it happened to be higher, then when we coupled with size and earnings per share control variable measures. In terms of price change, it is also sensitive to asset turnover and liquidity measures. Finally, when we consider results connected to bank risk profiles, we conclude that there are changes in volatility in terms of overall and systematic risk. We observe that banks are particularly effective, in terms of overall volatility reduction, earrings, and short leverage metrics.

The main contribution of our paper to previous studies is twofold. For our best knowledge, we are the first to discriminate the reaction by a large set of control variables describing the economic status of financial companies, so that there may be differences in the response across banks. The title of this paper goes in this direction. Second, we argue that this kind of monetary policy interventions influences not only stock prices of financial companies, but also their risk profiles, as well as systematic risk, that is the most interesting component in periods of financial turbulence (Bali et al. 2012; Campbell et al. 2005; Savor et al. 2016).

This paper consists of following parts. A literature survey is included in the next Sect. 5.2. We present our data and empirical design in Sect. 5.3 and our main results in Sect. 5.4. In Sect. 5.5, we summarize our findings and discuss their policy implications.

5.2 Literature Review

Short selling is a common tool to be used when periods of crises are coming. The practice of borrowing shares and selling them at a lower price should be studied in its influence on different economic and financial processes, such as market liquidity, volatility and market price. The consequences of short selling, especially under stressful market conditions, require some tests on market downturns due to the ban. That is why our research is related to a number of existing studies, which confirm our statements and provide ideas on stabilizing the market.

Beber and Pagano (2013) found that bans were detrimental for liquidity (even for financial stocks, where bans are associated with large bid-ask spreads), in the most degree for stocks with small capitalization and no listed options, slowed down price discovery mostly on bear markets and failed to support prices. Moreover, they found that the adverse liquidity effect of bans was stronger for stocks without listed options. The effect of short selling bans on liquidity is measured by the quoted percentage bid-ask spread and the Amihud illiquidity ratio; the effect on the speed of price discovery is done by capturing the extent to which individual stock returns correlate with past market returns; and the effect on the overpricing stocks is measured by the excess returns on stocks subject to bans. They use regression analyses to measure short sale restrictions and base the bid-ask spread models on adverse selection and inventory holding risk. Furthermore, the bans failed to support prices with the exception that may be explained by the confounding effect of the concomitant TARP announcement of the US financial stocks.

In contrary, Appel and Fohlin (2010) show that bans can improve market liquidity and lower volatility. They found that bans did not harm but even improved market quality, based on effective spreads and volatility. They build a model based on idea, that the bid-ask spread is lower, when regulators impose a ban on short selling and when only those who already own a stock can sell it. Their results, received by the use of panel regressions, suggested that short sellers were more likely to trade on information, the limits on short selling reduced information transmission and price discovery and ban reduced liquidity. Their observation of the impact of the short selling ban on stock volatility demonstrated that imposing of short selling bans reduced volatility in equity markets. Moreover, they found that bans improved liquidity and reduced volatility. The lifting of the ban led to increase the volatility of financial stocks in relation to non-financial stocks.

The effect of short selling on volatility requires deep attention, especially in times of financial crises. Mattarocci and Sampagnaro (2010) examine whether the short selling bans from financial companies of Italian Stock Exchange affected the daily volatility and returns of the shares. They suggest a different impact of the short selling prohibition, which depends on focus on risk or performance of bank shares to the ban. They use a dual methodological approach, which is the analysis of standard deviations pre- and post-restriction, and analysis of asymmetric conditional volatility by ANOVA and GARCH. They proved that volatility increases in most of the stocks, covered by the ban, and there is a direct relationship between the increase in volatility and prohibitions, imposed by the authority despite the original market function of the ban. Moreover, they suggest that elimination of short selling can actually trigger market instability. Short selling can be used for correction of market trends and prevention of market bubbles.

Charoenrook and Daouk (2005) checked if short selling restrictions have no effect on skewness and if it declines with introduction of options trading. They found that the absence of short selling reduces liquidity and found no evidence that short selling disrupts orderly markets by causing panic selling, high volatility or market crashes. They proved that short sales increased market quality. By the use of panel regression and event study, authors conclude that short sales enhance market quality and affect market returns.

Initially, short selling was implemented in order to reduce the negative pressure on financial market stocks and supposed to end in a lower volatility. In fact, according to another research paper (Schwartz and Norris 2009), the market behaved in an opposite way and brought a short-term increase in volatility for all observed firms. Moreover, as it turned out, small firms were affected in the days just after the ban, while large ones felt its influence before and during the ban implementation.

It is worth of saying that short selling has a direct impact on risk, which requires further careful studies. Felix et al. (2014) examined how the European short sale ban affected jump and contagion risk of banned and non-banned stocks. It resulted in the evidence that short positions in banned stocks decreased while they increased for non-banned stocks. On using extreme value theory and implied volatility skews, they found that jump risk abruptly rose for all stocks and contagion risk decreased for banned stocks and increased for non-banned stocks after imposition of the ban. They showed that the increase in jump risk was caused by the imposition of the ban itself, rather than by information flow, options trading volumes and stock-specific factors. They show that the increased risk levels are especially evident for the banned financial stocks. An increased jump risk may provoke financial contagion and increase systematic risk. They found that the contagion risk dropped for banned stocks after the ban. So, their results proved that short sale bans reduced contagion risk in the financial sector.

Some following studies suggest that short sale bans do not impact stock prices and can even contribute to their decline and negatively impact on market quality. For example, Helmes et al. (2010) proved that imposing constraints on short selling reduce trading activity, increase bid-ask spreads and price volatility, which was done with the use of univariate and multivariate fixed effects panel regressions.

Boehmer et al. (2013) studied emergency order (SEC decision in 2008) that temporarily banned about 1000 financial stocks. They found that the ban affected larger stocks in a greater degree than the small quartile stocks of firms. It ended in a low market quality, as it was measured by quoted spreads, effective spreads, and volatility. Authors checked the hypotheses by the following fact. If shorting is banned, bid-ask spreads would narrow, because liquidity providers face less adverse selection. On the other side, they questioned how a shorting ban can influence market quality, if short sellers are important liquidity providers. They describe the effects of shorting ban graphically and in firm-pair fixed effect panel regressions. They prove that shorting ban eliminates a substantial subset of trading activity and it might worsen market liquidity.

Battalio et al. (2012) focus on investors, who short stocks for longer periods, because they are overpriced according to them. They are studying the effect of short selling bans of 2008. They examine the link between market downturns and short selling; evaluate evidence on the bans' effectiveness in limiting share price declines of 2008 and the costs imposed by these bans. To measure the impact of short selling on stock prices, regression models are used. Authors conclude by saying that bans seem to have unwanted effects of raising trading costs, lowering market liquidity and preventing short sellers from cases of fraud and earnings manipulation, however, they do not drive price declines on markets.

If the ratio of informed to uninformed short sellers rises, prices react more negatively to unexpected short interest news (Kolasinski et al. 2013). They examine the market response (around 1000 US financial stocks) to short interest announcements and find that rule changes increase the ratio of informed to uninformed short sellers. They find that the negative relation between returns and changes in short volume becomes stronger during the ban. The price reaction to one standard deviation increases in the ratio of short to total volume and becomes more negative by economically and statistically significant points. They use the Diamond and Verrecchia (1987) empirical model, which predicts an increase of information content of short sales and causes prices to better reflect private information, which they call the "short restriction" effect.

Short selling ban can lead to inflation in banned stocks when buyers have to pay more during the period of the ban. The previous analyses of effects of the ban on short selling of US financial stocks imposed by the SEC in September 2008 (Harris et al. 2013) showed that price inflation was found to be lower for stocks with greater short interest before the ban. Moreover, they found that price inflation is the strongest for stocks, where no listed options trade. The estimation is done with the use of the factor-analytic model, where they compare the actual and predicted banned stock index returns in two separate timeframes outside of the ban period.

The effect of short selling ban can be different for financial and non-financial firms (Hasan et al. 2010). They find that during the crises period, the short selling of financial firms stock was not much greater than of non-financial firms when short sellers rationally short sold the financial company stocks with the greatest subprime and insolvency risk exposures. Moreover, they investigated whether short selling activity rationally reflected financial companies' insolvency risk exposure with the use of a direct measure of the exposure to the subprime market.

Grullon et al. (2015) found that the increase of short selling brings price fall, affects asset prices and impacts on financing and investment decisions. He proved that even "the uptick rule can have a significant effect on the equity prices of financially constrained firms and appear to be a binding constraint on the equilibrium level of short selling." Moreover, he discovered that when removed, short selling influences short selling activity and stock prices "even before the actual suspension of the constraints."

5.3 Data and Methodology

In this section, we present the research design to measure the impact of short selling bans on financial companies. We have implemented several methods investigating the reaction of banks to short selling bans in terms of stock price reaction and checking what has happened from the risk side. In Table 5.2, we show the relevant event date of short selling bans.

First, we conducted a descriptive analysis by observing what was going on at different firm fundamentals for certain periods back and forth with respect to the dates of the interventions of short selling bans. We then wondered what effect can be observed on the stock price, as a proxy for the entire banking firm value, when the action of the short selling ban is implemented. We perform pooled regressions to understand what banks reacted better and worse with respect to their fundamental firms. To this end, we run two models (Mod1 and Mod2) as follows:

$$\begin{aligned}\text{Mod1}: P_{i,t} = \alpha + \sum_j \beta_j X_{j,i,t} + \sum_j \lambda_j W_{j,i,t} + \sum_k \gamma \text{Exp}_{k,i,t} \\ + \sum_k \delta \text{Lev}_{k,i,t} + \sum_k \xi \text{Size}_{k,i,t} + \varepsilon_{i,t}\end{aligned} \quad (5.1)$$

where the dependent variable in the model is the stock price considered at the end of selling ban period, for the i-th stocks. We considered also a dynamic version of the Eq. 5.1, as follows:

$$\begin{aligned}\text{Mod2}: \Delta P_{i,t} = \alpha + \sum_j \beta_j \Delta X_{j,i,t} + \sum_j \lambda_j \Delta W_{j,i,t} + \sum_k \gamma \Delta \text{Exp}_{k,i,t} \\ + \sum_k \delta \Delta \text{Lev}_{k,i,t} + \sum_k \xi \Delta \text{Size}_{k,i,t} + \varepsilon_{i,t}\end{aligned} \quad (5.2)$$

where $\Delta P_{i,t}$ represents the change of stock price between the start of short selling restrictions and the same observations one year ahead for the i-th banks. Same interpretation counts for all the other independent variables. $X_{j,i,t}$ is a vector of control variables accounting for the level of Profitability (Asset_Turnover, EPS_Annualized, Ebit, EPS_Growth, Grossmargin, Return_On_Asset, Return_On_Cap); $W_{j,i,t}$ is a vector of variables representing the level of firm's Liquidity (CF_CASH_FROM_OPER, CF_NET_INC); $\delta Lev_{k,i,t}$ includes control variables accounting for Leverage (CURRATIO, LTBTBT); $\text{Exp}_{k,i,t}$ is a vector of control variables, stands for Expectations (BEST_ANALYST, BEST_TARGET_PRICE); and lastly $\xi Size_{k,i,t}$ is a vector accounting for Size control variables (CURR_MAR_CAP, TOT_COM_EQY) of each i-th stock taking into account (see Table 5.1 for the description of variables).

Table 5.1 Fundamental variables description

Variable	Description
ASSET_TURNOVER	Asset turnover ratio is the ratio of the value of a company's sales or revenues generated relative to the value of its assets
CUR MARKET CAP	Current market capitalization and means a total value of all outstanding shares of a company
CUR_RATIO	Current ratio and indicates whether a company is able to pay its obligations
EBIT	Earnings before interest expenses and income taxes
EPS_ANNUALIZED	Earnings per share in last fiscal year
EPS_GROWTH	The raise or down of earnings before extraordinary items, when making a comparison between the observed current period and the same time last year
LT_DEBT_TO_TOT_ASSET	All interest-bearing financial obligations that are not due within a year
RETURN_ON_ASSET	Return_on_asset stands for ROA and shows how profitable a company is in relation to its total asset
TOT_COMMON_EQY	Represents an equity measure, which counts only the common stockholders without the preferred ones
CF_NET_INC	Stands for cash flow on net income and explains the ratio between a stock's price and its cash flow per share
RETURN_ON_CAP	Return_On_Cap is a metric that measures the return that an investment generates for capital contributors. It is a proxy of ROE, a measure of a corporation's profitability by revealing how much profit a company generates with the money shareholders have invested
GROSS_MARGIN	It represents the percent of total sales revenue that the company retains after incurring the direct costs associated with producing the goods and services sold by a company
CF_CASH_FROM_OPER	Cf_Cash_From_Oper represents Cash Flow from Operating activities
BEST_ANALYZED	Best_Analyst represents the consensus rating based on analyst recommendations
BEST_TARGET_PRICE	Best_Target_Price consists in analyst price short-term forecast

This table reports fundamental variables description. *Source* Authors' elaboration

When it comes to control variables, we mention some details about the use of different analysis levels and their role in explaining effects on stock price changes.

Profitability: These variables are used to estimate the impact of profitability measure on stock price changes. We expect a positive relationship between profitability and stock price changes. Asset turnover ratio is the ratio of the value of a company's sales or revenues generated relative to the value of its assets. Ferrer and Tang (2016) find a positive relation between changes in stock prices and asset turnover ratio; their results show that asset turnover ratio, coupled with other financial ratios, would have a positive impact on the year-on-year change in stock price. Also, Earnings before interest expenses and income taxes, Earning per Share, Gross Margin, Return on Asset (ratio of net income to total assets) and Return on Capital (ratio of net income to capital) might be included in profitability indicators. Under this perspective, many studies have analyzed the effect of banking business diversification on profitability and the relation on stock prices, but their evidences are often contradictory (Maudos 2017).

Leverage: The capital structure is arguably one of the most important decisions a company face. On using these variables, we estimate the effect of leverage changes (debt/capital structures) on stock prices. Current Ratio is given by the ratio of current assets and current liabilities and indicates whether a company is able to pay its obligations. This indicator represents both Leverage and Liquidity indicators, following Ferrer and Tang (2016). The impact on stock price (Shieh et al. 2012), regarding the US market, depends on market characteristics and momentum effect. LT_DEBT_TO_TOT_ASSET considers all interest-bearing financial obligations, that are not due within a year on total asset, and may represent another leverage measure. Cai and Zhang (2011) find a negative effect of the change in a firm's leverage ratio on its stock prices for non-financial firms. However, the evidences provided (on a dataset that consists of 20 US banks) by Papanikolaou and Wolff (2014) indicate that leverage contributes to both total bank risk and systemic risk and increases risks and volatility.

Size: Through these variables, we analyze the impact of banks' size on stock price changes. Current market capitalization, current enterprises value, and common equity represent the size of companies. Using the vector autoregressive (VAR) process on US monthly stock market data (from 1926 to 2006), Ho et al. (2011) find a highly and negative relationship between small and large cap stock prices with a cyclical pattern.

Liquidity: Cash flow from operating activities and cash flow from net income represent a liquidity measure in *stricto sensu*. Khan et al. (2016) investigate the relation between funding liquidity and banks' risk for US bank holding from 1986 to 2014 and find that banks facing lower funding liquidity risk take more risk or more instability of stock price changes.

Expectation: The nature of expectation variables is seen through the following. Based on a sample of 23,632 analyst recommendations of 1106 banks, Premti et al. (2016) find that analyst recommendations are more informative for riskier banks and subject to a higher degree of information asymmetry. The impact on stock prices is unpredictable and depends on analysis period.

To analyze the impact of short selling restrictions from risk side, we investigated, via pooled regressions, what was going on with overall and systematic risks in the presence of short selling restrictions. Focus on such fundamental firms is more effective in limiting the risk for banks.

To be specific, we select all stocks belonging to local market banking index and we run two models as follows:

$$\begin{aligned}\text{Mod3} : \Delta\text{OverallRIsk}_{i,t} = \alpha + \sum_j \beta_j \Delta X_{j,i,t} + \sum_j \lambda_j \Delta W_{j,i,t} + \sum_k \gamma \Delta\text{Exp}_{k,i,t} \\ + \sum_k \delta \Delta\text{Lev}_{k,i,t} + \sum_k \xi \Delta\text{Size}_{k,i,t} + \varepsilon_{i,t}\end{aligned} \quad (5.3)$$

$$\begin{aligned}\text{Mod4} : \Delta Syst_{i,t} = \alpha + \sum_j \beta_j \Delta X_{j,i,t} + \sum_j \lambda_j \Delta W_{j,i,t} + \sum_k \gamma \Delta\text{Exp}_{k,i,t} \\ + \sum_k \delta \Delta\text{Lev}_{k,i,t} + \sum_k \xi \Delta\text{Size}_{k,i,t} + \varepsilon_{i,t}\end{aligned} \quad (5.4)$$

where $\text{OverallRIsk}_{i,t}$ represents standard deviations computed in an estimation window of 252 days, $\text{Syst}_{i,t}$ stands for systematic risk, also known as "undiversifiable risk," affecting the overall market, not just a particular stock or industry.

Following Damodaran's approach (1999), we use the following formula to determine the systematic risk for *i*-th securities:

$$\text{syst}_i = \beta_i * \sigma_{\text{mkt}} \tag{5.5}$$

where syst_i is the systematic risk for *i*-th security, σ_{mkt} the standard deviation of market return, β_i is the Beta regression (OLS method) calculated as:

$$\text{r}_i = \alpha_i + \beta_i \text{r}_{\text{mkt}} \tag{5.6}$$

where r_i is the return of *i*-th security and r_{mkt} the return of market. The unsystematic risk is obtained as:

$$\text{unsyst}_i = \sqrt{\sigma_i^2 - \text{syst}_i} \tag{5.7}$$

where σ_i^2 represented the variance of the return of *i*-th security.

In order to avoid outliers, namely extremely deviant cases with Cook's D greater than 1, we perform robust regression using iteratively reweighted least squares.

Data are collected from various sources. For the period from January 2009 to December 2013, we draw information from specific national FSA agency regarding the period of short selling restrictions (see Table 5.2 for viewing specific event dates). Single stock and general index prices are downloaded by Datastream. Fundamental firms are extracted by Bloomberg.

The sample from our analysis is composed of 82 banking companies of USA—Standard & Poor's 500 Index. It covers the period from January 2005 to December 2014. Our dataset consists of daily observations, total returns, and fundamental balance sheet data. All-time series are obtained

Table 5.2 Short selling ban interventions in US financial sector

Country	Authority	From	Till	Type of restriction	Exceptions	Type of targeted firms
USA	(FSC) Securities and Exchange Commission (SEC)	07/21/2008	08/20/2008	Naked short selling ban (mandatory pre-borrowing)	Market makers	Financial institutions

This table reports Short Selling Ban Interventions in US Financial Sector. *Source* Authors' elaboration starting from single country FSA web site

Table 5.3 Descriptive statistics

	n° stocks	Best analyst rating	Best target	cash flow	Cash flow net income	Curr enterprise value	Current market	Current ratio %	Debt to total asset	Common equity	EPS annual %	EPS growth	ROA %	ROC %	Daily return
Mean	82	3.68	60.36	768.06	381.66	57,366.10	24,711.63	1.60	16.46	19,374.12	1.37	48.93	2.99	6.84	0.06%
Standard deviation	82	0.43	90.10	6615.95	1811.55	161,409.85	39,128.80	1.14	15.52	36,271.12	40.48	473.98	5.69	13.60	0.07%
Skewness	82	−0.15	10.12	11	4	39	38	3.54	33.33	38.18	3.99	2.19	7.54	16.20	0.10
Kurtosis	82	2.63	131.75	82.43	568.13	27.40	15.88	20.65	4.89	15.26	1605.35	143.75	29.34	123.64	3.02

This table provides the panel data descriptive statistics for the sample used in our elaboration for the period of January 2006–December 2013. The analyses and the values contained in the table are developed starting from daily observations. The variable *Best Analyst Rating* is calculated as a weighted average of opinions of various analysts (5 = buy; 4 = high performance; 3 = hold; 2 = low performance; 1 = sell) and indicates the analyst recommendation and their consensus on single stock. The variable *Best Target* indicates the projected analyst price level. The variables *Cash Flow, Cash Flow Net Income, Current Enterprise Value, Current Market and Common Equity* represent the fundamental balance sheet information. The variable *Debt to Total Asset* indicates the ratio between Total Asset and Debt. *EPS Annual %* and *EPS Growth* represent the earning per share and the rate of growth of earning per share, respectively. *ROA %* and *ROC%* indicate, respectively, the Return On Asset and the Return On Capital. *Daily Return* is the daily stock return. *Zeta Altman* represents the Altman Z-score for predicting bankruptcy from Bloomberg. Table 5.3 provides an overview of the descriptive statistics associated with the banned financial stocks.

Table 5.3 contains the mean, standard deviation, skewness and kurtosis values of the fundamental variables used in the analysis organized by: expectation (Best Analyst Rating and Best Target Price), corporate liquidity (Cash Flow and Cash Flow Net Income), enterprises values (Current Enterprise Value and Current Market Capitalisation), leverage (Current Ratio and Debt to Total Asset) and performance (Common Equity, EPS Annual %, EPS Growth, ROA %, ROC % and Daily Return) and risk (Zeta Altman). Daily closing stock prices for individual financial institutions and for market indices are also retrieved from Bloomberg.

5.4 Empirical Results

We present empirical results according to the logic showed above. In Sect. 5.4.1, we present banks' fundamental analysis, then in Sect. 5.4.2 we report empirical results in terms of stock price reaction. Then we conclude in Sect. 5.4.3, considering risk analysis in terms of both overall and systematic measures.

5.4.1 Banks' Fundamental Analysis

We performed our test by considering fundamental variables related to each specific bank, listed in the US Sp500 Financial Index, and in terms of 1 year before the event and 1 and 2 years after the event. Specifically, we aimed to reach our research objective, that is, to explore the stock price performance in these countries in their response to stock short selling ban announcements, as it is a remedy to be used by central banks in order to provide a stable situation on the market and control over the price decline. The analysis contains 14 variables, where every variable corresponds to a certain year of analysis and is grouped according to its characteristics, e.g., Profitability (ASSET_TURNOVER, EBIT, EPS_ANNUALIZED, EPS_GROWTH, RETURN_ON_ASSET, RETURN_ON_CAP, GROSS_MARGIN),

Leverage (CURR_RATIO, LT_DEBT_TO_TOT_ASSET), Liquidity (CF_CASH_FROM_OPER, CF_NET_INC), and Size (CURR_MAR_CAP, CURR_ENT_VAL, TOT_COM_EQY). We were measuring stock price reaction to two dates of announcements of short selling ban (initial and final date).

On following the presentation of fundamental variables in Sect. 5.2, we provide our main results and policy implications from descriptive statistics analysis contained in Table 5.4.

Profitability: We started our observation from how did short selling restrictions affect profitability indices. ASSET_TURNOVER demonstrated decline in the US profitability indices in their reaction to short selling ban announcements for both observed event dates, which was followed by their reduction in the first year after the ban in the short term and got growing meaning only for EPS_ANNUALIZED, ROA and ROC 2 years after the ban, that means that the US market needed some time in order to respond to short selling ban, however, in the year of announcement in the short term, it did not bring any improvement in the US profitability fundamentals.

Leverage: Furthermore, we decided to explore the reaction of leverage fundamentals to short selling ban. The US leverage fundamentals showed that CURR_RATIO demonstrates price decline to short selling in the short term, in contrast, there are very little changes in the long term. As for LT_DEBT_TO_TOT_ASSET, it was raised in the short period, however, without any big changes in the long term.

Size: Size fundamentals were influenced by short selling restrictions in the following way. We should notice reduction of both CURR_MAR_CAP and CURR_ENT_VAL size variables for the US banks in the short term. At the same time, it is worth of saying that there are no improvements of size fundamentals for the US banks in the long term. We can conclude that short selling did not cause many improvements in firm's size.

Liquidity: Then, we observed liquidity fundamentals of our sample countries, in their reaction to short selling ban. We found that short selling caused a rise of the US firms' liquidity by its announcement in a short-term perspective for CF_CASH_FROM_OPER. However, it ended in a general reduction of indices in the long time. CF_NET_INC

Table 5.4 Fundamental firms' analysis

Years	t = −1	t = 0	t = +1	t = +2
Profitability				
ASSET_TURNOVER	0.23	0.21	0.19	0.19
	0.23	0.21	0.19	0.19
EBIT	938.25	556.77	386.83	372.86
	919.59	515.64	386.83	372.86
EPS_ANNUALIZED	5.74	0.19	1.55	2.02
	5.76	0.07	1.55	2.02
EPS_GROWTH	50.12	−3.16	−23.46	60.81
	50.71	−3.29	−23.46	60.81
RETURN_ON_ASSET	4.44	3.57	0.27	2.18
	4.44	3.57	0.27	2.18
RETURN_ON_CAP	10.80	8.10	0.61	5.59
	10.80	8.09	0.61	5.59
GROSS_MARGIN	3.20	3.04	2.97	3.41
	3.20	3.04	2.97	3.41
Leverage				
CURR_RATIO	0.22	0.16	0.18	0.18
	0.22	0.16	0.18	0.18
LT_DEBT_TO_TOT_ASSET	14.53	16.01	17.30	16.97
	14.54	16.01	17.30	16.97
Liquidity				
CF_CASH_FROM_OPER	49.92	1971.30	1027.80	1496.51
	127.58	1979.57	1027.80	1496.51
CF_NET_INC	651.18	299.36	313.96	379.25
	644.86	289.08	313.96	379.25
Size				
CURR_MAR_CAP	28980.29	22269.71	17460.62	22158.81
	29440.91	22250.52	19768.79	20582.19
CURR_ENT_VAL	54697.59	44384.54	34065.30	39443.27
	54712.16	43427.62	35349.04	38765.32
TOT_COM_EQY	15474.20	15629.03	15695.61	19413.22
	15430.28	15654.07	15695.61	19413.22

This table provides the fundamental firms' descriptive statistics for all the banks listed in US general index according to time (years), ahead and back, corresponding to short selling restrictions period. The first line of each variable corresponding to the observation detected at the day (t = 0) of short selling ban start, or 1 year before (t = −1) or 1 and 2 years (t = +1, t = +2) ahead, respectively. The second line of each variable reports variable values corresponding to the observation detected at the day (t = 0) of short selling ban end, or 1 year before (t = −1) or 1 and 2 years (t = +1, t = +2). The variables are grouped according to firm fundamental characteristics and legend of each variable is provided by Table 5.1

reduced indices of US banks (first announcement), but caused raises of US firm fundamentals in the long time.

Our analyses of how short ban restrictions affected firm fundamentals in US banking system showed that it did not cause any big improvements in profitability of firms, leverage and liquidity, as well as no much positive effect on firm size. So, short selling ban did not bring the results, that might have been expected by official bodies, when implementing it in the short-time period and did not cause lots of changes in the long-time period. For sure, the effectiveness of short selling is a key point for policy makers on their decisions to see if it can bring serious improvements in firm's characteristics. However, it is very important for policy makers to pay attention to a local level, as our results are not the same for the observed countries. Moreover, we would like to underline that some variables show a greater sensitivity to firm fundamentals than the others. To tell more, it turned out that short selling brought almost no improvements on firm's fundamentals at the time of its closing date and only slight changes can be seen in 2-year time.

5.4.2 Stock Price Reaction

Next, we decided to study the reaction of bank stocks, therefore, their price response to final date of short selling and the change of the price (between the final and the initial date).

The results about the price changes (see Table 5.5) at the end of the ban period (we refer in the text as Mod1) and 1 year after the end of the ban interventions (we refer in the text as Mod2) are more interesting. This part of the analysis is a novel in the literature.

The situation of price change 1 year later the short selling ban closing (Mod2) involves the following considerations. The characteristics of our country samples, by a number of banks, are as follows: We consider 82 banks listed in US Sp500 Financial Index, while the average value of the stock price change a year after the short selling ban closure is −42%. The first reading exhibits that American banks have shown a price fall.

Profitability: When considering ROA as a profitability indicator, its contribution (which is normally expected to be positive) seems not to be

Table 5.5 Stock price change

USA	Size		Profitability		Leverage		Liquidity		Expectations		Full model	
	Coeff.	St. Dev	Coeff.	St. Dev	Coeff.	St. Dev	Coeff.	St. Dev	Coeff.	St. Dev	Coeff.	St. Dev
Price final date												
f_cur_mkcapt	−0.0004	0.0004									0.0004***	0.0002
f_tot_com	−0.0005**	0.0002									0.0015***	0.0004
f_assetturnover			−38.8896	31.9368							−38.8896	31.9368
f_ebit			−0.0006	0.0012							−0.0012	0.0018
f_EPS_an			0.5083***	0.1823							2.4566***	0.1233
f_EPS_growth			0.0130	0.0148							0.0094***	0.0084
f_grossmargfn			0.1996	0.2230							−1.8838	2.6300
f_roa			0.4266	0.7047							−0.4468	0.6564
f_roc			−0.0458	0.2060							0.2180	0.3410
f_curratio					-3.1233	5.3238					−7.1038	12.8120
f_lt_db_t					0.0231	0.1099					0.0737	0.3591
f_cf_net							0.0004	0.0005			0.0018***	0.0007
f_cf_in							0.0044***	0.0030			−0.0205***	0.0043
f_best_an									0.7887***	0.0451	−5.8691***	1.6420
f_best_targ_price									−7.5403***	1.6376	0.7887***	0.0451
Delta price												
d_cur_mkcapt	0.0028***	0.0004									0.0004***	0.0002
d_tot_com	0.0001	0.0001									0.0001	0.0001
d_assetturnover			−27.6598	44.3376							−27.6598	44.3376
d_ebit			−0.0013**	0.0006							−0.0013**	0.0006
d_EPS_an			0.5968***	0.1695							0.5968***	0.1695
d_EPS_growth			0.0043***	0.0030							0.0043***	0.0030
d_grossmargin			−0.8629	0.8499							−0.8629	0.8499
d_roa			0.2803***	0.2281							0.2803***	0.2281
d_roc			−0.0734	0.1142							−0.0734	0.1142
d_curratio					17.5205	30.3783					−2.2000	4.0666

(continued)

Table 5.5 (continued)

USA	Size		Profitability		Leverage		Liquidity		Expectations		Full model	
	Coeff.	St. Dev	Coeff.	St. Dev	Coeff.	St. Dev	Coeff.	St. Dev	Coeff.	St. Dev	Coeff.	St. Dev
d_lt_db_t					−1.7512	1.3282					−0.3937*	0.1977
d_cf_net_in							0.0001	0.0006			0.0001	0.0002
d_cf_cash_in							−0.0260***	0.0033			−0.0038***	0.0010
d_best_an									−2.3662	1.8207	−3.9638***	1.5300
d_best_targ_price									0.6246919***	0.0137	0.6719***	0.0397

In this table, we report the effect it can be observed on the stock price, as a proxy for the entire banking firm value, when the action of the short selling ban is implemented. To this end, we perform pooled regressions to understand what banks reacted better and worse with respect to their fundamental firms

Mod1 : $P_{i,t} = \alpha + \sum_j \beta_j X_{j,i,t} + \sum_j \lambda_j W_{j,i,t} + \sum_k \gamma \text{Exp}_{k,i,t} + \sum_k \delta \text{Lev}_{k,i,t} + \sum_k \xi \text{Size}_{k,i,t} + \varepsilon_{i,t}$ where the dependent variable in the model is the stock price considered at the end of selling ban period, for the i-th stocks, $X_{j,i,t}$ is a vector of control variables accounting for the level of Profitability (ASSET_TURNOVER, EPS_ANNUALIZED, EBIT, EPS_GROWTH, GROSSMARGIN, RETURN_ON_ASSET, RETURN_ON_CAP), $W_{j,i,t}$ is a vector of variables representing the level of firm Liquidity (CF_CASH_FROM_OPER, CF_NET_INC), $\delta \text{Lev}_{k,i,t}$ includes control variables accounting for Leverage (CURRATIO, LTBTBT), $\text{Exp}_{k,i,t}$ is a vector of control variables, stands for Expectations (BEST_ANALYST, BEST_TARGET_PRICE) and lastly $\xi Size_{k,i,t}$ is a vector accounting for Size control variables (CURR_MAR_CAP, TOT_COM_EQY) of each i-th stock taking into account. We considered also a dynamic version of the Eq. 5.1, as follows

Mod2 : $\Delta P_{i,t} = \alpha + \sum_j \beta_j \Delta X_{j,i,t} + \sum_j \lambda_j \Delta W_{j,i,t} + \sum_k \gamma \Delta Exp_{k,i,t} + \sum_k \delta \Delta Lev_{k,i,t} + \sum_k \xi \Delta Size_{k,i,t} + \varepsilon_{i,t}$ where $\Delta P_{i,t}$ represents the change of stock price between the start of short selling restrictions and the same observations 1 year ahead for the i-th banks. Same interpretation counts for all the other independent variables. ***, **, * denote that estimates are statistically significant at the 1, 5 and 10% levels estimated by market participants, especially for Mod1. While a positive and significant contribution is provided by EPS indicators for two models, classical profitability variables and those related to the levels of earnings are not effective in contrasting the price fall.

Leverage: Results highlight a positive contribution to the containment of the price fall for the degree of leverage in Mod2 through long term and for total asset ratio.

Size: Evidence shows the importance of current market capitalization as a size variable and its positive contribution to stock price in both Mod1 and Mod2, while common equity does not provide a significant contribution to the explanation of stock price changes in two models.

Liquidity: The contributions of liquidity variables to stock (Mod1) and stock price changes (Mod2) are ambiguous and depend on the type of indicator used. Using cash flow from net income, the impact is positive on both models.

Expectations: The contribution of analysts' expectations is positive, in the sense of contribution to the price reduction due to the variation of recommendation, i.e., increasing the level of recommendation on individual securities is an increase of the reduction of the price fall. Even a long-term debt improved results in a better price change.

In the model used to measure the sensitivity of the price change 1 year from the closing of the ban, some information useful for policy makers comes out. In particular, there are considerations about the results coupled with the size variable and mostly to those related to cash levels and those related to the expectations of the analysts in the sense of recommendation issued. It seems that policy makers should pay more attention to the size and to the banks' liquidity levels, rather than to profitability variables.

5.4.3 Risk Analysis: Total and Systematic Risk

When making our analyses about the effect of short selling on stock price risk attitude, we divided our results into overall and systematic risk measure (see Table 5.6).

Table 5.6 Total and systematic risk analysis

Panel B USA	Size		Profitability		Leverage		Liquidity		Expectations		Full model	
	Coeff.	St. Dev	Coeff.	St. Dev	Coeff.	St. Dev	Coeff.	St. Dev	Coeff.	St. Dev	Coeff.	St. Dev
Overall risk												
d_cur_mkcapt	0**	0									0.0000	0.0000
d_tot_com	0	0									0.0000	0.0000
d_assetturnover			0.1173***	0.0662							0.1173***	0.0662
d_ebit			0	0							0.0000	0.0000
d_EPS_an			−0.0004**	0.0002							−0.0014*	0.0008
d_EPS_growth			0***	0							0.0000***	0.0000
d_grossmargin			−0.0001	0.0039							0.0008	0.0038
d_roa			0.0026***	0.0010							0.0020***	0.0010
d_roc			−0.0020***	0.0005							−0.0019***	0.0005
d_curratio					−0.0207	0.0211					−0.0034	0.0184
d_lt_db_t					0.001691***	0.0009					0.0008	0.0009
d_cf_net							0	0.0000			0.0000	0.0000
d_cf_in							0.0000	0.0000			0.0000***	0.0000
d_best_an									−0.0203***	0.0062	−0.0110	0.0069
d_best_targ_price									−0.0001**	0.0000	−0.0003	0.0002
Systematic risk												
d_cur_mkcapt	0.0000	0.0000									0	0
d_tot_com	0.0000	0.0000									0***	0
d_assetturnover			0.0585***	0.0314							0.0616***	0.0305
d_ebit			0.0000	0.0000							0	0
d_EPS_an			−0.0001	0.0001							−0.0009***	0.0004
d_EPS_growth			0**	0.0000							0	0
d_grossmargin			−0.0006	0.0019							−0.0003	0.0018
d_roa			0.0009***	0.0005							0.0006***	0.0005
d_roc			−0.0007***	0.0002							−0.0006***	0.0002

(continued)

Table 5.6 (continued)

Panel B USA	Size		Profitability		Leverage		Liquidity		Expectations		Full model	
	Coeff.	St. Dev	Coeff.	St. Dev	Coeff.	St. Dev	Coeff.	St. Dev	Coeff.	St. Dev	Coeff.	St. Dev
d_curratio					−0.0109	0.0090					−0.0050	0.0087
d_lt_db_t					0.0007***	0.0004					0.0004	0.0004
d_cf_net_in							0	0			0	0
d_cf_cash_in							0	0			0***	0
d_best_an									−0.0052*	0.0029	−0.0005	0.0033
d_best_targ_price									0	0	−0.0002***	0.0001

In this table, we report the effect of short selling restrictions on total and systematic risk. To this end, we perform pooled regressions to understand what banks reacted better and worse with respect to fundamental firms

$\text{Mod 3}: \Delta\text{OverallRIsk}_{i,t} = \alpha + \sum_j \beta_j \Delta X_{j,i,t} + \sum_j \lambda_j \Delta W_{j,i,t} + \sum_k \gamma \Delta\text{Exp}_{k,i,t} + \sum_k \delta\Delta\text{Lev}_{k,i,t} + \sum_k \xi\Delta\text{Size}_{k,i,t} + \varepsilon_{i,t}$ and $\text{Mod 4}: \Delta\text{Syst}_{i,t} = \alpha + \sum_j \beta_j \Delta X_{j,i,t} + \sum_j \lambda_j \Delta W_{j,i,t} + \sum_k \gamma \Delta\text{Exp}_{k,i,t} + \sum_k \delta\Delta\text{Lev}_{k,i,t} + \sum_k \xi\Delta\text{Size}_{k,i,t} + \varepsilon_{i,t}$ where $\text{OverallRIsk}_{i,t}$ represents standard deviations computed in an estimation window of 252 days; $\text{Syst}_{i,t}$ stands for systematic risk, also known as "undiversifiable risk," affecting the overall market, not just a particular stock or industry; $X_{j,i,t}$ is a vector of control variables accounting for the level of Profitability (ASSET_TURNOVER, EPS_ANNUALIZED, EBIT, EPS_GROWTH, GROSSMARGIN, RETURN_ON_ASSET, RETURN_ON_CAP); $W_{j,i,t}$ is a vector of variables representing the level of firm Liquidity (CF_CASH_FROM_OPER, CF_NET_INC); $\delta\text{Lev}_{k,i,t}$ includes control variables accounting for Leverage (CURRATIO, LTBTBT); $\text{Exp}_{k,i,t}$ is a vector of control variables, stands for Expectations (BEST_ANALYST, BEST_TARGET_PRICE); and lastly $\xi\text{Size}_{k,i,t}$ is a vector accounting for Size control variables (CURR_MAR_CAP, TOT_COM_EQY) of each *i*-th stock taking into account (d_ represents the difference of the variable values at the beginning and 1 year after the short selling ban). ***, **, * denote that estimates are statistically significant at the 1, 5 and 10% levels

With regard to overall risk and systematic risk dynamic models, hereafter, we expose some main findings. We focus in particular on the category of variables that from present analysis, they result the most effective in the containment of overall and systemic risk component.

Profitability: US banks appear to be effective in reducing the overall risk by increasing the level of earnings per share annualized. The growth of earnings per share is also statistically significant in the reduction of overall risk. Therefore, the policy makers must pay deep attention to dynamics of earnings of banks, in order to better understand their impact on the local banking system and decisions of short selling ban. Also, the increase of profitability in terms of ROC is effective in the overall risk containment. The increase in ROA is not effective in overall risk containment. So, the American banking system seems to be more sensitive in reducing the risk on profitability return, calculated on bank capital. Also, there is an evidence of the effectiveness of ROC ratio, as well as of the overall risk. The increase of asset turnover results in increase of both overall and systematic risk components. As for systematic risk, it contains a specific risk component in relation to increase in earnings per share annualized level, so it is related to overall risk too.

Liquidity: From our results, we evidence the increase of liquidity in terms of cash flow. It appears to have a non-restraining effect of the overall risk.

Expectations: Even the increase in target price, expressed by analysts, is useful in the containment of the systematic risk.

Overall, we can conclude that policy makers of the US banks must keep an eye on earnings and profitability variables in terms of ROC, as fundamental firm, which is more effective in containing the overall and systematic risk. These findings appear to be worthy of being considered by local policy makers when they want to analyze the potential effects of their decisions about short selling ban on the local banking system.

5.5 Discussion and Limitations of the Study

The use of short selling ban in different countries caught high attention of policy modeling. The attitude to it was split into two points of view, whether such actions could stabilize the market or not, and raised some doubts concerning a speculative character of policy implementations and rationality. It resulted in a certain influence on stock demand and reduced *stock prices in a different degree in every country. Our paper is one of the first ones trying to* explain the evidence of different bank price reactions in terms of stock market conditions. Therefore, the degree of the appropriate level of policy actions aimed to smoother the selling ban pressure could be discussed if stock market and bank characteristics are well-known by policy institutions. Recent events about Brexit gave room, worldwide, for debating about the effectiveness and convenience of policy measures such short selling bans. From the evidence of occurred trading days, it is clear to see a noticeable increase in volatility on global markets. Therefore, banks got record trading volumes when immediate aftermath of Brexit and when usual trading levels were increased up to 10 times and brought commissions 10 times more. Investors are seen very concerned about banking which is expressed in large selling of bank stocks worldwide. There was a risk-off trading on financial markets when investors returned back to the less volatile asset class. At the same time, banks experienced extremely negative volatility events, because their value shrinks and their capability to continue their traditional banking activities was concerned. Indeed, the price fall corresponds to a destruction of the value of banks, and it also influences the future lending policy.

For these reasons, it is very important to investigate what can happen to banks under the short selling ban regime, in terms of both potential destruction of value and increase in volatility. To this end, in this section, we try to light policy implications related to our results. To understand better how these situations can be read in light of short selling ban measures, it is useful to start by summarizing our results and then identify the policy ideas related to various evidence we found in the same order we present in empirical result section. With respect to fundamental firm analysis, and focusing just on ban periods, for the US banks, we do not observe any improvement in the profitability indices. It might also be due to the short period taken into account. Also, 1 year later the start of the ban period, we have no evidence of improvement. Likewise, there is slight or no improvement with regard to the level of leverage and liquidity. On analyzing these results from a policy maker's point of view, authorities should think of implementing this intervention in market conditions not much compromised. In fact, we observe improvements neither in profitability nor in leverage and liquidity bank conditions. It makes us realize that short selling ban actions cannot be implemented to achieve improvements in economic characteristics of the banks. They can only become buffer actions temporary stressful conditions of market volatility.

When it comes to analysis of price changes in the end of the ban period and 1 year after the end of ban interventions, we conclude that it is very important for policy makers to be aware of, which bank characteristics are particularly sensitive to short selling ban, before it actually starts.

When we analyze the specific characteristics of banks to decide which fundamental firm should be considered, we turn to overall response in terms of stock price change, return results and unpredicted evidences.

To be specific, we found that the classical profitability variables (ROA, ROC and EBIT) and those related to the levels of earnings are not effective in contrasting the price fall. In addition, evidences suggest that policy makers consider positive contribution of recommendation (as market expectation) on stock price. Therefore, the policy maker must not pay too much attention to the current banks' profitability, before taking actions on ban restriction.

In fact, he should be focused on checking the banks' health, by considering the most long-term debt (as leverage indicator) and levels of liquidity (measured by cash flow from net income). These two fundamental firms in fact, in the present context, have shown their effectiveness in supporting the stock price. Policy makers should also pay attention to the size of the bank, measured by market capitalization, due to the fact that the bigger the market size, the higher the stock price. Under this perspective, it might be useful to hypothesize differentiated short selling interventions according to the size of the bank.

For volatility containment that is connected with stock price fall, it is usually the second milestone to the base of the interventions of short selling ban. Specifically, policy makers must pay deep attention to the dynamics of an indicator of profitability, the earnings (EPS annualized and growth) of banks, in order to reduce the impact of the overall risk on the local banking system. Under this perspective, policy makers should also consider the increase of profitability to be effective in terms of ROC, when in the overall risk containment. Our evidences could be of some interest also in the perspective of recent stress test exercises. Since stress test is conducted on the assumption of a static balance sheet that is made by banks with respect to the P&L, revenue, and costs, it all should be in line with the constraints of zero growth and a stable business mix. Under this perspective, it might be interesting to national policy makers to understand how banks react to short selling bans, and mostly, what kind of fundamentals are there for different market reactions under a short selling ban regime. Since short selling restrictions are implemented in high volatility and price fall scenario, its analysis could enrich the knowledge of how banking systems could react in adverse conditions that represent the same logic on which stress test exercises are based on.

We conclude this study by presenting some limitations of present analysis. We think that we mostly deal with two kinds of limitations. From one side, the ban period occurs in a limited time period, so we face the limited data variability that means, changes in firm fundamental occur in months and so, if we deal with a very short period of time, this means that we have limited availability in changing of fundamental firm data. This could, in some way, affect estimations we obtain by running statistical models. In this context, we could also have some difficulties (the most serious of the previous case to tell the truth) in using macro variables that in some ways could be useful in describing local banking systems. From the other side, we have a well-known problem of an analyst interested in the estimation of a treatment effect of a given policy program. Here we try to perform ex-post evaluation of policy actions (namely short selling bans) via evidence-based statistical analysis. From a statistical point of view, some recent studies (see, e.g., Cerulli 2012) claim that it needs to perform counterfactual causal analysis in order to better discriminate evidences coming out by performing econometric models. In our case, we do not think it is useful to perform counter-factual analysis, because we focus only on one sector (banking indeed), and ban measures we examined were focused on a single sector. We prefer to think of our evidence as descriptive statistics results and not as casual effects of a certain policy action, because in this case, we would have to approach, even with limitations, what we have already discussed but with different statistical tools.

References

Appel I., and C. Fohlin. 2010. Shooting the messenger? *The Impact of Short Sale Bans in Times of Crisis*. Pennsylvania: Department of Finance, the Wharton School, University of Pennsylvania, 1–35.

Bali, Turan G., Stephen J. Brown, and Mustafa Onur Caglayan. 2012. Systematic risk and the cross section of hedge fund returns. *Journal of Financial Economics* 106 (1): 114–131.

Battalio, Robert H., Hamid Mehran, and Paul H. Schultz. 2012. "Market declines: What is accomplished by banning short-selling?" Permanent DOI at https://www.newyorkfed.org/medialibrary/media/research/current_issues/ci18-5.pdf.

Beber, A., and Macro Pagano. 2013. Short-selling bans around the world: Evidence from the 2007–2009 crisis. *Journal of Finance* 68: 343–381.

Boehmer, E., C.M. Jones, and X. Zhang. 2013. Shackling short sellers: The 2008 shorting ban. *The Review of Financial Studies* 26 (6): 1363–1400.

Cai J., and Z. Zhang. 2011. Leverage change, debt overhang, and stock prices. *Journal of Corporate Finance* 17 (3): 391–402, ISSN 0929-1199, http://dx.doi.org/10.1016/j.jcorpfin.2010.12.003.

Campbell, John Y., Christophe Polk, and Tuomo, Vuolteenaho. 2005. Growth or glamour? Fundamentals and systematic risk in stock returns. National Bureau of Economic Research No. w11389.

Cerulli, Giovanni. 2012. "ivtreatreg: A new STATA routine for estimating binary treatment models with heterogeneous response to treatment under observable and unobservable selection." CNR-Ceris Working Papers 03/12.

Charoenrook A., and H. Daouk. 2005. *A study of market-wide short-selling restrictions*. New York: Department of Applied Economics and Management, Cornell University 1–43.

Diamond, Douglas W., and Robert E. Verrecchia. 1987. Constraints on short-selling and asset price adjustment to private information. *Journal of Financial Economics* 18 (2), 277–311.

Felix L., Kräussl R., and P. Stork. 2014. The 2011 European short sale ban: An option market perspective. LSF Research Working Paper Series, 14 (2), 1–45.

Ferrer, R.C., and A. Tang. 2016. An empirical investigation of the impact of financial ratios and business combination on stock price among the service firms in the Philippines. *Academy of Accounting and Financial Studies Journal* 20 (2): 104–115.

Grullon G., S. Michenaud, and J. Weston. 2015. The real effects of short-selling constraints. *The Review of Financial Studies* 28 (6): 1737–1767.

Harris L.E., Namvar E., Phillips B. 2013. Price inflation and wealth transfer during the 2008 SEC short-sale ban. *Journal of Investment Management* 2: 1–43.

Hasan I., N. Massoud, A. Saunders, and K. Song. 2010. *Should short-selling be restricted during a financial crisis?* 1–48. Stern School of Business, New York University: New York University.

Helmes, Uwe, Julia Henker, and Thomas Henker. 2010. "The effect of the ban on short selling on market efficiency and volatility." Permanent DOI at http://epublications.bond.edu.au/cgi/viewcontent.cgi?article=1532&context=business_pubs.

Ho, K.Y., B.D. Ernst, and Z.Y. Zhang. 2011. Assessing the dynamic relationship between small and large cap stock prices. *MODSIM 2011—19th International Congress on Modelling and Simulation—Sustaining Our Future: Understanding and Living with Uncertainty*, p. 1554.

Khan M.S., Harald Scheule, and E. Wu. 2016. Funding liquidity and bank risk taking. *Journal of Banking & Finance*, Available online 21 Sept 2016, ISSN 0378-4266, http://dx.doi.org/10.1016/j.jbankfin.2016.09.005.

Kolasinski, Adam C., Adam Reed, and Jacob R. Thornock. 2013. Can short restrictions actually increase informed short selling? *Financial Management* 42 (1), 155–181.

Mattarocci G., and G. Sampagnaro. 2010. Financial crisis and short selling: Do regulatory bans really work? Evidence from the italian market. *Academy of Accounting and Financial Studies Journal* 14 (4): 1–23.

Maudos, J. 2017. Income structure, profitability and risk in the European banking sector: The impact of the crisis. *Research in International Business and Finance* 39: 85–101, Part A, ISSN 0275-5319, http://dx.doi.org/10.1016/j.ribaf.2016.07.034.

Papanikolaou N.I., and C.C.P. Wolff. 2014, Oct. The role of on- and off-balance-sheet leverage of banks in the late 2000s crisis. *Journal of Financial Stability* 14: 3–22, ISSN 1572-3089, http://dx.doi.org/10.1016/j.jfs.2013.12.003.

Premti A., L. Garcia-Feijoo, and J. Madura. 2016. Information content of analyst recommendations in the banking industry. *International Review of Financial Analysis*, Available online 21 Nov 2016, ISSN 1057–5219, http://dx.doi.org/10.1016/j.irfa.2016.11.005.

Savor, Pavel, and Mungo Wilson. 2016. Earnings announcements and systematic risk. *The Journal of Finance* 71 (1): 83–138.

Schwartz L., and K. Norris. 2009. The impact of temporary short selling restrictions on the volatility of financial stock prices: does firm size matter? In *Academy of Business Education, Proceedings* 10 (19).

Shieh, S.-J., C.-Y. Lin, and P.-H. Ho. 2012. Large changes in stock prices: Market, liquidity, and momentum effect. *Quarterly Review of Economics and Finance* 52 (2): 183–197.

6

Reputational Risk in Banking: Important to Whom?

Ewa Miklaszewska and Krzysztof Kil

6.1 Introduction

Protecting a financial institution's reputation is among the most significant challenges facing financial firms, and trust in the integrity of the financial sector is the cornerstone of its stability and growth. The financial crisis of 2007–2009 and the post-crisis restructuring period have brought an increased interest in the reputational risk, particularly in the banking and financial sector. Crisis and post-crisis restructuring always results in an increased interest in the issues of trust and corporate culture, as scandals and excesses of the pre-crisis period come to light, and the amounts spent to rescue banks raise public opposition (Walter 2013). Moreover, as the empirical research has indicated, the reputational risk increases with the scale and profitability of banks, making the subject even more relevant in a global system characterized by a highly

E. Miklaszewska (✉) · K. Kil
Cracow University of Economics, Kraków, Poland
e-mail: uumiklas@cyf-kr.edu.pl

G. Chesini et al. (eds.), *The Business of Banking*, Palgrave Macmillan Studies in Banking and Financial Institutions, DOI 10.1007/978-3-319-54894-4_6

concentrated banking markets (Fiordelisi et al. 2011). The crisis caused multibillion losses and revealed problems with strategic priorities and the failure of risk management systems in large global banks. Consequently, there has been a renewed interest in the creation of stable and functional risk culture in global banks. Thus, the aim of this chapter is to analyze why reputational risk is important for banks, and what are the incentives to manage it.

Reputational risk is often analyzed within an operational risk framework. The Basel Committee (BCBS 2001) described the latter as one of the three main categories of banking risks and defined it as a possibility of direct or indirect loss resulting from inadequate or failed internal processes, actions of people or systems, or losses related to the impact of external events. Although the definition was quite broad, the reputational risk, as well as the strategic one, has not been included. The methodology to manage and measure operational risk has been advancing rapidly in recent years, fueled by a number of well-publicized scandals (the bankruptcy of Barings, problems of Société Générale due to rogue traders and the Allied Irish Bank, and UBS due to unauthorized trading), and also, huge sums paid by banks and insurance companies after 2008 crisis to settle allegations of sales abuses illustrate the point. However, as it took over a decade to develop an acceptable infrastructure for operational risk management, the reputational risk is only at the beginning of a similar process.

Reputational risk is not a new concept, but the efforts to manage it as a self-standing type of risk and not within an operational risk framework are quite recent. However, it is more difficult to manage reputational risk than other risk categories, as it is difficult to define and quantify, or separate it from the impact of other events (ACE 2013). Consequently, in the empirical part, this chapter proposes a methodology to measure reputational risk, based on the bank stakeholders' perspective. The reputational risk is approximated by an integrated indicator: Stakeholder Reputation Score (SRS). Then, panel regression models are used to examine its impact on bank performance, for listed banks in Central and Eastern Europe (CEE-11). The aim of the empirical part is to analyze whether there is a reputational premium, i.e., what are the incentives to manage the reputational risk in banks.

The chapter is organized as follows: Sects. 2–3 review the approaches to define the reputational risk, Sect. 4 analyzes the literature on factors causing reputational risk, Sect. 5 reviews the approaches to measure reputational risk, Sect. 6 describes the empirical methodology and summarizes the results of the panel data models aiming at measuring the reputational performance premium for CEE banks, approximating reputational risk by Shareholder Reputational Score, and the last section concludes the chapter.

6.2 Reputational Risk from a Regulatory Perspective

Risk appears with every banking product and operation, and managing risk constitutes an everyday bank activity. Risk can be defined as uncertainty concerning the return or outcome of an investment or an action. Risk management is a process by which managers identify, assess, monitor, and control risks associated with financial institutions' activities (Koch and MacDonald 2015). Its objective is to minimize negative effects on the financial result and capital of a bank. However, in financial institutions, risk can be treated both as a threat and also as an opportunity (Marcinkowska 2014). Banks manage risk at many levels, taking account of both macro- and micro-factors, in many cases external to the decisions taken by bank. In many cases, risk is interconnected, both within a bank and in the whole system. Risk management encompasses the process of identifying risks to the bank, measuring exposures, ensuring that an effective capital monitoring program is in place, monitoring risk exposures and corresponding capital needs on an ongoing basis, taking steps to control or mitigate risk exposures, and reporting to senior management and the board on the bank's risk exposures and capital positions (BCBS 2011). In the future, the new challenges will be coming from expanding regulations, raising customers' expectations due to technological progress and the emergence of new types of risks (McKinsey 2015).

Historically, the efforts in managing risk by banks tend to focus on credit and market risk. However, risk management in banking has been transformed over the past decade, largely in response to regulations that emerged from the global financial crisis. Reputation risk was not included in the recommendations of the Basel Committee on the modeling of risk in the banking sector. Basel II (2004) and Basel III (2010) kept reputational risk out of pillar one capital requirement, and reputational risk is currently not subject to any specific capital requirements in the EU. Capital Requirements Directives applicable to EU countries require only that the competent authorities evaluate reputational risks arising from securitization transactions and that financial institutions develop methodologies to assess the possible impact of reputational risk on funding positions (Dey 2016). In the USA, reputational risk is one of the Federal Reserve System's categories of safety and soundness and fiduciary risk (credit, market, liquidity, operational, legal, and reputational) and one of the three categories of compliance risk (Business Insurance 2016).

Reputational risk—damage to an organization through loss of its reputation—can arise as a consequence of operational failures, as well as from other events. Both operational and reputational risks belong to a similar area, as operational problems can have negative consequences for bank reputation, affecting client satisfaction and shareholder value. However, those risks can also include a broader set of incidents, such as fraud, privacy protection, legal risks, and physical (e.g., infrastructure shutdown) or environmental risks. In light of the significant number of recent operational risk-related losses incurred by banks, in June 2011, the Basel Committee published the "Principles for the Sound Management of Operational Risk," which incorporated the lessons from the financial crisis. The eleven principles cover governance, risk management environment and the role of disclosure, and address the three lines of defense: business line management, an independent operational risk management function, and an independent review. In 2014, the Committee conducted the review in the form of a questionnaire, involving 60 systemically important banks in 20 countries, in which the banks self-assessed their implementation of the principles. A key finding of the review was that banks have made insufficient progress in implementing the principles (BCBS 2014). Hence, in 2014, the Basel Committee proposed a revision to its operational risk framework that set out a new approach for calculating operational risk capital. In addition, the Financial Stability Board stressed the importance of operational risk in the post-crisis environment, defining it as a synthetic one, including people risk, outsourcing risk, internal and external fraud, money laundering, and technology risk (FSB 2012).

In 2009, the Basel Committee passed the document addressing the need to strengthen risk management by banks, in which the reputational risk was defined as a multidimensional process, based on the perception of other market participants (BCBS 2009). Reputational risk was explained as the actual or potential risk related to earnings or capital, arising from negative perception of financial institutions by the current and potential stakeholders (customers, counterparties, shareholders, employees, investors, debt-holders, market analysts, other relevant parties, or regulators) that can adversely affect a bank's ability to maintain existing, or establish new, business relationships and its continued access to sources of funding, including the interbank market or the securitization processes. In this document, the Basel Committee stressed the need to manage reputation risk, identifying its sources and taking it into account when testing the resilience of a bank business model to external shocks (BCBS 2009). The Fed's *Commercial Bank Examination Manual* defines reputational risk as "the potential that negative publicity regarding an institution's business practices, whether true or not, will cause a decline in the customer base, costly litigation or revenue reductions" (Business Insurance 2016).

6.3 Reputational Risk as Internal and External Factor

Risk management is result oriented, with different priorities given to avoidance of operational and reputational problems and a different time horizon for maximizing the value of the company. The reputational risk is associated with faulty strategy, poor management and leadership, or a wrong system of incentives, inadequate supervision, and problematic corporate culture. Reputational risk can be defined as the risk of economic losses associated with a negative image of the bank by the clients, supervisors, regulators, and the public. This and similar definitions stressed that reputational risk is multidimensional and reflects the perception of other market participants.

It can also be defined as the risk to bank goodwill, which is not associated with deterioration of book value and is typically reflected in a falling stock price (Walter 2013). There is also a problem of time frame. In most cases, the effects of a scandal or unexpected loss are immediate. The loss is seen as a signal that the company has a weak control environment. Shareholders may also sell shares if they believe that future losses are inevitable. However, there are also cases of more prolonged problems with corporate culture, which gradually erode customers' and business partners' trust. In some cases, reputational problems have a negative impact on the financial results, but there are also the opposite cases (Marcinkowska 2013).

Reputational risk is not regulation or compliance driven, but determined by stakeholder expectations. Steinhoff and Sprengel (2014) observed that risk awareness is probably the most important factor for risk reduction, so it should be placed inside the corporate governance framework, particularly in "who is responsible for what" approach. However, corporate culture is also a very broad concept and can be defined in many ways (Guiso et al. 2006). The development of corporate culture is a continuous process, where the results are visible in the long term. Its definitions emphasize that it rests on a set of values shared by a community, which affects its organization and motivates behavior within the organization (Carretta and Sargiacomo 2016). The period of crisis often results in an increased interest in corporate governance; however, changes in prudential regulations correcting errors in risk management are usually easier than the long-term changes in the corporate culture of market participants (Walter 2013). However, there are some mechanisms which can be used in enhancing trust, such as codes of ethics, internal anti-fraud systems, independent ethics audits, and reputational indices. Indirect measures involve membership of professional associations or self-regulatory organizations, which protect the reputation and discipline among its members, setting standards in codes of conduct and developing mechanisms of better risk assessment processes (Morris and Vines 2014; Marcinkowska 2013).

Reputational risk is usually due not to incidental events, but is the result of long-term poor decision-making processes. The causes are often linked to the pressures on results, the asymmetry of the profit-to-risk ratio, conflict of interest related to the complexity of bank business models, and compensations based on bonuses (Walter 2013). Financial services differ significantly from the industrial sector. Key stakeholders of banks are depositors, creditors, and the government (insurance). As banks are financed largely through debt, shareholders have a lesser importance than in corporations. However, bank governance prioritizes shareholder interests, particularly when ownership is concentrated in institutional investors with a large risk tolerance. Consequently, governance of financial institutions may accept excessive operational risk, which may erode shareholder wealth and may fail to meet the expectation of other stakeholders (Dow 2014).

Inside the banking sector, reputation is often treated in the same way as a "brand," i.e., an intangible asset that can be impaired by operational mistakes or inappropriate behavior. In this approach, reputational risk is a derivative risk, arising as a result of damaging action (Steinhoff and Sprengel 2014). Reputation may also serve as a cushion against losses, i.e., companies with a better reputation suffered less severe declines in market value during the crisis periods although the empirical evidence varies in this respect—in some cases good reputation softens the impact of failures; in others, it may be dangerous, as other objective indicators of strength, such as capital or liquidity, may seem irrelevant. The third way is not to treat it as an asset, nor as a kind of equity capital, but as a set of obligations toward stakeholders, which have to be fulfilled (Steinhoff and Sprengel 2014). Thus, reputation can be summed up as having three main manifestations:

- reputation as asset (stakeholders' goodwill),
- reputation as liability (stakeholders' expectations), and
- reputation as capital (buffer against failure, helping to maintain goodwill when failing to meet expectations).

The impact of reputation on performance is a direct consequence of the interaction of those domains (Steinhoff and Sprengel 2014).

6.4 Reputational Risk in Global Surveys

The strategy of the largest global banks has evolved from simple, commercial institutions, providing selected services for a specific customer segment, to complex conglomerates, serving millions of customers in many countries. Traditionally, the financial services industry worked according to easily understandable principles, with clearly defined risk profiles, but in the last 20 years those divisions were blurred, and new players, such as hedge and equity funds, were offering para-banking services (Rajan 2005). However, the strategy of a "financial supermarket" and a "too big to fail" scale turned out to be very risky. Although among the top causes of the global financial crisis was a systemic risk associated with the activities of large global banks, after the crisis, their role has been further strengthened. In many countries, post-crisis restructuring took a form of mergers and acquisitions, particularly of investment banks by the universal ones in the USA or merging the nationalized banks to control losses (the Netherlands and the UK). So the question of managing the reputation risk in the process of acquisition is another important challenge (Schoenmaker 2011; Dermine 2006).

The 2008 financial crisis had a significant effect on bank reputation and trust, and only recently can we observe a gradual rebound of trust: Financial services have recorded an 8-point increase from 43% in 2012 to 51% in 2016 on a global basis. Financial services, however, are still the least trusted industry among those surveyed by the Edelman Trust Barometer (2016). Inside the industry, employees are more trusted than senior executives and CEOs to communicate about topics like financial earnings, crises, and the treatment of customers. In the USA, the Reputation Institute compared the financial industry problems with past reputation of tobacco firms. In the post-crisis period, the financial sector has been obliged to pay an incredible amount of litigation expenses, with the most notable being JP Morgan paying a 13 billion dollar settlement to the US government over behavior leading to the crisis in 2014, Deutsche Bank investigated for tax evasion and money laundering, in addition to Libor fixing in 2012, or large banks fined for the Libor scandal in 2015. However, in 2016 for the first time, the large banks have risen in the US ranking—of the 33 banks evaluated, ten banks had an "excellent" reputation among their customers, compared to eight in 2015 (American Banker 2016). Other surveys have also shown that inside the banking industry, the best reputation has divisions related to new technologies, e.g., Internet banking and ATM, though not telephone banking (Ernst and Young 2014).

As early as in 2005, the Economist Intelligence Unit Report observed that protecting a firm's reputation is the most important and difficult task facing a firm's managers and reported that in a survey of 269 senior executives, responsible for managing risk, reputational risk emerged as the most significant threat to business out of a choice of 13 categories of risk. Reputational risk was defined as an event that undermined public trust in bank products or brand (The Economist 2005). Reputation is based on aggregate past experience; however, it is directed toward the future and reflects the expectations concerning the firm (Edelman Trust Barometer 2014). Customers satisfied with the services of the bank have a greater loyalty which helps to improve the bank image and its competitive position (Fiordelisi and Molyneux 2009). In contrast, problems with bank reputation can lead to (Eccles et al. 2007):

- loss of current or prospective customers,
- loss of employees or managers in the organization,
- departure of current or future business partners, and
- an increase in the cost of financing through a loan or capital markets.

The growing awareness of reputational risk is reflected in an annual survey conducted by the European Banking Authority and reported in "*Risk Assessment of the European Banks.*" This document includes a section on reputational risk, particularly assessing its impact on consumer confidence (EBA 2014, 2015, 2016). The reports showed a growing awareness of the reputational risk in the European banking sector, as indicated by 33% of responding banks in 2013, 44% in 2014, and 68%

in 2015. Numerous case studies and empirical studies showed that reputational risk is particularly important for large global banks and those with relatively low capitalization, so it should be an important subject of supervisory concern. According to EBA reports, particularly a detrimental impact on consumers had failures with regard to rate benchmark-setting processes, the misselling of banking products, and more recently misconduct related to foreign exchange rates, violations of trade sanctions and redress for payment protection insurance, and floors for mortgage loans at variable interest rates. The scope of identified detrimental business practices remains wide and misconduct costs remain high. The share of banks indicating that they have paid out more than one billion euros in compensation, litigation, and similar payments increased in 2015 to 32% of participating banks (16% in 2014 and only 8% in 2013) (EBA 2014, 2015, 2016). Efforts to adjust culture and risk governance are the most widely considered approach to address reputational and legal risks (85% in 2016), an increase from less than 50% of respondents in previous surveys. However, in the 2016 Report, only about 10% of surveyed banks indicated their intention to adjust products and business models in an effort to address reputational and legal risks.

Kaiser (2014) analyzes two surveys conducted by KPMG among the G-SIBs (the Global Systemically Important Banks) in 2013 and 2014 and responded to by ten banks and a survey of the German banks, responded to by 18 institutions, 13 of which belong to the 20 biggest German banks in 2012. In the surveys, 60% of both global and German banks asserted that reputational risk stands on its own, rather than being a consequential risk, or triggers to other risks; however, most banks did not include it in their risk inventory and admitted that it is not explicitly addressed in their risk strategy. Another question showed that only 55% of the G-SIBs and 60% of the German banks prioritized their stakeholders, in order to manage reputational risk more efficiently. German banks gave the highest priority to customers, while global banks gave top priorities to customers, employees, and regulators. The surveys demonstrated that banks put the main emphasis on the self-assessment of reputational risk, only supplementary emphasis on expert opinions, interviews with senior management, and analysis of press and social media, and that they register and report losses due to reputational risk mainly as a part of an operational risk database, so although banks were aware of the need to include reputational risk in their overall risk mapping, in everyday life, they dealt with it in an operational risk management framework.

6.5 Problems with Measurement of the Reputational Risk

Efforts to manage operational risk have been successfully quantified in the last decade, but for reputational risk, the typical approach is still to monitor it inside the broadly defined “risk culture.” What gets measured gets managed (Diermeier 2008), but quantification of reputation risk is extremely difficult as there is no universally accepted methodology and the concept is broad. If we define reputational risk as unexpected losses due to the reaction of stakeholders to an altered perception of an institution (Kaiser 2014), there are many possible ways of approximating this risk. Moreover, reputational risk does not act in isolation and, on the contrary, is interrelated to many other types of risks. Some sources of gain/loss in the reputational capital include economic performance, stakeholder interface, and legal interface, which can be reflected in client flight, loss of market share, investor flight and increase of cost of capital, and talent flight and increase of contracting costs (Walter 2016). Assuming that reputational risk is managed through strong corporate governance, another approach is to create indexes which measure the quality of firms’ corporate governance structure and link it to stock price-based performance of the company, assuming that the change in corporate governance index is a signal of quality of firm management (Fox et al. 2016).

Empirical studies typically focus on various surveys, case studies, or media coverage of detrimental events. There is also a lack of tools to link reputational risk with financial performance, and it is unclear how reputation risk can impact capital (Diermeier 2008). In many companies, reputational problems are still considered rather as a problem of public relations than a strategic one, and the response is frequently inadequate to the scale of the damage. The problem of reputational risk measurement is still aggravated for CEE banks, as the stock markets are not efficient in discounting information, so the panel data models using stock market information may be misleading.

Assessing reputational risk is most often not an objective process, but rather it is a subjective assessment that could reflect a number of different factors. Reputation could be perceived as an intangible asset, synonymous with goodwill, which is difficult to measure and quantify. Consistently strong earnings, a trustworthy board of directors and senior management, loyal and content branch employees, and a strong customer base are just a few examples of positive factors that contribute to a bank's good reputation (Business Insurance 2016).

Establishing a strong reputation provides a competitive advantage. A good reputation strengthens a company's market position and increases shareholder value. It can even help attract top talent. Communication between a bank and its stakeholders can be the foundation for a strong reputation. Bank examiners may consider whether an institution responds to customer concerns; whether the stock analyst recommends buying or selling and why; and what the shareholders, employees, or general public are saying about the institution. They also consider whether the institution is expanding outside its normal geographical area and is supportive of the community. On-site, examiners will talk to both bank employees and management to get a sense of corporate ethics. Examiners will assess whether an institution's expertise is adequate and controls are in place to oversee growth if the institution should engage in riskier products or enter into new business lines (Brown 2016).

Also, the agencies, such as Standard & Poor's, Moody's, and Fitch, have significantly increased their emphasis on reputational risks related to corporate governance. The rating agency's primary focus is the ability and willingness of an entity to make full and timely payment of debt service on its financial obligations. However, a damaged reputation can significantly affect the performance and, ultimately, the ability to borrow capital. For example, S&P issued a statement saying that costs associated with the Costa Concordia disaster had negatively affected the firm's operating performance in 2012. Another example of the importance of reputation in obtaining the rating score is public universities in the USA, which rely heavily on their reputation and brand as a strategic asset (Business Insurance 2016).

A measure that is sometimes used is the difference between the immediate costs of a crisis and damage to a firm's market capitalization in the period following a crisis event (ACE 2013). Another frequent approach in modeling reputational risk is to analyze it within an operational risk framework, assuming that operational loss events can lead to significant reputational losses, and to check the impact of bank reputational problems on bank market capitalization (Perry and De Fontnouvelle 2005). The reputational loss is defined as market value loss that exceeds announced operational loss (Eckert and Gatzer 2015). Another frequent approach is to conduct an event study analysis of the impact of operational loss events on the market values of financial institutions by examining a firm's stock price reaction to the announcement of particular operational loss events such as internal frauds, estimating the Reputational Value at Risk at a given confidence level, which represents the economic capital needed to cover reputational losses over a specified period (Micocci et al. 2009).

6.6 Empirical Analysis of the Reputational Risk in the CEE Banking

Reputation can be perceived not only as a problem, but as an asset, contributing to a performance premium. The empirical part adopts this approach, examining the relationship between an indicator of the reputational risk (Shareholder Reputational Score) and bank performance. To test the role of reputational risk for bank performance in CEE-11 countries, the panel data model with fixed effects was used (with Hausman and Breusch-Pagana tests), based on individual bank data from Bankscope. In the sample, 42 banks listed at CEE stock exchanges were analyzed (15 from Poland, 12 from Croatia, 4 from Bulgaria and Slovakia, 3 from Romania, and 1 from the Czech Rep., Hungary, Lithuania, and Slovenia), for which the rating information from at least one of the three major agencies: Standard & Poor's Rating Services, Moody's Investors Service Inc., or Fitch Ratings Ltd., was available.

The first step was to construct an index of reputational risk; the following one was to test its impact on bank performance. In the model, reputation risk was represented by a three-dimensional, synthetic index: Stakeholder Reputation Score (SRS). The index is based on the perspectives of three major bank stakeholders, according to the following formula:

SRS: (a) market participant perspective + (b) client perspective + (c) investor perspective.

Those three perspectives were approximated by:

SRS: (a) credit agencies' bank ratings + (b) deposit growth + (c) bank stock returns.

There is a long debate on the relevance of the rating information and rating agencies' credibility, particularly after the global crisis (Grothe 2013; Eckert and Gatzer 2015), but nevertheless credit rating encompasses a broach range of information. Credit ratings express credit rating agencies' forward-looking opinion about the creditworthiness of an obligor—the capacity and willingness to meet its financial obligations in full and on time (S&P 2016) and represent an evaluation of the qualitative and quantitative information on the prospective debtor. In the model, the ratings were employed both at a country level (CR) and at the bank level, included in the SRS index.

The three dimensions in SRS (a, b, and c) were calculated as follows:

a. ratings: scores from major credit agencies were used and the average score (arithmetic mean, in points) was established as in Table 6.2, on a scale of 1–16, adjusted by rating perspective of ±0.5% points; a stable outlook did not cause adjustments in the assessment;
b. deposits: the annual growth rate of current deposits from the non-financial sector was used (converted to points); and
c. stock return: the annual rate of return from bank stock was used, adjust by splits and dividends paid (in points) (Table 6.1).

Table 6.1 Scoring scale used in the model

Rating agency assessment			Model score
S&P	Fitch	Moody's	
AAA	AAA	Aaa	16
AA+	AA+	Aa1	15
AA	AA	Aa2	14
AA−	AA−	Aa3	13
A+	A+	A1	12
A	A	A2	11
A−	A−	A3	10
BBB+	BBB+	Baa1	9
BBB	BBB	Baa2	8
BBB−	BBB−	Baa3	7
BB+	BB+	Ba1	6
BB	BB	Ba2	5
BB−	BB−	Ba3	4
B+	B+	B1	3
B	B	B2	2
B−	B−	B3	1

Point values of the three dimensions (a, b, and c) of the SRS were calculated by assigning each year a numerical value to each decile for each indicator and for the whole group, in the following way:

- 0 points for the median for the entire group in a given year;
- from −5 to −1 respectively for deciles from 1 to 5; and
- from 1 to 5 respectively for deciles from 6 to 10.

Consequently, the SRS index ranges from −15 to +15 points for the three indicators and represents an approximation of the bank's reputational risk.

The next step was to run a panel data model, for the period 2009–2014. The dependent variables were the long-term, comprehensive indicator: Multi-Level Performance Score (MLPS) and the short-term, simple indicator: Return on Equity (ROE). MLPS was defined as the sum of points awarded in five key areas for long-term evaluation of bank performance: three performance indicators (ROE, cost-to-income ratio and loans-to-asset ratio) and two sustainability indicators (Z-score and NPL) (Miklaszewska and Kil 2015). Thus, MLPS = ROE + C/I + L/A + Z-score + NPL.

Table 6.2 Description of explanatory variables

Symbol	Description	Rationale/Data source
a. Macroeconomic variables		
Δ GDP	Real GDP growth rate (%)	Macroeconomic business cycle (World Bank: World Development Indicators)
HHI	Herfindahl-Hirschman index for credit institutions	Banking market concentration (BSCEE Review and ECB Database)
SB	Total bank assets (% of GDP)	Size of the banking sector (Raiffeisen Research 2015)
CR	Country LT credit rating	Country credit standing (Bankscope, rating agencies' internet sites)
b. Bank-level variables (data source: Bankscope)		
ln_TA	Logarithm of total assets (in USD)	Bank size
SRS	Reputational risk index	Approximation of reputational risk
L_D	Loans-to-Deposits ratio	Bank funding risk
NeII_NoIOI	Net interest income/ Total non-interest operating income	Income diversification (bank business model)
S_TA	Securities/Total Assets	Market risk
LA_DSTF	Liquid assets/Deposits and short-term funding	Liquidity risk

The score was calculated as follows: For each indicator, the whole group was divided into ten deciles, and the median value is 0 (neutral); each subsequent deciles above the median for the ROE, L/A, and Z-score ranged from 1 to 5, and each successive deciles below the median had negative value and ranged from −1 to −5. For C/I and NPLs, the signs were the opposite. This indicator has a simple interpretation: The higher the value of the MLP score, the better the assessment of the bank's results. The panel data model with fixed effects was used, which measured the impact of reputation risk (approximated by the SRS score) on bank performance, measured by the comprehensive index Multi-Level Performance Score (MLPS) and profitability indicator (ROE). For robustness, bank stock rate of return (RR) as dependent variable was also tested, but the SRS was insignificant for that model. The explanatory variables are defined in Table 6.2.

The results of estimations for the reputational effects on bank performance are summarized in Tables 6.3 (for the comprehensive MLPS) and 6.4 (for the ROE).

Table 6.3 Panel data estimations for MLPS, CEE-11, 2009–2014

Control variables		
const	−79,050	
	0.121	
Δ GDP	0.369	*
	0.068	
HHI	−249,297	*
	0.078	
SB	2351	
	0.827	
CR	−3789	***
	0.008	
ln_TA	7173	**
	0.030	
SRS	−0.265	**
	0.011	
L_D	0.218	***
	0.000	
NeII_NoIOI	−0.012	**
	0.017	
S_TA	−0.039	
	0.688	
LA_DSTF	0.178	**
	0.026	
R^2	0.856	
R^2 corrected	0.837	

Note ***, **, * correspond to 1%, 5%, and 10% significance level
Source Own calculation

The estimation results presented in Tables 6.3 and 6.4 indicate that analyzing bank performance, both approximated by short-term ROE and by a comprehensive MLP score, the index of bank reputation SCR (similarly like the country's rating CR on a macroeconomic level) not only has a positive impact, but on the contrary affects bank performance strongly negatively, similarly as the HHI concentration index. Factors with a positive impact on bank performance were the size of the bank, its financing strategy, the asset risks, and the high level of GDP growth. Thus, the empirical results are contrary to the expectations: For CEE-11 stock-listed banks, large risky banks with low reputational score were best placed for best results, both in a short-term (ROE) and in a long-term (MLPS) perspective.

Table 6.4 Panel data estimations for ROE, CEE 2009–2014

Control variables	2009–2014	
const	−187,278	*
	0.082	
Δ GDP	0.121	
	0.747	
HHI	−504,163	*
	0.076	
SB	21,042	
	0.288	
CR	−2037	
	0.424	
ln_TA	12,325	*
	0.072	
SRS	−0.357	*
	0.081	
L_D	0.168	**
	0.048	
NeII_NoIOI	−0.003	
	0.672	
S_TA	0.488	**
	0.012	
LA_DSTF	0.292	*
	0.067	
R^2	0.639	
R2 corrected	0.489	

Note ***, **, * correspond to 1%, 5%, and 10% significance level
Source Own calculation

6.7 Conclusion

The reputational risk literature and surveys, analyzed in this chapter, suggested that banks should treat reputational risk as a separate class of risk and analyze it beyond the framework of operational risk and corporate governance. It should not be narrowed down to "public relation" response to crisis events, but treated as a strategic type of risk, with a strong potential to harm the value of the company.

However, as the reputational literature and many case studies indicate, it is very difficult to categorize and quantify reputational risk, as it can arise as a consequence of other risks and many events. The panel data models for listed banks in CEE-11 countries, analyzed in this chapter, have also indicated that proper management of reputational risk may not be important (and even harmful) for an assessment of bank performance, which may explain why many banks dealt with reputational risk mainly in the context of minimizing loss after a scandal. Consequently, there seem to be incentives to disregard reputational risk in an operational and strategic bank management and deal with it only with crisis events.

References

ACE. 2013. *Reputation at Risk.* London. www.acegroup.com/global-assets/documents/EuropeCorporate/ThoughtLeadership/ace_reputation_at_risk_july_2013.pdf.

American Banker. 2016. *Survey of Bank Reputation.* www.americanbanker.com.

BCBS—Basel Committee on Banking Supervision. 2001, January. *Consultative Document: Operational Risk*, BIS.

BCBS—Basel Committee on Banking Supervision. 2009, July. *Proposed Enhancements to the Basel II Framework. Consultative Document Bank for International Settlement.*

BCBS—Basel Committee on Banking Supervision. 2011, June. *Principles for the Sound Management of Operational Risk*, BIS.

BCBS—Basel Committee on Banking Supervision. 2014, October. *Review of the Principles for the Sound Management of Operational Risk.*

Brown, W.J. 2016. *Understanding Reputational Risk: Identify, Measure, and Mitigate the Risk*, www.philadelphiafed.org/bank-resources/publications/src-insights/2007/fourth-quarter/q4si1_07.

Business Insurance. 2016, August 1st. *Reputation Risk in Focus at Credit Rating Agencies.*

Carretta, A., and M. Sargiacomo, (eds.). 2016. *Doing Banking in Italy: Governance, Risk, Accounting and Auditing Issues.* Milano: McGraw Hill.

Dermine, J. 2006. European Banking Integration: Don't Put the Cart Before the Horse. *Financial Markets, Institutions & Instruments* 15 (2): 57–106.

Dey, S.K. (2016). *Reputational Risk in Banking—The Current Approach and a Way Ahead*, TCS Financial Solutions, www.tcs.com.

Diermeier, D. 2008, March. Measuring and Managing Reputational Risk. *Risk Management*, 12 (3).

Dow, S. 2014. *Managing Stakeholder Expectations*. Reputational Risk Management in Financial Institutions: Risk Books Incisive Media Investments Ltd.

Eccles, R., S. Newquist, and R. Schatz. 2007, February. Reputation and its Risk. *Harvard Business Review*.

Eckert, Ch. and N. Gatzer. 2015. *Modeling Operational Risk Incorporating Reputational Risk: An Integrated Analysis for Financial Firms*. FAU Working Paper, www.vwrm.rw.fau.de/files/2016/05/Reputation_Risk_2015-08-14_WP.pdf.

Edelman Trust Barometer. 2014, 2016. *Trust in Financial Services*. www.edelman.com/insights/intellectual-property/2016-edelman-trust-barometer/state-of-trust/trust-in-financial-services-trust-rebound.

European Banking Authority. 2014, 2015, 2016. *Risk Assessment of the European Banking System*. https://www.eba.europa.eu/documents.

Ernst and Young. 2014. *Building a Better Working World*. Global Consumer Banking Survey.

Fiordelisi, F., and P. Molyneux. 2009. *Shareholder Value in Banking*. Basingstoke: Palgrave Macmillan.

Fiordelisi, F., S. Soana, and P. Schwizer. 2013, May. The Determinants of Reputational Risk in the Banking Sector. *Journal of Banking & Finance* 37 (5): 1359–1371.

Fox, M.B., J.R. Gilson, and D. Palia. 2016, August. *Corporate Governance Changes as a Signal: Contextualizing the Performance Link*. Working Paper 323, European Governance Institute.

FSB. 2012. *Increasing the Intensity and Effectiveness of SIFI Supervision Progress Report to the G20 Ministers and Governors*. www.fsb.org/wp-content/uploads/r_121031ab.pdf.

Grothe, M. 2013, December. *Market Pricing of Credit Rating Signals*. ECB: Working Paper no. 1623.

Guiso, L., P. Sapienza, and L. Zingales. 2006. Does Culture Affect Economic Outcomes? *Journal of Economic Perspectives* 20 (2): 22–48.

Kaiser, T. 2014. Reputational Risk Management across the World: a Survey of Current Practices. In: *Reputational Risk Management in Financial Institutions*, London: Risk Books Incisive Media Investments Ltd.

Koch, T.W., and S. MacDonald. 2015. *Bank Management*. Boston: Cengage Learning.

Marcinkowska, M. 2013. *Kapitał relacyjny banku: Kształtowanie relacji banku z otoczeniem*. t. I, Łódź: Wydawnictwo Uniwersytetu Łódzkiego.

Marcinkowska, M. 2014. *Corporate governance w bankach, teoria i praktyka*. Łódź: Wydawnictwo Uniwersytetu Łódzkiego.

McKinsey. 2015, December. *The Future of Bank Risk Management*, McKinsey Working Papers on Risk, McKinsey & Company.

Micocci, M., G. Masala, G. Cannas and G Flore. 2009. *Reputational Effects of Operational Risk Events for Financial Institutions*, University of Cagliari Working Paper, http://www.actuaries.org/AFIR/Colloquia/Rome2/Micocci_Masala_Cannas_Flore.pdf.

Miklaszewska, E. and K. Kil. 2015. The Impact of the 2008 Crisis on the Banking Sectors of the CEE-11 Countries: Multi Level Performance Index as a Synthetic Measure of Bank Risk Adjusted Performance. *Econometrics*, 4 (50).

Morris, N., and D. Vines. 2014. *Capital Failure: Rebuilding Trust in Financial Services*. Oxford: Oxford University Press.

Perry, J., and P. De Fontnouvelle. 2005, October. Measuring Reputational Risk: The Market Reaction to Operational Loss Announcements, Federal Reserve Bank of Boston.

Raiffeisen Research. 2015, June. *CEE Banking Sector Report*.

Rajan, R. 2005, November. *Has Financial Development Made the World Riskier?* Working Paper Series 11728, NBER. http://www.nber.org/papers/w11728.

Schoenmaker, D. 2011, April. *The European Banking Landscape after the Crisis*. Policy Paper, 12, DSF.

S&P: Standard & Poor's Ratings Definitions 2016, February 1. www.standardandpoors.com/ratingsdirect.

Steinhoff, C., and R. Sprengel. 2014. *Governance as the Starting Point for a Reputational Risk-Management Process*. Reputational Risk Management in Financial Institutions, London: Risk Books Incisive Media Investments Ltd.

The Economist. 2005, December. Reputation: Risk of Risks. *The Economist Intelligence Unit*.

Walter, I. 2013. Reputational Risk and Financial Crisis. In: *Global Asset Management*, eds. M. Pinedo and I. Walter. New York: Palgrave Macmillan.

Walter, I. 2016, February. Reputational Risk and Large International Banks. *Financial Market Portfolio Management*, 30 (1): 1–17.

7

The Business Model of Banks: A Review of the Theoretical and Empirical Literature

Stefano Cosma, Riccardo Ferretti, Elisabetta Gualandri, Andrea Landi and Valeria Venturelli

7.1 Introduction

The business model (BM) has become a key concept in banking literature. The topic's relevance is due to the impact of the crisis on bank profitability and risk levels, leading to new challenges for bank managers, analysts and regulators.

S. Cosma · R. Ferretti · E. Gualandri (✉) · A. Landi · V. Venturelli
University of Modena and Reggio Emilia, Modena, Italy
e-mail: elisabetta.gualandri@unimore.it

S. Cosma
e-mail: stefano.cosma@unimore.it

R. Ferretti
e-mail: riccardo.ferretti@unimore.it

A. Landi
e-mail: andrea.landi@unimore.it

V. Venturelli
e-mail: valeria.venturelli@unimore.it

G. Chesini et al. (eds.), *The Business of Banking*, Palgrave Macmillan Studies in Banking and Financial Institutions, DOI 10.1007/978-3-319-54894-4_7

From the managerial point of view, the crisis has caused an in-depth review of banks' strategies and enhanced their ability to change/adapt both their business mix and their market positioning in the different strategic areas where they compete.

In the years since the outbreak of the crisis, three main drivers have spurred a significant change in banks' strategic plans.

Firstly, a new adverse economic context, with a combination of slow economic growth and historically low levels of interest rates. Both phenomena depress the prospects for traditional bank intermediation, since they lead to less, higher-risk lending while simultaneously squeezing profit margins on the loans–deposits circuit.

Secondly, the re-regulation introduced in the wake of the crisis is triggering strategic changes in BMs to adapt balance sheet structures to new regulatory requirements: liquidity, high-quality capital, more stable funding resources and bail-inable debt.

A third driver concerns the structural configuration of the main banking systems, which affects banks' ability to handle the fast pace of technological innovation and its impact on products and distribution channels.

This Darwinian economic context opens the question of which banks are in the best position to succeed and, at the same time, which banks are going to become the victims of this much more competitive arena.

Business model analysis (BMA) has become the conceptual framework used by analysts and regulators in the attempt to identify banks' main strategic behaviours and their implications in terms of competitiveness and future performance and stability.

As far as banking regulation and supervision are concerned, BMA is the basis for a proactive response and aims to reveal the key vulnerabilities of the different banking business models (BBM). This conceptual framework, embedded in the Supervisory Review and Evaluation Process (SREP), has a central role in the 2015 and 2016 Thematic Review by the Single Supervisory Mechanism (SSM). In banking supervision, BMA is an important tool for revealing a bank's main vulnerabilities in the short run and the viability and sustainability of its strategic plans in the short and medium terms. The supervisory assessment not only regards the risks each bank has undertaken and therefore its vulnerability (idiosyncratic risk in a microprudential perspective), but also its contribution to systemic risk, in a macroprudential perspective.

For financial analysts and investors, the BM is an important factor in the evaluation of banks' ability to create value. In a phase of high financial market volatility and high equity capital needs, it is crucial to understand how the market assesses and evaluates a bank's restructuring process and its changes in strategies and business mix.

A key issue in BMA is the identification of banks' BM types: which variables and typical characteristics should be considered? Can these variables be clustered into relatively homogeneous groups to develop a peer analysis aimed at identifying the relative strengths and weaknesses of different BMs?

These questions are at the centre of recent banking literature, which has revealed wide differences in the approaches used to classify the strategic variables on which BM definition is based. This diversity originates from conceptual schemes that are not always made explicit in the literature and this means that results are not always easily comparable.

Our review of banking business model (BBM) literature aims to deepen and specify the definition of BMs by drawing on the main concepts adopted in strategic management literature.

Relying on a definition of BM that takes into account what banks do and how they do it, we classify the plurality of contributions that address the subject of banking BM themes and summarise our main findings. In doing this, we specify the nexus linking BM literature with other approaches to bank strategic choices, mainly in diversification studies.

Lastly, we relate the main pointers obtained from the literature reviewed to the assessment scheme adopted by supervisory authorities to evaluate the viability, sustainability and key vulnerabilities of banks' current BMs.

7.2 The Definition of Business Model

In management literature, the use of BM analysis has increased significantly since the mid-nineties under the pressure of technological innovation and the expansion of traditional competitive areas through virtual networks.

The BM concept has been examined in depth in different fields of economic literature, such as Information and Communication

Technologies (ICTs) and e-business management, organisation theory and strategy studies. This variety of approaches implies that, even now, there is not a widely accepted definition of BM and there are many meanings of the keywords "business model" (Klang et al. 2014).

7.2.1 ICT and e-Business Stream

In the last two decades, the BM has become a focal concept for researchers in the e-business stream; they consider it as a way of analysing competitive behaviour and explaining firms' performance in competitive environments characterised both by intensive use of ICTs in production and distribution processes and by a rise in the importance of stakeholder networks (suppliers, partners, customers, etc.) in value creation.

This literature has developed a BM concept that aims to embrace all the elements and relationships that enable IT-based or Internet-based firms to generate value. It follows the idea that the system (a sort of *gestalt*) creates more value than the sum of its individual parts and the BM is essential to enhance it (Amit and Zott 2001; Zott et al. 2011). Therefore, according to these analyses, a BM is interpreted as a representation of the set of decisions, activities and relationships between them that explain how an organisation creates, delivers (to its stakeholders, including customers) and captures value (Osterwalder and Pigneur 2012), building a sustainable competitive advantage in specific markets (Morris et al. 2005).

Often these contributions tend to give greater emphasis to specific components of this systemic representation. Some stress how firms generate value, i.e. the value proposition (Baden-Fuller and Haefliger 2013), or how they optimise the cost/revenue structure (i.e. value capture); others focus on the way in which relationships with the enterprise's network (suppliers, customers, delivery channels, partners, competitors) increase value.

Notwithstanding the different focus on BM components, there is consensus on the idea that BM has value at the corporate level and offers a useful holistic perspective for understanding not only what businesses firms do (e.g. what products and services they produce to serve the needs of customers in addressable market spaces) but also how they do it (e.g. how they bridge resources and product markets in serving the needs of customers). So that BM becomes a new unit of analysis which puts emphasis on a firm's activity system to create value as well as to capture it (Zott et al. 2011).

7.2.2 Organisational Theories and Resource-Based View

In organisation theory, the BM concept has been developed as an integrated presentation of the company, in order to contribute to process management and process-based organisation design. Not much has been published from the organisational point of view, and the role of this approach is marginal in comparison with the management or strategy streams. In these works, the BM concept focuses to a greater extent on the business's operational aspects and value creation within the firm. In this stream of the literature, the BM generally refers to the firm overall and its structural components (Wirtz 2011). It has been seen as a tool for the abstraction of an entire company and its architecture.

Various works within the e-business stream concentrate on the components of a systemic representation of the firm, with a resource-based view (RBV) approach, considering the firm as a combination of resources and competences. A RBV approach is also used by Osterwalder (2004) in his BM ontology, in order to represent the knowledge and exchanges of both tangible and intangible resources (competences, services, etc.) between organisational players to identify the ways in which the firm generates value (Chen et al. 2014). However, resources only represent a firm's potential. They are necessary but not sufficient for success. Competitive advantage derives from the ability of the company in its entirety to activate, coordinate and integrate resources to achieve performances better than those of its competitors (Penrose 1959).

Although useful for representing a firm's organisation, the RBV is insufficient to describe the ability to generate value without the aid of a BM. Resources in themselves do not generate value for the customer; value is generated by relationships and transactions with the customer based on them. DaSilva and Trkman (2014) define the BM as a representation of "a specific combination of resources" which through transactions generate value for both customers and the organisation, combining the RBV with transaction cost economics. The resource-based approach runs through many works, but its theoretical rationale has difficulty in understanding how a BM is able to create value in a way that differs from other management literature concepts (DaSilva and Trkman 2014). One BM theory, in which a firm's organisational outcomes are affected by managerial competences, expertise, ability to learn and execution, is very appealing. Nevertheless, in the literature, there is no agreement on the nature of the individual components and this approach does not clearly explain the contribution of internal resources and cannot be precisely distinguished from managerial literature (George and Bock 2011).

7.2.3 Strategy Stream

Traditionally, the strategy stream approach relates a company's creation of value to its ability to identify a strategy (or combination of strategies) able to provide a competitive advantage.

Taking the competitive environment as a reference, strategy is the creation of a unique, valuable position for the firm through the development of a competitive advantage. Strategy involves a different set of activities and the choice of the specific way in which the firm competes (Porter 1996; Teece 2010). It is useful to analyse the concept of strategy on two different levels.

At the first level, there is a corporate strategy (Ansoff 1965), which concerns the choice of the size and diversification of the company's business portfolio. This level involves the definition of the various strategic business areas (SBAs) which reflect the product–market–technology combination chosen.

Corporate strategy refers to the firm's high-order (first level) long-term choices in terms of diversification, vertical integration, internationalisation, growth (acquisitions and new ventures), size, governance structures, capital allocation to the different SBAs and disinvestment. It answers the question "Where are we going to compete?"

At the second level, there is the business strategy, which identifies how to compete and how to achieve competitive advantage in each SBA. The business strategy's specific objective is the sustainable competitive advantage a company can achieve and the relationship between that advantage and the industry, by which it is defended. It answers the question "How are we going to compete?"

The SBA identifies the actual (physical or virtual) situation where the business strategy is applied. It is a combination of customers, products and internal resources, where the specific internal relations need a particular entrepreneurial and strategic approach.

Within the "strategy stream", two different meanings of BM can be identified.

On the one hand, in a more operational perspective, the BM is a way of representing and analysing (and, not least, validating, through analysis of internal consistency) the value generated by the strategies, and on the other hand, it is a way of maximising value through the best operational structure and articulation (Shafer et al. 2005). Business strategies focus on the market and external competition, while the BM concentrates on the ability to optimise the business internally and/or within the network. It defines the activities through which the objectives defined by the business strategies can be pursued to improve or optimise competitive advantage (Mottura 2011).

An alternative systemic perspective positions the BM closer to strategy. It can be defined as the concrete choices that derive from the actual combination of corporate/business strategies and the various activities and economic levers involved (price variables, control of costs, customer segments, quality, distribution channels, degree of relationship, technology, productive processes, etc.).

This second approach provides the rationale for connecting the key company strategic choices to their main consequences. BM is the representation of a subset of key choices implemented and their main consequences. Choosing a specific BM (policies, assets and governance) means choosing a specific way of operating and creating and capturing value for the firm's stakeholders. Strategic choices establish the BM. Therefore, the BM is not the strategy, but is the direct result of the strategy a firm implements (Casadesus-Masanell and Ricart 2010).

7.2.4 Strategic Groups

According to the strategy stream literature, one way to analyse the firm within a specific industry is to compare its performance with that of its main competitors, in order to identify any strategic groups. The literature tells us that a strategic group is made up of firms which follow the same or similar behaviour along key strategic dimensions, with regard to specific criteria such as product range, size, internationalisation, technology and vertical integration (Porter 1996).

The group of firms builds mobility barriers on these key strategic dimensions and the investments they require to separate the individual group from the external competition. These barriers help to explain firms' competitive advantage, their performance and the effects of the external context on their profitability.

Recent empirical literature has led to the identification of the strategic group with the BM, as in the large number of studies which employ cluster analysis to group similar strategic behaviours and performance. The empirical results of these analyses are controversial, and their methodology is not always considered effective for analysing differences in firms' performance within the strategic group (Short et al. 2007; Leask 2004).

The employment of cluster analysis has usually focused on economic variables which only provide a very indirect, sketchy picture of actual strategies, and therefore, the attempt to classify firms' strategies on the basis of very broad differences between firms is able to identify general but not specific strategies.

At the same time, the finer the classification criteria used, the more homogeneous but also the narrower the groups become in terms of profitability and strategic behaviour. Moreover, when the analysis deals with strategies as context specific, as specific actual choices bounded by available resources, competitive position, management attitude to risk and industry structure, the strategic group BM is replaced by the individual firm.

In Fig. 7.1, we classify the different approaches in management literature with respect to BM definitions, in order to assess their usefulness

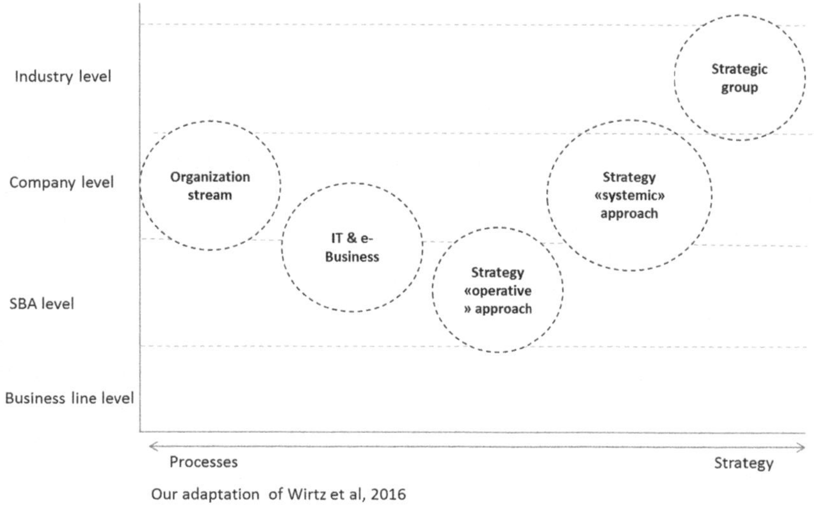

Fig. 7.1 BM definition: the different approaches in the management literature

in relation to the firm's operations. They are arranged on two axes: we place the operational/strategic level on the horizontal axis and the firm's level of organisation, from industrial sector through to individual lines of business, on the vertical axis.

7.3 The BBM Literature

Following the broad conceptual perspective of strategic management studies and its adaptation to bank strategic studies, we review and classify the BBM literature, taking as reference a definition which considers the set of both bank portfolio choices and management abilities intended to exploit market positioning in the different business areas.

Portfolio choices are indicated by the different mix of SBAs, which reflects how "first level long-term strategies" (like growth, diversification, internationalisation and attitude to risk) translate into organisational features of different combinations of products/customers/resources. These strategies, also referred to as *corporate strategies*, reflect the firm's history, its experience and capabilities and the competitive context.

Long-term strategies—stable in a stable economic context—were stressed in the pre-crisis era when banks set their strategic plans against the prospect of continuous growth in the demand for financial services. Then, after the crisis burst, retrenchment and a consequent deep revision of growth, diversification and internationalisation strategies prevailed, along with a strengthening of capital positions. This was followed by significant changes in the business mix, which affected the composition of banks' assets and liabilities as well as their earnings.

At a second strategic level, we set *business strategies*, the managerial choices that pursue revenue enhancement through customer segmentation and product differentiation, cost efficiency and risk management in the different business areas, capturing value from the business mix adopted. How these strategies are successfully implemented will depend on the specific managerial abilities of the bank's organisation.

Both long-term and business strategies are affected by macroeconomic, competitive and regulatory variables. These context variables have ex ante effects on banks' strategies and their BMs in so far as they influence the hypothesis the strategic plans are based on. Ex post they directly affect the way in which business strategies achieve the targeted results.

In Fig. 7.2, we show the different strategic levels through which we represent the concept of the BM. This schema enables us to classify the main contributions to BBM literature and underline how the different approaches focus on a different identification of strategic variables.

An initial classification of the literature is based on the different emphasis placed on the identification of bank peer groups sharing similar BMs.

Several studies follow the literature on strategic groups and aim to find evidence of how the banking industry can be classified using just a few different bank BMs with different performance with respect to economic and financial context.

The main characteristic of these studies is the distinction between what the bank is doing and how the bank is doing it, so that business composition is identified with the BM concept, whereas other strategic variables are considered as the outcome of portfolio choices. Under our

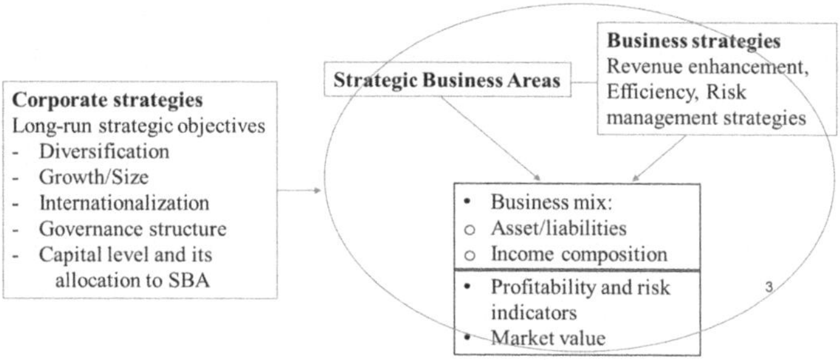

Fig. 7.2 Strategic components of banking business model (BBM)

schema, this approach implies a representation of the BM in terms of SBAs, which are approximated by asset/liabilities and/or income composition, whereas business strategies are implicitly evaluated in the outcome analysis. It is important to underline that this definition of BM can lead to the attribution of performance results to the business mix even when the former are due to the bank's skill in managing the single business areas.

This approach can be traced in the work of Ayadi and Groen (2014) and Ayadi et al. (2016a). Following the pioneering work of Passmore (1985) and Amel and Rhoades (1988), these authors employ a two-stage procedure for the BM analysis of European banks. The first step adopts cluster analysis to group banks on the basis of asset and liability composition. Then, they evaluate how the bank clusters perform with respect to a very broad set of indicators concerning both performance results and strategic behaviours such as risk exposure, loan growth and internationalisation. Six indicators of asset and funding composition used in cluster analysis identify four large, distinct groups that differ from each other in their retail and financial market orientations. A comparison between bank clusters on the basis of risk-return frontier confirms that investment banks have higher risk and volatility, while diversified retail banks seemed to perform better during the financial crisis thanks to their higher revenue stability.

Roengpitya et al. (2014) also use the cluster algorithm, along with the adoption of some selection criteria and balance sheet ratios, to classify the BMs of a large sample of listed and non-listed banks from 34 countries, during 2005–2013. They compare three distinct bank clusters with respect to outcome variables. When valued in terms of performance, the retail-funded group (high share of loans on total assets and high reliance on deposits) displays the highest average level and the lowest variability of profitability over time. The trading banks (half of the assets in tradable securities and predominantly funded in the wholesale market) are the group with the highest volatility of return on equity and cost base. The wholesale-funded group stands between the other two groups in terms of return levels and volatility. The study finds significant shifts across different BMs before and after the crisis: two-fifths of the banks classified as wholesale funded or trading in 2007 ended up with a retail-funded BM in 2013. The performance statistics show that the change in banks' BM induced a prevailing worsening in profitability.

A different result with respect to migration between bank clusters over time is shown by a study presented in the ECB Financial Stability Review (2016) in the classification of European banks during 2007–2014. Comparing the bank clusters based on size, asset/liability and income composition indicators, they find that most banks remained in the same group, revealing "sticky" BMs which have difficulty in adapting to a changing environment or the anticipation of stress.

De Meo et al. (2016) adopt an original fuzzy clustering technique based on a broad set of asset/liability mix indicators of listed and non-listed European banks (77 for 15 countries) for 2006–2014. They identify three main clusters of banks: retail, diversified and investment banks. Each group was then subdivided on the basis of four EBA classification criteria (systemic relevance, dimension, organisational complexity and cross-border activity) considered by the authors to be attributes of strategic choices. Among the eight resultant peer groups, retail banks show the highest return on assets in the years preceding the financial crisis but the worst performances at the peak of the sovereign debt crisis, due to the deterioration in credit quality. Among them, small banks with limited cross-border exposure and a low degree of income diversification (non-complex retail banks) were hardest hit by the increasing credit risk. The study analyses the effects of macroeconomic variables on the performance of the different peer groups: as expected, economic growth, yield curve and sovereign risk are the most significant variables affecting retail banks, whereas due to their dependence on non-interest income, investment and diversified banks displayed a significant exposure to financial markets. One methodological aspect of the analysis must be underlined: probabilistic clustering tends to make the performances of different BBM more similar, a sign that bank-specific strategies may be more important than membership of a strategic group in explaining bank performance.

The specificity of bank strategies is the focus of Mergaert and Vennet's (2016) analysis. They define BM in terms of the strategic variables that reflect the management's long-term choices (latent strategies) with regard to asset and liability composition, capitalisation, income structure and the bank's risk profile. The common variances of these variables define two broad BBM: retail and diversified. The authors underline the fact that these models are graduated and use common factor analysis to evaluate both how these long-term strategies are implemented and their impact on performance. The authors conclude that there is a substantial variation in the effects of the BM between different bank types and show that retail-oriented banks perform better in terms of both profitability and stability and that diversification improves profitability, but also increases the likelihood of distress.

A different approach to the grouping of European banks is employed by Bonaccorsi et al. (2016). They classify 112 significant European banks following a step procedure based on threshold values of balance sheet parameters including size, lending propensity and international credit exposure. The authors use data published by the European Banking Authority (EBA) and the European Central Bank (ECB) further to the comprehensive assessment, which allows them to define portfolio composition by counterpart type, showing that large domestic and other lending banks are more exposed towards SMEs and retail real estate secured loans than large international or diversified banks. This composition explains the higher level of profitability of lending banks but also their greater cyclical sensitivity. The study points to macroeconomic conditions as the main driver of current differences in profitability across bank types, whereas riskiness seems to reflect both differences in borrowers' risk profiles and the extent to which banks use IRB models. In particular, the ratio between risk-weighted and unweighted exposure (risk density) is lower for large banks able to both tailor riskiness to each individual position more effectively and, in some cases, manipulate risk weights, thus creating a bias towards lower risk density.

How the management of risk weights is linked to banks' chosen BM is the theme of the study by Ayadi et al. (2016b). Applying the Ayadi et al. (2016a) cluster approach and using the same group classification, the authors provide evidence of the different degree of regulatory arbitrage across bank BMs. Notably, IRB adoption seems to have a positive effect on the riskiness of retail diversified banks, signalling that regulatory arbitrage is occurring within this banking BM.

An alternative strand of BBM literature adopts a wide definition of BM that combines portfolio choices with many other business and context variables. According to our schema, this approach has the merit of considering many strategic aspects of a BM, although these studies often fail to make a clear distinction between long-term strategies, business mix and business strategies.

A second feature of these studies is their emphasis on banks' different strategic behaviours rather than the identification of strategic groups. In some cases, BM variables are compared across the main institutional bank groups or considering different bank sizes.

A further characteristic of this approach is the focus on bank riskiness and the identification of which BM variables most affect bank vulnerability. The focus on risk reflects the perspective of bank supervisors and their concern for the consequences of bank strategies on default events.

This approach is central to the work of Altunbas et al. (2011), who use a broad set of bank characteristics to identify BMs. Three risk measures of a large sample of European and US banks are regressed on groups of indicators collected in the pre-crisis period. These should denote different banks' BMs: asset, funding and income composition variables along with indicators like loan growth, capital ratio, total assets and a number of variables that account for major macroeconomic and institutional factors. Therefore, their definition of BM includes business mix variables along with some other strategic variables concerning growth, capitalisation and size. These strategic variables, along with the reliance on short-term market funding, are statistically significant in explaining bank distress. The main indication concerns the significant, high impact on banks' risk of the aggressive expansion in loan growth in the pre-crisis years, as evidence of the relaxation of credit standards and a deterioration in asset quality. In addition, the ratio of loans to total assets is positively related to bank risk as well as bank size. With regard to funding and income composition, the study finds evidence that relying on deposit funding reduces the probability of a bank rescue, whereas non-interest income reduces the likelihood of distress during the crisis. Conversely, the use of wholesale funding increases the bank's risk.

Köhler (2014) follows a similar approach, relating Z-logscore to business mix and loan growth variables for a large sample of European banks. The analysis evaluates the relationship to the main institutional bank categories: commercial, saving and cooperative, and investment banks, with a focus on listed banks. In Köhler (2015), the same risk indicator is regressed on two main business mix variables (non-interest income share and non-deposit funding as a fraction of total assets) and then integrated with many other control variables. The approach is similar to that adopted by Demirguc-Kunt and Huizinga (2010) for an international sample of 1334 banks in 101 countries leading up to the 2008 financial crisis. The econometric study by Köhler confirms some results found in the bank diversification literature, which point to the risk of shifting a bank's operations onto the financial markets (securities and wholesale fund market). For savings and cooperative banks, a larger share of their income from non-traditional activities generates more return stability, but the banks themselves become less stable due to the increase in their share of non-deposit funding. This contrasts with investment banks, which become riskier when they increase their non-interest income and will be significantly more stable if their share of non-deposit funding rises. This may be because retail and investment banks diversify in different ways. The latter derive most of their non-interest income from securities-related activities that incorporate a market risk, whereas the former earn their diversification revenue mainly from banking-related services. This signals the importance of keeping these two fundamentally different types of activities separate when studying the relationship between bank risk and diversification (DeYoung and Torna 2013; Brighi and Venturelli 2014). Along with diversification, lending growth is also an important determinant of bank risk that significantly differs across countries, due to both the different aggregate credit growth and the reduction in bank lending standards and collateral requirements during booms.

A ECB study (2016) of a sample of 143 Euro area banking groups during 1995–2014 also regresses the z-score variable on several bank-specific BM characteristics, including some business mix measures (including retail ratio, income diversification and short-term borrowing), cost-to-income ratio, a leverage ratio and size. Other explanatory variables regard macroeconomic conditions and structural market features. Pre-crisis, income diversification is associated with higher default risk, whereas during and after the onset of the financial crisis more diversified banks displayed lower default risk levels. During the whole period, a higher default risk for global systemically important financial institutions (G-SIBs) contrasted with an overall reduction in riskiness for smaller, less complex banks. This result is in line with Köhler's findings that diversification is beneficial up to a point, beyond which banking group complexity is prejudicial to bank stability. Increasing recourse to short-term borrowing also has significant riskiness implications for G-SIBs, whereas if they shift their funding mix towards deposits, they are able to reduce their risk exposure.

The bulk of these studies focuses on the nexus between BM variables and individual bank risk, and only a few of them deal with the effects of strategic choices on systemic risk.

An analysis of the nexus between BM variables and measures of individual and systemic bank risk based on market values is proposed by Van Oordt and Zhou (2014), who rely on stock market data from CRSP of US Bank Holding Companies from 1991 to 2011. Drawing on the literature on market risk, the authors identify two aspects of banks' systemic risk: bank tail risk and the linkage between a bank's tail risk and severe shocks in the financial system. As expected, they find a stronger dependence between large banks and systemic risk, with a positive association between size and sensitivity to severe shocks in the financial system (approximated by severe changes in the financial sector index). The same positive relationship with severe financial shocks is found for non-interest income share, confirming that banks' involvement in these activities is relevant not only for microprudential but also for macroprudential regulation. With regard to asset/liability composition, the study points out that lending-focused BMs are significantly associated with higher levels of tail risk, but with lower systemic linkage. For the deposits-to-assets ratio, they find similar results on the relationship to financial shocks. Growth strategies are associated with an increase in sensitivity to large shocks in the financial system, whereas banks with higher capital ratios show a significantly lower exposure to systemic risk.

As already underlined, the analysis of the interrelations between systemic risk and some main bank characteristics has considerable implications for regulation: the breakdown of systemic risk clearly indicates that regulators must choose the right balance between micro- and macroprudential objectives.

7.4 The Literature on Bank Diversification: The Nexus with BBM Analysis

The review provided above demonstrates that the literature on bank BMs is closely linked to that on diversification strategies. The link clearly emerges from the empirical analysis centred on the nexus between diversification activities and measures of banks' performance, with the former usually approximated by asset/liability and income composition indicators and in particular by the distinction between net interest income and non-interest components. These measures thus highlight the scope of corporate strategy, or in other terms, the results of the strategic portfolio banks decide to develop. At the same time, the so-called control variables (i.e. size, economic efficiency and risk profile) used in diversification studies can be considered as a proxy for bank choices at the business strategy level.

If the focus is on the main commercial banks, it is reasonable to assume that the differences in their BMs concern mainly the different intensity with which the functional diversification[1] process, in terms of an array of products and services and customer segments, has been carried out. In recent decades, the development of financial markets and the increasing complementarity between the banking and securities segments of financial intermediation have contributed to the characterisation of banks' BMs: the securitisation process is emblematic of this change. In many countries, the development of the asset management business has been favoured by banks' diversification strategies. Banks are also the main investors in bonds and in particular have continued to play an important role in the coverage of sovereign debt.

For these banks, decisions about their BM and the competitive advantages that may result are interwoven with key strategic decisions concerning size/growth and diversification.

The goal of achieving optimum size and exploiting economies of scope in the offering of a wider range of products and services was central to the strategies of many banks, at least until the outbreak of the financial crisis. In retrospect, it is easy to see that this approach was based on an overestimation of the prospects for growth in the demand for banking products and services, and a clear underestimation of the operational complexity and risk profile related to larger size and wider SBAs.

From a theoretical point of view, the existing banking literature focuses on the question "should banks diversify their portfolios or should they specialise?" since both pros and cons can be identified. Among the recognised benefits, the possibility of exploiting economies of scope may lead to an increase in performance through cost savings or revenue improvements (Teece 1982; Herring and Santomero 1990; Llewellyn 1996; Klein and Saidenberg 1997; Campa and Kedia 2002; Elsas et al. 2010), along with a reduction in the degree of information asymmetry (Diamond 1984, 1991; Rajan 1992; Stein 2002) and the agency costs of managerial discretion (Stulz 1990; Stein 1997; Gertner et al. 1994). These benefits have to be traded off against the costs associated with diversification. In particular, increasing the size and scope of a bank's activities introduces the "cost of complexity", which at some point may outweigh the benefits that can be achieved (Rajan et al. 2000; Graham et al. 2002). Moreover, diversified institutions can suffer (DeYoung and Roland 2001) from earnings volatility, lower switching costs for clients and higher operational and financial leverage (Demsetz and Strahan 1997; DeYoung and Roland 2001), increasing the volatility of earnings and hampering risk-adjusted performance measures.

While the theoretical literature has effectively addressed the reasons for and economic effects of greater diversification of business, empirical studies only estimate the implications of functional diversification at a general level, by testing the nexus between some aggregated indicators of business mix and measures of banks performance.

Most studies are centred on the US banking industry, following the implementation of Gramm Leach Bliley in 1999. With few exceptions,[2] these contributions find that a shift towards non-interest activities worsens the risk-return trade-off because the costs of diversification outweigh the benefits, mainly due to the increased volatility of these activities (DeYoung and Roland 2001; Stiroh 2004; Stiroh and Rumble 2006; Laeven and Levine 2007; Goddard et al. 2008); moreover, this finding is valid for both financial holding companies and smaller institutions such as credit unions.

Fewer studies deal with European banks and those which are available provide similar results regarding the effect of diversification on bank performance. Among them, Mercieca et al. (2007), examining a sample of 755 small European banks for the period 1997–2003, find that small European banks do not gain from their diversification strategy because the higher volatility of net interest income outweighs the benefits of diversification, implying lower risk-adjusted returns, and this is linked to small banks' lack of expertise in managing new lines of business. Lepetit et al. (2008) find that for a set of European banks from 14 countries during 1996–2012, expansion into non-interest income-generating activities displays higher risk and higher insolvency, and this is particularly true for smaller banks and those driven by commission and fee activities. Baele et al. (2007), using a sample of listed banks from 17 European countries during 1989–2004, confirm Stiroh's finding (2006) that banks that rely more on non-interest sources of income have systematically higher market betas and hence higher systematic risk.

These findings may be affected on the one hand by measurement problems linked to the definition of diversification used and on the other hand by the lack of consideration of the possible interaction between diversification and banks' other characteristics.

In this sense, the degree of information granularity disclosed by banks in relation to the nature of fee-based revenues allows a more precise evaluation of the nexus between diversification and performance and can affect the final results.

Gallo et al. (1996) showed the importance of distinguishing between the different components of non-interest income. In particular, combining bank and mutual fund activities improved the profitability and reduced the risk of US bank holding companies during 1987–1994.

More recently, DeYoung and Rice (2004), DeYoung and Torna (2013) recognise that different fee-generating activities show different production and risk-return characteristics and hence are likely to have different impacts on the probability of financial distress and insolvency. The authors identify three categories of non-interest income, and the results point out that higher involvement in asset-based non-traditional activities such as venture capital, investment banking and asset securitisation is associated with higher probability of failure for financially distressed US banks and that an increase in pure fee-based non-traditional activities such as securities brokerage and insurance sales reduced the probability that banks would fail during the crisis.

The recent studies on the diversification of Italian banks benefit from detailed, public data on bank income composition. Cotugno and Stefanelli (2012) use a panel data set comprising 4038 observations relative to Italian banks for 2005–2010 and find a positive relationship between product diversification and bank performance, also in terms of risk-adjusted measures. On a sample of 145 Italian banks during 2006–2008, Vallascas et al. (2012) reveals that institutions that were diversified within narrow activity classes before the financial crisis experienced large declines in performance during it. By contrast, diversification across broad activity classes, such as lending and capital market activities, did not cause performance losses during the crisis. Brighi and Venturelli

(2016) use bank-level data on 491 Italian banks during 2006–2012 to investigate the impact of functional and geographical diversification on bank performance during the 2008 financial and the 2010 sovereign debt crises. Both crises negatively affected bank profitability, but banks that were more diversified, in terms of both revenue and geographical diversification, were less penalised in terms of risk-adjusted profitability. Results differ for the sample of mutual and non-mutual banks, with the former benefiting more from geographical and the latter from functional diversification.

The importance of the degree of information disclosure is captured well in a recent study by Williams (2016), which models the relationship between bank revenue composition and bank risk using data drawn from the confidential regulatory returns of Australian banks. At first glance, consistently with previous international evidence, it is seen that banks with lower levels of non-interest income as a proportion of total bank revenue and higher revenue concentration are less risky, but at the same time, some types of non-interest income are risk reducing when the effects of bank specialisation are considered. To study this in greater detail, bank revenue is broken into six categories, and the results underline the existence of some portfolio diversification benefits from trading and investment income.

Turning to the theory that findings relating to diversification may be influenced by a failure to consider interactions between diversification and banks' other long-term choices, the possible effect of interaction between size and diversification is accurately described in De Jonghe et al. (2015). Examining a panel of 16,507 bank-year observations, distributed over 15 years and 76 countries, the authors identify a negative interaction between size and non-interest income in their relationship with systemic risk. In other terms, non-interest income reduces large banks' systemic risk exposures, whereas it increases those of small banks. In particular, small banks are more likely to lack the expertise needed to handle a wide array of products and services or manage complex financial products. Moreover, they are not subject to in-depth external scrutiny, so they may be more inclined to engage in riskier activities; on the other hand, larger banks are typically subject to more external scrutiny, which may discourage excessive risk taking, and they can count on more sophisticated risk management techniques and a more experienced management team. So the concepts of size and scope should not be analysed in isolation, since they are strictly interrelated.

Summing up, the results of diversification studies are strongly influenced by the consideration of the nature of non-interest income and the simultaneous interaction with banks' long-term choices. As a consequence, BMA cannot limit its scope to the same metrics used in the diversification literature, since from the heterogeneity of the results it is clear that there is an optimal mix between size, risk and revenue diversification that calls for an integrated approach extended to the analysis of diversification, which is just one component of BMA. These findings also influence the measurement aspect of BMA; from a methodological point of view, BMA requires the implementation of techniques that enable the simultaneous consideration of the different dimensions involved: long-term strategies, business mix and business strategies.

7.5 Banks' Key Vulnerabilities in the Supervisory Assessment Scheme

The analysis of the recent developments in BBM literature suggests interesting key points on the conceptual framework adopted by supervisory authorities: how they are approaching this theme and to what extent they share the perspectives emerging from the studies discussed above.

To this end, it is first of all interesting to trace the birth and evolution of BMA as a proactive supervisory instrument.

The increasing interest of supervisory authorities in BMA stems from the crisis (2007–2008). BMA was pioneered in the UK after the Northern Rock crisis and the failure of the "light supervision" applied by the Financial Services Authorities (FSA). The Turner Report (FSA 2009) named the FSA's supervisory approach, based on the idea that BM risks were better assessed and balanced with returns by top management and boards of directors (BoD) than by bank regulators and supervisors, as one of the causes of the crisis. "Light supervision" was focused mainly on the operation of appropriate systems and controls within the supervised institutions. Changes in the supervisory philosophy were put in place from 2009 onward, with the introduction of a more intrusive, systemic revised approach to be implemented by a new authority: the Prudential Regulation Authority (PRA), operative since 2013. The revised supervisory approach is based on an "Intensive Supervision" model with the pendulum shifting from trust in market discipline, with supervisory intervention mainly after something had gone wrong, to a proactive regulatory and supervisory action, with a forward-looking perspective (Moloney 2012).

Within the new approach, PRA (Bank of England FSA 2012) gives an important role to BMA as a proactive, forward-looking instrument with two main aims: from an idiosyncratic point of view, to examine the threats to the viability of a bank's BM and its key vulnerabilities; from a systemic point of view, to identify possible adverse effects on other participants in the system from the way in which the institution conducts its business. The key aspects for identification of a bank's vulnerabilities are an assessment of its sources of revenues, the related risks and funding, and the analysis of its strategy and the business plan. The second step is peer analysis to identify each bank's position within its strategic group and evaluate any outlier BMs and management practices, and their contribution to systemic risk.

BMA is now embedded in the SREP, Pillar II of the Basel Capital Accord, and is intended to reveal a bank's key vulnerabilities in the short run and the viability and sustainability of its strategic plans in the short and medium term. The aim of BMA is to assess not only each bank's risks and therefore its vulnerability, meaning its idiosyncratic risk in a microprudential perspective, but also its contribution to systemic risk, in a macroprudential perspective. Within this framework, BMA was introduced by the EBA (2014), as the first of four key elements, followed by the assessment of internal governance and institution-wide control arrangements, risks to capital and adequacy of capital to cover these risks, and risks to liquidity and adequacy of liquidity resources to cover these risks.

The ECB also identified BMA as a key area of the supervisory activity of the SSM in its Thematic Review in 2015 (ECB Banking Supervision

2015) and in greater detail in 2016. Under EBA Guidelines (EBA 2014; ECB Banking Supervision 2016), the elements of BM analysis are: identification of banks' main activities; assessment of the business environment; analysis of the forward-looking strategy and financial plans; assessment of the BM's viability (within one year), sustainability (within three years) and sustainability over the cycle (more than three years); and assessment of key vulnerabilities (Lautenschlager 2016; ECB Banking Supervision 2016). Through this analysis, the supervisors aim to understand the implications of BM characteristics for banks' overall riskiness. The peer analysis follows.

The SSM approach is based on both quantitative and qualitative analysis and should incorporate a forward-looking perspective, linked to financial planning, business plan analysis and macroeconomic and market trends. The scheme of analysis identified by the EBA is quite exhaustive, and different aspects are considered when focusing on the BM adopted by each bank, with the aim of revealing its viability, sustainability and key vulnerabilities due to risk assumptions. The specific levels of granularity of information on different aspects, product/business lines, breakdown of income and cost streams, impairment provisions and key ratios required by the SSM are not disclosed; the criteria for the definition of peer groups, and the banks included, are also not officially disclosed. The BMA of supervisory authorities is currently being developed from basic to more sophisticated analysis.

Interesting points for consideration emerge from the scheme of analysis provided by the EBA guidelines (2014), concerning the theoretical and methodological framework underlying the work of the supervisory authorities, also in relation to the main findings of the theoretical and empirical literature on BMA, set out above.

One initial comment relates to the methodological approach of the SREP, where BMA precedes and supports the three subsequent analysis stages, assessment of governance, ICAAP and ILLAP. BMA (EBA 2014) is intended to pinpoint the determinants of BMs and the adequacy of their returns over time, while the other three areas analyse risks, risk management models and risk governance. In fact, the assessment of these areas should aid in the overall assessment of the viability of the current BM and the sustainability of the strategies, the main objective of BMA, which, therefore, should combine with rather than complementing an evaluation that investigates the strong and weak points of the BM adopted at the various strategic levels. Thus, a holistic approach is needed in BM evaluation, linking risk analysis to the main strategic areas, both corporate, where the guidelines for the types and amounts of risk to be taken are decided, and at the business strategy level, with regard to risk management in the various business areas. Above all, it is essential to maintain a close connection between business mix decisions, the allocation of resources and risk management. A multidimensional, transverse approach is the way to strengthen the final synthetic evaluation, with banks classified into four groups and an additional class for "*failing or likely to fail*" institutions, for which specific supervisory measures must be defined for each bank.

Another point of reflection stems from an assessment of the BM's sustainability and viability through two levels of analysis: "corporate/first level long-run strategies" and "business strategic level", related to managerial choices concerning revenue enhancement policies, cost efficiency objectives and risk management processes. The first level of analysis should consider a time span long enough to take into account changes in the economic cycle, which are intertwined with and determine strategic corporate choices, such as growth, internationalisation and diversification before the crisis, and deleveraging, capital saving and different sources of funding after the crisis. This approach could help to strengthen a forward-looking approach, preventing the static assessment of corporate strategies in terms of profitability and risk assumption. One example is the different negative impact of the two phases of the crisis on bank performance in Europe: in 2008–2009 notably higher for wholesale and investment than for retail banks; the opposite after 2012 with lower profitability for retail banks mainly serving the SME segment, worst affected by the economic recession. Moreover, this latter effect was more serious in peripheral countries than in core countries with better economic trends. This last finding is also relevant for country-specific factors that should be taken into account when explaining lower bank profitability. Since macroeconomic conditions seem to be the main driver of current differences in profitability across the country bank binomial

(Bonaccorsi et al. 2016), a key question arises concerning the effectiveness of peer analysis for taking these factors into account.

A further reflection arising from the literature review concerns the different behaviour of banks in relation to their size and diversification and the different analysis required by regulators. This distinction is evident from the BMA developed by the ECB for significant banks and that adopted by the National Competent Authorities (NCAs) for less significant banks. In the first case, a high degree of granularity of information at the second strategic level is a key element in verifying the sustainability of corporate strategies, especially for systemic banks displaying high complexity in the BMA conceptual framework. Peer analysis must carefully consider banks' different dimensions in terms of complexity and diversification: the granularity required is a strong argument in favour of one bank-one BM. For these banks, given the variety of their strategic choices, a rough definition of clusters, based on too few overly generic variables, could lead to a misallocation of banks and/or an inadequate framework for their evaluation (Gualandri 2016). On the other hand, a less complex BMA approach is envisaged by the NCAs, with lower granularity, for the large amount of small banks with a higher degree of homogeneity of strategies and asset mix.

Another consideration is that capital adequacy is a key element considered by supervisory authorities, bank management and also the market from slightly different but complementary perspectives. Supervisors evaluate capital strength for its effect on idiosyncratic and systemic risks, managers as a basis for strategic decisions such as growth and diversification. In the new regulatory context, the level of capital and its allocation become a more long-term strategic variable, strictly interrelated with corporate strategies. As a consequence, from the supervisory point of view the forward-looking perspective adopted in BMA should be reinforced with a further analysis aimed at evaluating the market's capacity to absorb capital-intensive strategies (Calomiris and Nissim 2014). Analysis based on market value measures may be used to highlight the nexus and distinction between BM variables and measures of individual and systemic bank risk. In particular, recent research has identified a stronger relationship between large banks and systemic risk, with a positive association between size and sensitivity to severe shocks in the financial system.

The capital, corporate strategy nexus clearly reveals how regulation may influence strategic choices, especially those regarding portfolio mix and risk assumption and management, determining an important linkage between diversification and regulatory arbitrage. In the literature, this theme is exemplified by capital arbitrage behaviour affecting levels of risk density, which is determined at a twofold level: at the corporate strategy level, the focus is on strategic areas requiring less capital absorption than others, while at the business strategies level the management of risk weights depends on the BM adopted. Peer analysis may give supervisors some indicators of possible regulatory arbitrage across BMs via Basel risk weights manipulation. This kind of analysis could help SSM in the targeted review of internal models (TRIM) to assess the reliability and comparability of internal rating systems and models. The project is scheduled by 2019.

Finally, the two perspectives of micro- and macroregulations should be deepened and cross-analysed to appreciate, at the microlevel, the viability and sustainability of a bank's BM and, at the macrolevel, each bank's contribution to systemic risk. To this end, in a supervisory perspective, appropriate BM diversification within the system is an important factor in reducing risk arising from external shocks. A key point is the definition of the characteristics and composition of peer groups as already underlined, where more in-depth analysis is required on systemic banks. Information on BM variety is fairly significant, especially in the case of systemic banks where variety helps to reduce systemic risk.

7.6 Conclusions

Evolving market conditions, technological innovations, regulatory changes and current monetary policy stances challenge the sustainability of banks' BMs. The "business model question" is increasingly grabbing the attention of bank managers, regulators, investors and financial analysts. The need to use the BM concept as a tool for analysing a bank's performance and assessing its viability requires, first of all, a clear understanding of what "business model" means, since the existing literature does not offer a uniform picture.

We start by drawing on strategic management studies to deepen and specify the concepts of corporate strategy, business strategy and BM. Three different strands of the literature deal with BMs: IT and e-business, strategy and strategic groups. In the first, the BM symbolises how a firm creates, distributes and captures value; in this holistic perspective, BM and business strategy often overlap. In the second field of studies, strategy, the foundation of competitive advantage and value creation, is implemented at two levels: corporate (what) and business (how). Corporate strategy delineates the breadth and diversification of the company's business portfolio in terms of SBAs; it is the set of high-order (first level) long-term choices such as growth, size, governance structures, diversification and internationalisation. Business strategy (second level) identifies how to achieve competitive advantage in each SBA. Some scholars see a clear distinction between strategy and BM: strategy focuses on the market and external competition, while BM has a more operative nature, focusing on the internal consistency of strategic choices (operative approach). For others, BM and strategy are different but strongly related, since BM is the direct result of a firm's implemented strategy (systemic approach). A systemic approach is detectable in the latter strand as well, but with reference to groups of companies with similar strategies (strategic groups) instead of single firms. Cluster analysis of data at the firm level is adopted to identify strategic groups; since the input data are usually the result of both strategic and operative choices, the overlap between strategy and BM is amplified.

This theoretical framework guides our review of the BBM literature. In banking, corporate strategy (what) leads to SBA choices reflected in the business mix (asset & liability composition and income composition), while business strategy (how) relates to the management of revenues, efficiency and risk in each SBA. Business mix and business strategy are the components of the BM and the factors affecting performance indicators (profitability, risk levels, market value).

The first group of studies we review can be traced to the strategic group literature, in its attempt to classify banks in a small number of BM archetypes with different performances. However, this approach is based on a distinction of *what* the bank is doing (proxied by asset/liabilities and/or income composition), from *how* the bank is doing it (revenue enhancement, efficiency and risk management strategies), so that the BM concept overlaps with the business mix, whereas other strategic variables (revenues, efficiency and risk strategies) are implicitly regarded and evaluated as outcomes of portfolio choices. This BM definition can lead to the attribution of performance results to the business mix and obscure the role played by the bank's skill in managing the individual business area.

A second stream of the BM literature in banking relies on a wide definition of BM that combines corporate and business strategies with context variables, but fails to make a clear distinction between long-term strategies, business mix and business strategies. The primary aim of this approach is to identify which BM variables affect banks' vulnerability, reflecting the supervisors' concerns for the consequences of bank strategies on default events. Most studies deal with the risk of individual banks. When the analysis extends to systemic risk, important implications for regulators emerge: some BM variables have opposite effects on a bank's tail risk and its exposure to severe shocks in the financial system, signalling the need for the right balance between micro- and macro-prudential objectives.

The BBM literature is clearly linked to that exploring diversification strategies. On the one hand, both consider the business mix, particularly the distinction between interest and non-interest income. On the other hand, some control variables (i.e. efficiency and risk profile) popular in diversification studies may represent the business strategy level. As a consequence, our review extends to the literature on diversification in banking to gain additional insights into the BM debate by considering the pros and cons of diversification.

BM analysis has recently become a supervisory tool. After tracing the birth and evolution of BMA as a proactive supervisory instrument, we propose some reflections on the scheme adopted by the supervisory authorities to evaluate the viability, sustainability and key vulnerabilities of banks' current BMs.

Overall, the main lessons stemming from our review of the literature and the supervisory viewpoint are the following.

- The literature on bank BMs applies the concepts developed in the strategic management field with some difficulties. The BM is often restricted to the business mix (cluster approach). When the definition of BM is more holistic, there are flaws in the recognition of the different strategic levels (corporate and business).
- Empirically, the degree of reliance on retail deposits and their contribution to the funding of loans are the most significant elements of the business mix in defining strategic groups.
- In our perspective, the shift towards retail funding as a way of dealing with the shrinking of the wholesale market due to the financial crisis is more a change in growth strategy and risk appetite than in business mix (SBAs tend to be quite stable).
- BBM sustainability has to be evaluated over a time span long enough to cover entire business and financial cycles. The BM most resilient in the first wave of the financial crisis (retail banks with loans oriented to SMEs) has been the worst performer in the subsequent economic slowdown.
- In the banking system, as in industry, dichotomous strategies are emerging: to respond to the crisis some banks are restricting their size and scope of activities, others are growing through M&A. The cluster approach does not seem sufficiently effective in capturing this trend.
- The availability of equity capital heavily influences banks' corporate strategy. From this point of view, listed banks and banks with capital market access have a competitive advantage. At the same time, the market evaluation of banks' securities (debt and equity) is important both in influencing banks' strategies and for bank supervisors.
- BM complexity depends on size. Small banks usually have homogenous strategic behaviours and business mix, while big banks tend to adopt specific BMs that require more detailed information to be analysed.
- In a large proportion of the BBM literature and in diversification studies, business mix is proxied by income composition. In general, greater diversification means greater risk, not always rewarded with higher profitability. However, diversification in terms of non-interest income share seems to be beneficial when commissions and fees come from traditional banking services and detrimental if they derive from

asset-based non-traditional activities such as venture capital, investment banking and asset securitisation. Therefore, the granularity of data on the income from services is essential for analysing the influence of BM on bank risk.

BMA perspectives rely on the intersection between the literature on BMs and the literature on diversification to get a more integrated representation of banking, able to explore both corporate and business strategies and their connections. At the same time, more detailed data are needed to allow a deeper understanding of the different elements that define banks' BMs.

This holistic and systemic approach to BM valuation is only partially detectable in the SREP guidelines, where the BM is one of the four areas under assessment (alongside internal governance and institution-wide control arrangements, capital adequacy and adequacy of liquidity), rather than representing the framework for the risk profile analysis of corporate and business strategic choices, with a limited view on how business mix and risk and resource management interact.

On the subject of better BM disclosure, it is worthwhile mentioning the recent (July 2016) statement of the Financial Reporting Council: "*We encourage clear disclosure of a company's business model as part of the strategic report, including a description of the main markets in which the company operates and its value chain*". This form of transparency helps both academic research and the judgements of analysts and investors, with positive effects on the information and signalling content of stock and bond market prices, useful for supervisory authorities in preventing crisis and for bank managers in acquiring market expectations.

Notes

1. In the literature (for a review see Rossi et al. 2009), diversification is analysed using two main parameters linked to income sources and geographical areas. The term functional diversification usually refers to the profile of the diversification between interest and non-interest bearing activities.
2. See Stiroh (2009) for a review of the literature.

References

Altunbas, Y., S. Manganelli, and D. Marques-Ibanez. 2011. Bank risk during the financial crisis—do business models matter? ECB, Working Paper Series, N. 1394, November.

Amel, D.F., and S.A. Rhoades. 1988. Strategic groups in banking. *The Review of Economics and Statistics* 70 (4): 685–689.

Amit, R., and C. Zott. 2001. Value creation in e-business. *Strategic Management Journal*, 22, 493–520.

Ansoff, H.I. 1965. *Corporate Strategy*. McGraw-Hill.

Ayadi, R.E., and W.P. de Groen. 2014. *Banking business models monitor 2014: Europe*. Montreal, Joint Centre for European Policy Studies (CEPS) and International Observatory on Financial Service Cooperatives (IOFSC) publication.

Ayadi, R.E., W.P. de Groen, I. Sassi, W. Mathlouthi, H. Rey, and O. Aubry. 2016a. *Banking business models monitor 2015: Europe*, Alphonse and Dorimène Desjardins International Institute for Cooperatives and International Observatory on Financial Service Cooperatives (IOFSC).

Ayadi, R., V. Pesic., and, G. Ferri. 2016b. Regulatory arbitrage in EU banking: Do business models matter? IRCCF Working Paper, Montreal.

Baden-Fuller, C., and S. Haefliger. 2013. Business models and technological innovation. *Long Range Planning* 46 (6): 419–426.

Baele, L., O. De Jonghe., and R. Vander Vennet. 2007. Does the stock market value bank diversification? *Journal of Banking & Finance*, 31(7), 1999–2023.

Bank of England and FSA. 2012. *The Bank of England, prudential regulation authority. The PRA's approach to banking supervision*, October, London.

Bonaccorsi di Patti, E., R. Felici., and F.M. Signoretti. 2016. *Euro area significant banks: Main differences and recent performance*. Bank of Italy, Questioni di economia e finanza, Occasional Papers, n. 306.

Brighi, P., and V. Venturelli. 2014. How do income diversification, firm size and capital ratio affect performance? Evidence for bank holding companies. *Applied Financial Economics* 24 (21): 1375–1392.

Brighi, P., and V. Venturelli. 2016. How functional and geographic diversification affect bank profitability during the crisis. *Finance Research Letters* 16: 1–10.

Calomiris, C.W., and D. Nissim. 2014. Crisis-related shifts in the market valuation of banking activities. *Journal of Financial Intermediation* 23 (3): 400–435.

Campa, J.M., and S. Kedia. 2002. Explaining the diversification discount. *The Journal of Finance* 57 (4): 1731–1762.

Casadesus-Masanell, R., and J.E. Ricart. 2010. From strategy to business models and onto tactics. *Long Range Planning* 43: 195–215.

Chen, L., J. Danbolt, and J. Holland. 2014. Rethinking bank business models: The role of intangibles. *Accounting, Auditing & Accountability Journal* 27: 563–589.

Cotugno, M., and V. Stefanelli. 2012. Geographical and product diversification during instability financial period: Good or bad for banks? Available at SSRN: http://ssrn.com/abstract=1989919 or http://dx.doi.org/10.2139/ssrn.1989919.

DaSilva, C.M., and P. Trkman. 2014. Business model: What it is and what it is not. *Long Range Planning* 47 (6): 379–389.

De Jonghe, O., M. Diepstraten, and G. Schepens. 2015. Banks' size, scope and systemic risk: What role for conflicts of interest? *Journal of Banking & Finance* 61: S3–S13.

De Meo, E., A. De Nicola, G. Lusignani., and L. Zicchino. 2016. *European banks in the XXI century: Are their business models sustainable?* (forthcoming).

Demirgüc-Kunt, A., and H. Huizinga. 2010. Bank activity and funding strategies: the impact on risk and returns. *Journal of Financial Economics*, 98 (3), 626–650.

Demsetz, R.S., and P.E. Strahan. 1997. Diversification, size, and risk at bank holding companies. *Journal of Money Credit and Banking* 29: 300–313.

DeYoung, R., and K.P. Roland. 2001. Product mix and earnings volatility at commercial banks: Evidence from a degree of total leverage model. *Journal of Financial Intermediation* 10 (1): 54–84.

DeYoung, R., and T. Rice. 2004. Noninterest income and financial performance at US commercial banks. *Financial Review* 39 (1): 101–127.

DeYoung, R., and G. Torna. 2013. Nontraditional banking activities and bank failures during the financial crisis. *Journal of Financial Intermediation* 22 (3): 397–421.

Diamond, D.W. 1984. Financial intermediation and delegated monitoring. *Review of Economic Studies* 51: 393–414.

Diamond, D.W. 1991. Monitoring and reputation: The choice between bank loans and directly placed debt. *Journal of Political Economy* 99: 689–721.

EBA. 2014. *Guidelines on common procedures and methodologies for the supervisory review and evaluation process (SREP)*, EBA/GL/2014/13, 19 December.

ECB Banking Supervision. 2015. *SSM SREP methodology booklet level playing field—High standards of supervision—Sound risk assessment.*
ECB Banking Supervision. 2016. *SSM priorities 2016*, January.
ECB. 2016. Recent trends in euro area banks' business models and implication for banking sector stability. *Financial Stability Review—Special Features*, May.
Elsas, R., A. Hackethal, and M. Holzhäuser. 2010. The anatomy of bank diversification. *Journal of Banking & Finance* 34 (6): 1274–1287.
FSA. 2009. *The Turner review. A regulatory response to the global banking crisis.* March, London.
Gallo, J.G., V.P. Apilado, and J.W. Kolari. 1996. Commercial bank mutual fund activities: Implications for bank risk and profitability. *Journal of Banking & Finance* 20 (10): 1775–1791.
George, G., and A.J. Bock. 2011. The business model in practice and its implications for entrepreneurship research. *Entrepreneurship Theory and Practice* 35: 83–111. doi:10.1111/j.1540-6520.2010.00424.x.
Gertner, R., D. Scharfstein, and J. Stein. 1994. Internal vs. external capital markets. *Quarterly Journal of Economics* 109: 1211–1230.
Goddard, J., D. McKillop, and O.J. Wilson. 2008. The diversification and financial performance of US credit unions. *Journal of Banking & Finance* 32 (9): 1836–1849.
Graham, J.R., M. L. Lemmon., and Wolf, J.G. 2002. Does corporate diversification destroy value? *The Journal of Finance*, 57 (2), 695–720.
Gualandri, E. 2016. Vigilanza unica: traguardi raggiunti e cantieri aperti. *Bancaria* 5: 2–18.
Herring, R.J., and A.M. Santomero. 1990. The corporate structure of financial conglomerates. *Journal of Financial Services Research* 4: 471–97.
Klang, D., M. Wallnöfer, and F. Hacklin. 2014. The business model paradox: A systematic review and exploration of antecedents. *International Journal of Management Reviews* 16: 454–478.
Klein, P.G., and M.R. Saidenberg. 1997. *Diversification, organization and efficiency: Evidence from bank holding companies*, mimeo.
Köhler, M. 2014. Does non-interest income make banks more risky? Retail-versus investment-oriented banks. *Review of Financial Economics* 23 (4): 182–193.
Köhler, M. 2015. Which banks are more risky? The impact of business models on bank stability. *Journal of Financial Stability* 16: 195–212.

Laeven, L., and R. Levine. 2007. Is there a diversification discount in financial conglomerates? *Journal of Financial Economics* 85 (2): 331–367.
Lautenschlager, S. 2016. *European banking supervision business model analysis*, CEO/CFO/CRO-Roundtable 7 July.
Leask, G. 2004. Is there still value in strategic group research? *Aston Business School research papers*, no. RP0404, Aston University, Birmingham (UK).
Lepetit, L., E. Nys, P. Rous, and A. Tarazi. 2008. Bank income structure and risk: An empirical analysis of European banks. *Journal of Banking & Finance* 32 (8): 1452–1467.
Llewellyn, D.T. 1996. Universal banking and the public interest: A British perspective. *Universal Banking: Financial System Design Reconsidered*, 161–204.
Mercieca, S., K. Schaeck, and S. Wolfe. 2007. Small European banks: Benefits from diversification? *Journal of Banking & Finance* 31 (7): 1975–1998.
Mergaerts, F., and R. Vander Vennet, R. 2016. Business models and bank performance: A long-term perspective. *Journal of Financial Stability*, 22, 57–75.
Moloney, N. 2012. *Supervision in the wake of the financial crisis. Achieving effective 'Law in Action'—A challenge for the EU*. In *Financial Regulation and Supervision. A Post-Crisis Analysis,* ed. E. Wymeersch, K.J. Hopt, and G. Ferrarini, Oxford University Press, Oxford.
Morris, M., M. Schindehutte, and J. Allen. 2005. The entrepreneur's business model: Toward a unified perspective. *Journal of Business Research* 58: 726–735.
Mottura, P. 2011. *Banche; strategie, organizzazione e concentrazioni*. Milano: Egea.
Osterwalder, A. 2004. The business model ontology-a proposition in a design science approach (2004), These Présentée à l'Ecole des Hautes Etudes Commerciales, de l'Université de Lausanne Universite de Lausanne.
Osterwalder, A., and Y. Pigneur. 2012. *Business model generation*. New York: Hoboken, John Wiley.
Passmore, S.W. 1985. Strategic groups and the profitability of banking. Research Paper 8501, Federal Reserve Bank of New York.
Penrose, E. 1959. *The theory of the growth of the firm*. Oxford: Oxford University Press.
Porter, M.E. 1996. What is strategy? *Harvard Business Review* 74 (6): 61–78.
Rajan, R., H. Servaes, and L. Zingales. 2000. The cost of diversity: The diversification discount and inefficient investment. *Journal of Finance* 55: 35–80.
Rajan, R.G. 1992. Insiders and outsiders: The choice between informed and arm's length debt. *The Journal of Finance XLVII* 4: 1367–1400.

Roengpitya, R., N.A. Tarashev, and K. Tsatsaronis. 2014. *Bank business models*, 55–65. Quarterly Review December: BIS.

Rossi, S.P., M.S. Schwaiger, and G. Winkler. 2009. How loan portfolio diversification affects risk, efficiency and capitalization: A managerial behavior model for Austrian banks. *Journal of Banking & Finance* 33 (12): 2218–2226.

Shafer, S.M., H.J. Smith, and J.C. Linder. 2005. The power of business models. *Business Horizons* 48 (3): 199–207.

Short, J.C., D.J. Ketchen, T.B. Palmer, and G.T. Hult. 2007. Firm, strategic group and industry influences on performance. *Strategic Management Journal* 28: 147–167.

Stein, J.C. 1997. Internal capital markets and the competition for corporate resources. *Journal of Finance* 52 (1): 111–133.

Stein, J.C. 2002. Information production and capital allocation: Decentralized versus hierarchical firms. *The Journal of Finance* 57: 1891–1921.

Stiroh, K.J. 2004. Diversification in banking: Is noninterest income the answer? *Journal of Money, Credit, and Banking* 36 (5): 853–882.

Stiroh, K.J. 2006. A portfolio view of banking with interest and noninterest activities. *Journal of Money, Credit, and Banking* 38 (5): 1351–1361.

Stiroh, K.J. 2009. Volatility accounting: A production perspective on increased economic stability. *Journal of the European Economic Association* 7: 671–696.

Stiroh, K., and A. Rumble. 2006. The dark side of diversification: The case of US financial holding companies. *Journal of Banking & Finance* 30 (8): 2131–2432.

Stulz, R. 1990. Managerial discretion and optimal financial policies. *Journal of Financial Economics* 26: 3–27.

Teece, D.J. 1982. Towards an economic theory of the multiproduct firm. *Journal of Economic Behavior & Organization* 3 (1): 39–63

Teece, D.J. 2010. Business models, business strategy and innovation. *Long Range Planning* 43: 172–194.

Vallascas, F., F. Crespi, F., and J. Hagendorff. 2012. *Income diversification and bank performance during the financial crisis*. Available at SSRN: http://ssrn.com/abstract=1793232 or http://dx.doi.org/10.2139/ssrn.1793232.

Van Oordt, M., and C. Zhou. 2014. Systemic risk and bank business models. WP No. 442, De Nederlandishe.

Williams, B. 2016. The impact of non interest income on bank risk in Australia. *Journal of Banking & Finance* 73: 16–37.

Wirtz, B.W., A. Pistoia, S. Ullrich, and V. Göttel. 2016. Business models: Origin, development and future research perspectives. *Long Range Planning* 49: 36–54.

Wirtz, B.W. 2011. *Business model management: Design instrument-success factor*. Wiesbaden: Gabler.

Zott, C., R. Amit, and L. Massa. 2011. The business model: Recent developments and future research. *Journal of Management* 37 (4): 1019–1042.

8

On European Deposit Protection Scheme(s)

Milena Migliavacca

8.1 Introduction

The stability of the banking sector has proven to be a crucial requisite for the overall stability of a nation's economy, particularly in recent years (Wheelock and Wilson 1995; Acharya 2009; Lambert et al. 2015). Financial safety nets are systems of legislative measures put in place to guarantee banks' stability (Demirgüç-Kunt and Huizinga 1999, 2004); one of the most relevant actors of a national safety net, along with the prudential regulator, the lender of last resort and the supervisory authority is the deposit protection scheme (DPS) (Laeven 2002; Schich 2008). DPSs are public authorities designed to reimburse depositors in place of their financial institution, when the latter is insolvent; within the European Union, they are in force in all Member States since 1994 (Directive 94/19/EC). This analysis focuses specifically on the DPSs across the EU28, as they have been recognised among the most effective

M. Migliavacca (✉)
Catholic University, Milan, Italy
e-mail: milena.migliavacca@unicatt.it

G. Chesini et al. (eds.), *The Business of Banking*, Palgrave Macmillan Studies in Banking and Financial Institutions, DOI 10.1007/978-3-319-54894-4_8

tools to temper investors' panic during the financial turmoil following both the global financial crisis and the European sovereign crisis and they are undergoing a major revision process (Demirgüç-Kunt et al. 2015).

The banking industry is particularly vulnerable to instabilities because of an intrinsic characteristic of its core business: the maturity transformation that leads to fractional-reserve banking. There is a physiological mismatching of volumes, interest rates and maturities between assets and liabilities in a bank's balance sheet, so only a fraction of bank deposits are available for immediate withdrawal. If the demand for deposits exceeds the fraction hold in a bank's account (as, for instance during a bank run), financial institutions cannot refund their depositors and the intervention of DPSs becomes necessary to prevent the depositors from losing the totality of their savings. DSPs safeguard the banking stability by acting contemporarily on the depositors' and the financial institutions' side. On one hand, they protect depositors against the unavailability of their deposits, and on the other hand, they protect banks from contagious runs; they may also provide additional liquidity to credit institutions during financial crises. These objectives contribute to the DPSs' *stabilisation* ultimate purpose. However, one of the costs of deposit insurance provision is the potential for *moral hazard*, as depositors have less incentive to monitor their bank managers' behaviour, knowing that their deposits are guaranteed by national funds (Gropp and Vesala 2004; Hovakimiam et al. 2003). Banks as well can engage in imprudent practices, secure in the knowledge that if the high-risk loans do not pay off, deposit insurance will shelter their principal (Demirgüç-Kunt and Kane 2002; Pennacchi 2006). Another subtle drawback of DPSs lays in the specific characteristics of the deposit insurance funds, which are largely left to the Member States' discretion, despite the constant harmonisation effort by the European legislator over the years (Carbo-Valverde et al. 2012), because such asymmetries may interfere with cross-country fair competition in the banking sector (Cordella and Yeyati 2002; Engineer et al. 2013). DPSs have been in the spotlight for both policy makers and scholars for decades, but particularly so after the global financial crisis and the following European sovereign crises. In this period, they have been the core topic of several empirical and theoretical contributions and went through significant legislative changes. There is a rich literature that analyses benefits and costs of explicit deposit insurance and looks for their optimal design (e.g. Diamond and Dybvig 1983; Pennacchi 1987; Kane 1995; and Pennacchi 2006) and two main streams stem from it: one that maintains that the stabilisation effect of DPSs prevails on moral hazard incentives (e.g. Diamond and Dybvig 1983) and another, which supports the opposite view (e.g. Pennacchi 2006). A handful of contributions (among others, Anginer et al. 2014), moreover, tries to refine the analysis by disentangling the prevailing effect in particular circumstances, such as the financial crisis. Anginer et al. (2014) provide evidence that the overall effect of an explicit deposit insurance mechanism is detrimental to the bank stability, but highlight a prevailing stabilising effect during financial turmoil as well.

Finally, among the most recent qualitative contributions, Cariboni et al. (2010) and Arnaboldi (2014) shed light on the effectiveness of the European DPSs during the crisis and their legal evolution.

This contribution provides an analytical overview of the DPSs set-up in the European Union Member States and analyses the main features of their design; it investigates the level of harmonisation reached by the DPSs within the EU28. According to the author, the way the features of the deposit insurance fund are combined may influence its prevailing effect (stabilising or risk-seeking); for instance, some DPS's characteristics, such as risk-based premia or *ex-ante* contribution may indeed mitigate the moral hazard that too generous DPS may trigger (Duan et al. 1992; Forssbaeck 2011).

The two main data sources exploited in the chapter are the 94/19/EC Directive and its development and the World Bank's Bank Regulation and Supervision Surveys. This chapter is structured as follows. In the second section, an overview of the reference Directives is given, along with a brief excursus on the DIS's features analysed. The third section details the status quo of the deposit insurance designs of the EU Member States and provides some insight into the most common features combinations and how they changed after the financial crisis. The final section draws some final remarks.

8.2 The Legal Framework

This paper aims at drawing a detailed overview of the DPSs in the EU28 by taking into account a number of features that characterise the national deposit insurance fund/s of the Member States. Information on the deposit insurance design has been mainly taken from the Bank Regulation and Supervision surveys. The Surveys, carried out by the World Bank, are a source of world-wide data on how banks are regulated and supervised, and they comprise a section dedicated to deposits protection schemes. The surveys have been carried out in 2001, 2003, 2007 and 2012 giving the chance to closely monitor the evolution of the DPSs over the years. For the sake of this analysis, nine features of the EU28 Member States' DPSs are taken into account (see Table 8.1).

*Coverage Limit_* indicates the extent of the investors' deposits coverage. Between 1994 and 2008, the coverage limit in the EU28 spanned from a minimum of €3400 (Romania) to a maximum of €103,291 (Italy). Some Member States, furthermore, granted blanket guarantees to depositors during the period 2008–2010. From 2009 on, the national coverage limits were harmonised to the common level of €50,000, raised to €100,000 in 2010, according to the EU-Directive 2009/14.

In each Member States, the deposit coverage limit is considered per account, in Euros.

*Coinsurance_* With coinsured deposits, account holders are explicitly insured for less than 100% of their savings, according to the national legislation. There has been much debate on this feature, designed as an incentive for depositors' monitoring. It might be questionable, though, in the first place, whether depositors have the necessary competences to carry out such an activity; moreover, as in the deposit insurance context, the banks themselves are the risk creators, high level of coinsurance may spur risk-seeking choices by the banks' management, so the net effect of this feature on the banks' moral hazard incentives remains unclear. After the financial crisis, though, Directive 2009/14/EC banned Coinsurance from the possible characteristics of deposit insurance funds.

*Fund Management_* EU Member States may choose whether their deposit insurance scheme is managed by the private sector, by the public

Table 8.1 Deposit protection scheme (DPS) features

Feature	Survey question	Comments
Coverage		
Coverage limit	What is the deposit insurance limit per account (in US$ and local currency)?	The maximum amount to which depositors can be reimbursed. Yearly values, in Euros
Coinsurance	Is there formal coinsurance? Yes?/No?	Coinsurance means that the depositor has to accept part of the risk for his/her own account, the presence of coinsurance increases the banks' MH incentives
Funding and management		
Fund management	The insurance fund is managed by (a) The private sector alone; (b) Jointly by private/public officials (c) The public sector alone	The moral hazard incentive is considered higher if the insurance fund is administered solely by banks
Source of funding	Funding is provided by a) Government; b) Banks c) Combination	According to the literature, the moral hazard incentive is considered higher when the funds are provided by the government or jointly by banks and government. Levies can typically be imposed upon banks, e.g. based on volume of insured deposits, and/or on the basis the risk profile of the bank
Ex-ante contribution	Is there an ex-ante fund/reserve to cover deposit insurance claims in the event of the failure of a member bank? Yes?/No?	"Ex-ante funds" implies the presence of an upfront amount of funds available to be used to compensate depositors, so it is expected to dampen the moral hazard incentives
Risk-adjustment	Do deposit insurance fees/premiums charged to banks vary, based on some assessment of risk? Yes?/No	According to the literature, Risk-based premia dampen the banks' MH incentives

(continued)

Table 8.1 (continued)

Intervention		
Intervention power	Does the deposit insurance agency/fund administrator have the following powers as part of its mandate? Bank intervention authority	This authority allows the agency to, e.g. issue cease and desist orders, impose a form of temporary administration which overrides management, replace managers, etc
Power to cancel	Does the deposit insurance authority by itself have the legal power to cancel or revoke deposit insurance for any participating bank?	The presence of this power reduces banks' MH incentives
Legal power	Can the deposit insurance agency/fund take legal action for violations of laws, regulations, and by-laws against bank directors or other bank officials? Yes?/No?	Legal action implies enforceable corrective action based on powers granted in law or regulation, providing direct powers to order action against individuals in the bank or its Board dampening the MH incentives

Notes This table summarises nine characteristics of DPSs analysed, divided up into three buckets: Coverage, Funding & Management and Intervention
Source Adapted from Bank regulation and Supervision surveys

sector or jointly by both of them. Pure private funding is expected to relax the discipline on DIS management and to leave room for possible banks' moral hazard incentives, which may be tempered if both private and public officials jointly manage the deposit insurance fund and are even more reduced if the public sector alone administers it.

*Source of Funding_* indicates whether the government, the banks or the two actors together fund the national DPS. The possible banks' moral hazard incentives decrease significantly if the source of funding is the banks themselves; in this case, in effect, taxpayers are not involved in bearing part or the whole risk arising from the deposits insurance funds' management decisions.

*Ex-ante Contribution_* the contributions to the deposit insurance fund can be collected on a regular basis to meet potential future obligations (*ex-ante* contribution) or only after a bank's failure (*ex-post*). Before Directive 2014/49/EU, 19 countries had *ex-ante* contributions (Belgium, Bulgaria, Croatia, Cyprus, Denmark, Finland, France, Germany, Greece, Hungary, Ireland, Latvia, Lithuania, Malta, Poland, Portugal, Romania, Slovakia and Spain). This option is considered among both scholars and practitioners to enhance the stabilising effect of DPSs and has, in effect, always been encouraged by the European Supervisory authorities (FSB 2012; Directive 2009/14/EC; IADI 2015), as the presence of readily accessible funds supports the clients' confidence. The difference between *ex-ante* and *ex-post* contribution, though, might not be stark, as in some Member States with *ex-post* contribution, there might be "virtual funds", not officially collected by the DPSs but privately set by the member banks. Another possible element of heterogeneity among the Member States with an *ex-ante* contribution system is the amount of the periodical contribution.

*Risk-based Contribution_* The contributions to the DPS are based on the degree of riskiness of each member, measured by a set of ad hoc indicators. The methodologies that assess the banks' risk may take into account the banks' business model, the level of total deposits or total liabilities, the different types of covered deposits or eligible deposits[1] and may vary across countries. Despite there might be room for unequal treatment, as the risk-weighting criteria are not homogeneous among the Member States, this feature is an effective way to minimise the moral hazard incentives on the banks' side and has been introduced as a mandatory feature of European DPSs since 2014 (Directive 2014/49/EU).

The three *Intervention Powers* reported in Table 8.1 refer to the supervisory agency's right to take actions against the management to restore the bank's solvency; these interventions comprise temporary administration, which overrides the bank's management, the exclusion of a bank from the national DPS and the possibility to take legal actions against the bank's management. The presence of these features serves as a rather powerful deterrent against banks' moral hazard, as confirmed by IADI (2014).

All the EU28 deposit insurance schemes are explicit, but may differ in the way the features described above are combined. DPSs' features have been designed to protect deposits, enhance depositor confidence and minimise bank-runs risk; with too generous schemes, though, the stabilising effect may be outweighed by banks' moral hazard incentives (Demirgüç-Kunt and Detragiache 2002; Barth et al. 2013; Angkinand and Wihlborg 2010; IADI 2013a, b, c, 2014).

In order to have a better understanding of the DPSs' design within the EU28, the features described by the World Bank's Bank Regulation and Supervision Surveys need to be considered within the legal framework in force. The first attempt to homogenise the deposit insurance regulation in the EU was the Directive 94/19/EC in 1994. The Directive ensured that the DPSs of the Member States had at least three main characteristics in common. All Member States needed to have at least one explicit DPS. If one bank went bankrupt, the national DGS would reimburse the account holders, and the minimum protection level was initially set to ECU 15,000 and then raised at ECU 20,000 on 01/01/2000. The third common feature among the EU Members' DPSs was payout time limits: 21 days for the deposit insurance authority to make the determination that a credit institution is unable to repay the depositors and three months for the actual reimbursement, with the possibility of extending this deadline up to nine months. Regarding this last point, however, the Directive did not specify the period in which depositors could submit the claim necessary to trigger the reimbursement process. The implementation of more stringent rules was left to the Member States, which were free to choose the categories of deposits/depositors to include in the DPS, how to finance and how to manage the fund/s and whether or not to resort to coinsurance; even among the Member States that apply coinsurance, the coinsured percentage of the deposits could significantly vary. The characteristics of the contributions themselves could vary, as well: members could choose between *ex-ante* and *ex-post* contributions and even among those countries, which chose the *ex-ante* method, the amount of resources periodically set aside could be heterogeneous, depending on the structure of the national banking industry and the legal role of the DPS, mainly. The payouts could be risk based or not, but once again, even among the Member States with risk-based contribution, the weighting coefficients were not harmonised. Each Member State, furthermore, could decide the intervention powers to leave to the supervisory authority. Even the coverage limit used to span within a wide range from the minimum guarantee of €20,000 in Romania to €103,291 in Italy. As in some countries the coinsurance was in force, the actual coverage could be even more heterogeneous, because the amount guaranteed could be lower than the coverage level, depending on the percentage of coinsurance. Finally, the Member States could exclude from the guarantee mechanism or lower the relative level of coverage of a number of typologies of deposits listed in the Directive. The Directive allowed considerable scope for Member States to design the DPSs, which were best in line with their national market conditions, but such freedom left room to distortions within those banking systems in which cross-country financial institutions coexisted. To address this issue, the Directive enforced the *topping-up* principle: the first attempt to homogenise the DPSs around Europe. According to this principle, the host country's conditions prevailed at national level, irrespectively of the origin of the hosted credit institutions and branches. The Directive on deposit guarantee schemes adopted in 1994 was substantially unchanged for 14 years, leaving the bulk of the DPSs' design to the single Member State's autonomous decision. This excessive discretionary power turned out to be detrimental to the financial stability, and the outburst of the global financial crisis forced the legislator to introduce the Amending Directive 2009/17/EC. In such a delicate moment, three main changes were made in order to boost depositors' confidence and limit contagious bank runs. The coverage limit was increased immediately to €50,000 and the Member States were asked to further raise the coverage for the aggregate deposits of each depositor to €100,000 by the end of December 2010. The Directive banned the use of coinsurance, as well. The third issue addressed is the payout time; the deadline for the determination of a bank's inability to repay depositors was reduced from 21 to 5 working days, and the repayment of claimed deposits was shortened from three months, extendible to nine months, to 20 working days; only under exceptional circumstances and after formal approval by the competent authorities, this deadline could be postponed by 10 more working days.

The Amending Directive represented an emergency measure; however, by comparing the information of World Bank's Bank Regulation and Supervision Surveys of 2003 and 2012, no major changes in the most qualifying features of the European DPSs emerge, as outlined in Table 8.2.

From a preliminary analysis, the substantial static of the DPSs' designs might surprise, given the shortcomings some Member States' DPSs faced during the most turbulent periods or the crisis. As a matter of fact, from the debate immediately following the outburst of the financial crisis, which led to the Amending Directive 2009/14/EC, the need for the deposit insurance regulation to be deeply renewed emerged clearly.

Because of the financial crisis, the need for timely negotiations impeded addressing the numerous open issues the European DPS framework suffered from, but at least three main areas of intervention were identified. Despite the need for a pan-European DPS began to be tangible, the proposal was rejected by nearly all stakeholders, so a detail cost/benefit analysis on the topic was encouraged. *Ex-ante*, risk-based contribution systems were promoted as well, even though the pro-cyclical effect of too heavy *ex-ante* contributions during times when banks were already in difficulty prompted further debate on this feature.

On 16 April 2014, the Directive 2014/49/EU answered to these unaddressed issues by introducing several changes; the most important one involved the contributions to the deposit insurance fund. Yearly *ex-ante* premia collection was introduced, and the target level of 0.8% for covered deposits was set to be reached by 2024. The Directive imposes, moreover, the contributions to DPSs to be based on the amount of covered deposits and the member's degree of risk, measured by a set of specific indicators assessed according to EBA's guidelines (2015). Member States are allowed to use their own risk-weighting method; however, these methods shall be approved by the national competent authority, and EBA should be informed, as well. Furthermore, the weighting techniques shall be revised 3 years after the entry into force of the Directive and every five years afterwards; the weights anyhow should reflect the risk profiles of the member credit institutions, including their different business models. Furthermore, a number of changes were introduced to simplify and speed up the depositors' reimbursement.

Table 8.2 Design features distribution across European countries

Country	AT		BE		BG		CY		CZ		DK		EE		FI		FR	
Feature/pre/post-crisis	pre	Post	pre	post	pre	post	pre	post	pre	post	pre	post	pre	post	pre	post	pre	post
Coinsurance	X		X				X		X								X	
DIS source of funding																		
Banks	X		X	X	X	X	X	X	X	X	X	X	X	X	X	X	X	X
Government or both		X																
Ex-ante premiums			X	X	X	X		X	X	X	X	X	X		X	X	X	X
Risk-adjusted premiums			X							X					X	X	X	X
DIS power of intervention on bank members				X														
DIS power to cancel members	X						X				X				X		X	
DIS legal power on bank management			X	X											X		X	X
DIS administration																		
Private sector	X	X	X												X	X	X	X
Public sector or jointly				X	X	X	X	X	X	X	X	X	X	X				

Country	DE		GR		HR		HU		IE		IT		LV		LT		LU		MT	
Feature/pre/post-crisis	pre	post	pre	post	pre	post	pre	post	pre	post	pre	Post	pre	post	pre	post	pre	post	Pre	post
Coinsurance	X				X		X		X				X		X		X		X	
DIS source of funding																				
Banks	X	X	X	X	X	X	X	X	X	X	X	X		X		X	X	X	X	X
Government or both													X		X					
Ex-ante premiums	X	X	X	X	X	X	X	X	X	X			X	X	X	X				X
Risk-adjusted premiums	X	X		X			X	X			X	X		X					X	
DIS power of intervention on bank members						X	X			X	X									
DIS power to cancel members		X	X	X			X	X	X	X	X			X	X		X	X		
DIS legal power on bank management	X					X				X			X	X				X	X	X
DIS administration																				
Private sector		X									X	X						X		
Public sector or jointly	X		X	X	X	X	X	X	X	X			X	X	X	X	X		X	X

Country	NL		PL		PT		RO		SK		SL		ES		SW		UK	
Feature/pre/post-crisis	pre	post	pre	post	pre	post	pre	post	pre	post	pre	post	pre	post	pre	post	pre	Post
Coinsurance	X		X		X				X		X		X				X	
DIS source of funding																		
Banks	X		X	X	X	X	X	X	X	X	X		X	X		–	X	X
Government or both		X										X			X	–		
Ex-ante premiums				X	X	X	X	X		X			X	X	X	X		
Risk-adjusted premiums					X	X									X	X		
DIS power of intervention on bank members									X		X	X						
DIS power to cancel members															X			X
DIS legal power on bank management									X		X	X	X	X		X	X	
DIS administration																		
Private sector												X						X
Public sector or jointly	X	X	X	X	X	X	X	X	X	X	X		X	X	X	X	X	

Source World Bank's Bank Regulation and Supervision Surveys (2003, 2012)

The payout time was sensibly shortened from 20 working days to 15 by the end of 2019, to 10 by the end of 2023 and to 7 from 2024 on; furthermore, during the transitional period, DGSs should ensure depositors to be able to have access to part of their deposits in order to cover their cost of living. Moreover, the scheme repays the depositors on its own initiative; no official application from depositors is needed.

The Member States should, then introduce periodical stress tests on their national DPSs, have in place adequate systems to determine potential criticalities and produce annual reports on their activities. EBA is supposed to carry out peer reviews in order to guarantee the resilience of national DPSs every five years, as well. If the deposit insurance fund's resources are not enough to cover claimed deposits, the Member States should furthermore ensure that their DPSs have in place adequate alternatives to have access to alternative short-term funding. In this case, extraordinary additional contributions may be imposed to banks or governments may step in the scene, whether they are officially among the DPS funders or not. The DPS, alternatively, can borrow financial resources from the market, usually from the European Central Bank. One further possible alternative funding source is for DPSs to borrow from one another, in order to create an informal network, that does not require changes in the national legal frameworks, but that might still lead the way towards a fully fledged European DPS. Even though the European DPSs harmonisation process began over twenty years ago and the Directive 2014/49/EU introduced much more stringent rules, there are still stark differences across the EU.

8.3 The EU Status Quo

In the EU28, there are almost forty different DPSs (see Table 8.3); usually each country has one DPS, which covers the deposits of all the banks in a country, however, more than one DPS may operate in a single state. This is the case of Austria (five DPSs), Germany (four DPSs), the Czech Republic and Spain (three DPSs) and Cyprus, Italy and Portugal (two DPSs). In these cases, a single deposit insurance fund is established for each typology of DPS. Usually, specific DPSs are set according to

Table 8.3 Deposit protection schemes (DPSs) in the EU28

Country	EU membership	Deposit insurance organisation
Austria	1995	Deposit Protection Company of the Austrian Commercial Banks Ltd
		O¨ sterreichische Raiffeisen-Einlagensicherung reg.Gen.m.b.H. (O¨ RE)
		AT3 Austria 3 Sparkassen-Haftungs Aktiengesellschaft
		AT4 Austria 4 Schulze-Delitzsch Haftungsgenossenschaft reg.Gen.m.b.H.
		AT5 Austria 5 Hypo-Haftungs-Gesellschaft m.b.H.
Belgium	1958	Fonds de Protection
Bulgaria	2007	Bulgarian Deposit Insurance Fund
Croatia	2013	State agency for deposit insurance and bank resolution
Cyprus	2004	Deposit Protection Scheme
		Deposit Protection Scheme for cooperative societies
Czech Republic	2004	Deposit Insurance Fund
Denmark	1973	The Guarantee Fund for Depositors and Investors
Estonia	2004	Deposit Guarantee Sectoral Fund
Finland	1995	Deposit Guarantee Fund
France	1958	Fonds de Garatie des Depots (FDG)
Germany	1958	Entschädigungseinrichtung deutscher Banken GmbH (EdB)
		VÖB-Entschädigungseinrichtung GmbH
		Entschädigungseinrichtung der Wertpapierhandelsunternehmen (EdW)
Greece	1981	Hellenic Deposit Guarantee Fund
Hungary	2004	National Deposit Insurance Fund (NDIF)
Ireland	1973	The Deposit Guarantee Scheme (DGS)
Italy	1958	Fondo Interbancario di Tutela dei Depositi (FITD)
		Fondo di Garanzia dei Depositanti del Credito Cooperativo
Latvia	2004	Deposit Guarantee Fund
Lithuania	2004	Valstybės įmonė "Indėlių ir investicijų draudimas"
Luxemburg	1958	Luxembourg Deposit Guarantee Association
Malta	2004	Depositor Compensation Scheme
Netherlands	1958	Depositogarantiestelsel
Poland	2004	Bankowy Fundusz Gwarancyjny (BFG)
Portugal	1986	Fundo de Garantia de Depósitos

(continued)

Table 8.3 (continued)

		Fundo de Garantia do Crédito Agrícola Mútuo
Romania	2007	Deposit Guarantee Fund in the banking system
Slovakia	2004	Deposit Protection Fund
Slovenia	2004	The central bank of the Republic of Slovenia
Spain	1986	Fondos de Garantía de Depósitos (FGD)
Sweden	1995	Swedish National Debt Office
UK	1973	Financial Services Compensation Scheme

Notes This table presents the national DPSs in each EU28 Member State

banks' specialisation and operate autonomously; the obligation to pay contributions and refund depositors applies primarily to the DPS to which the affected bank belongs to. In case the DPS in question is not able to refund the insolvent banks' depositors in full, the other national DPSs get involved in the reimbursement process. Only in the unlikely event that all the national DPSs are jointly not able to refund the claimed deposits, the firstly affected DPS should turn to alternative external sources of funding as, for instance, loans from public or private third parties. Finally, besides the official deposit insurance funds, additional so-called virtual funds can be established, as well on a voluntary base among groups of banks; this possibility increases significantly the complexity and homogeneity of DPS across the EU.

Over the past decades, DPSs have developed in quite heterogeneous ways in Europe, as most of the decisions regarding their characteristics were left to single Member States, hence the numerous different DPSs across the EU. The following brief overview of the current DPSs, according to the latest World Bank's Bank Regulation and Supervision Survey (2012), sheds light on the different design the EU28[2] Member States chose for their national DPSs.

Austria: In Austria, there is a legally autonomous deposit insurance agency, which does not have by itself any intervention authority, nor the possibility to revoke deposit insurance for any participating bank or take legal action against banks' directors and officials. The insurance funding is jointly provided by public and private institutions, according to a three-stage mechanism. At first, the DPS members are required to pay proportionate contributions; if a DPS is unable to reimburse the insured deposits in full, the other DPSs are obliged to make proportionate contributions in order to cover the shortfall. In case all the DPSs together are unable to pay out the claimed insured deposits in full, the primarily concerned DPS must issue debt securities in order to meet the remaining payment obligations. The Federal Minister of Finance may assume liabilities on behalf of the federal government, according to a special governmental authorisation and tops up the difference to the maximum insured amount. Despite the source of funding is both public and private, the private sector alone manages the fund. Foreign currency deposits, interbank deposits and deposits of the foreign subsidiaries of domestic banks are excluded from the coverage. The contributions to the deposit insurance fund, before the Directive 2014/49/EU was in force, were *ex-post* and not based on some assessment of the members' risk. After the financial crisis, Austria increased the amount of covered deposits, and during the most critical part of the crisis, the Austrian Government guaranteed in full the account holders' deposits and banks' debt.

Belgium: The Belgian banks alone contribute to the deposit insurance fund, which, though, is managed by both private and public officials. Even before the Directive 2014/49/EU was in force, the contributions to the insurance fund were periodical, but not risk based. The deposit insurance agency has both intervention authority and the power to take legal actions for the violation of its regulations and by-laws against bank directors and other officials. It cannot, though, cancel or revoke a bank's the membership to the DPS. The deposit insurance coverage is per depositors per institutions, and interbank deposits and deposits of foreign subsidiaries of domestic banks are excluded by the insurance mechanism.

Bulgaria: The DPS in Bulgaria is funded by banks only, but managed by both private and public actors. Even prior to Directive 2014/49/EU, the contributions to the insurance fund were periodical, but not risk based. The insurance authority has limited powers, and it cannot intervene against banks' officials or directors nor impose temporary administration; it is not allowed to revoke a membership from the respective DPS, either. From 2008 to 2010, the percentage of the total deposits of commercial banks covered by the DPS rose from 54.31 to 65.39% covering savings per depositor per institution, but excluding interbank deposits and deposits of both foreign subsidiaries and branches of national banks. In accordance with the Directive 2009/14, as a result of the global financial crisis, Bulgaria raised its coverage limit to €100,000.

Croatia: The claim for payment by the deposit insurance system is triggered by a court-declared bank's bankruptcy. The peculiarity of Croatian DPS is that the insurance fund is entirely funded by banks but exclusively managed by the public sector. The contributions to the fund have always been *ex-ante*, but not risk based until the Directive 2009/14 entered into force. The Croatian insurance authority can take legal action directly against banks' directors and officials in case they violate its regulations or by-laws; it can replace management and impose some form of temporary administration if necessary, as well.

Cyprus: The Cypriot DPS is funded by banks but jointly managed by banks and the public sector. Both a bank's bankruptcy and the banking supervisor's decision can trigger the deposits repayment claim. The Cypriot deposit insurance authority, which is a legally independent entity, is particularly week, regarding its intervention power: its authority in effect is limited to banks' examination. The participation in the deposit insurance system is not only compulsory for domestic banks, but for foreign bank subsidiaries and branches, as well; deposits of foreign subsidiaries of domestic banks, though, are excluded from the DPS. Banks had to periodically contribute to the deposit insurance fund, even before the Directive 2009/14 made it compulsory, but before the entry into force of the Directive, the periodical contributions did not depend on the members' riskiness. As a result of the global financial crisis, the contributions to the Cypriot DPS were increased, as well as the amount of guaranteed deposits.

Denmark: The Danish DPS guarantees deposits per depositor per institution up to a maximum of €40,000 increased to €100,000 in compliance to the Directive 2009/14. Only banks fund the DPS, which is, though, jointly managed with public officials. As in a number of EU28 Member States, the intervention power left to the deposit insurance authority is rather limited; they do not have intervention power, nor legal power against the banks' officials; they cannot exclude banks from the DPS or have access to information collected by the banking supervision, either. Domestic and foreign banks subsidiaries are included in the DPS, but foreign bank branches are not and the deposits of foreign branches of domestic banks are excluded from the Danish DPS, as well. Even before respectively Directive 2009/14/EC and 2014/49/EU, there was no coinsurance and the contributions to the fund were periodical (*ex-ante* regime).

Estonia: The Estonian DPS is jointly administered by banks and the public sector. The deposit insurance authority is an autonomous entity, but it only has the power to access to information collected by the banking supervisor and cannot directly intervene against the banks belonging to the national DPS. In Estonia, foreign banks' branches do not necessarily have to take part in the DPS; the participation is required to foreign bank subsidiaries, instead. The DPS is designed per deposit per institution, and before the Directive 2014/49/EU, the contributions to the fund were collected *ex-post* and were not risk adjusted.

Finland: The Finnish DPS is both funded and managed by banks. The intervention powers of the deposit insurance authority, moreover, are particularly limited; it only controls the reimbursement process. The possible moral hazard originating from these characteristics of the DPS is tempered by the lack of coinsurance, the *ex-ante* funding and the risk-based contributions that were in place even before Directive 2014/49/EU. The risk-adjusted premia are calibrated according to the participating bank's capital adequacy. In case the deposit insurance fund is not large enough to compensate the guaranteed deposits, it has to borrow money from the market, as no public intervention is due.

France: The insurance agency is a legally independent entity, in France; it does not have the power to take strong action to bring a bank back to solvency, nor revoke the DPS membership to a bank, but it can take legal action against banks' directors and other officials. This possibility tempers the possible moral hazard incentives arising from the fact that banks alone fund and administer the national DPS. Other than domestic banks, both foreign banks subsidiaries and branches are required to participate in the French DPS. Even before the respective directives were in force, the French DPS had no formal coinsurance, the deposit insurance reserve was funded *ex-ante* and the contributions were adjusted according to the members' riskiness, assessed on the participating banks' insured deposits level. Over and above the post-crisis measures put in place by the Directive 2009/14, the French DPS enlarged the typologies of exposures and depositors covered.

Germany: In Germany, there are four different typologies of deposit protection schemes. The statutory protection schemes are supervised by the Deposit Guarantee and Investor Compensation Act, which implements the respective EU-Directive. Two statutory protection systems are devoted to German commercial banks: the Entschädigungseinrichtung deutscher Banken (EdB) for private commercial banks, and the Entschädigungseinrichtung Öffentlicher Banken (VÖB) for public commercial banks. There are also voluntary protection schemes that supplement the statutorily required protection; for private commercial banks, a voluntary deposit protection fund is set up at the Association of German Banks, whereas for public commercial banks the corresponding voluntary deposit protection fund is set up at the Federal Association of Public Banks. Despite they are kept separated, both associations govern the respective statutory deposit funds and the voluntary deposit funds. Saving banks and cooperative banks are excluded from statutory deposit protection, but are covered by the protection schemes of the savings bank (DSGV) and cooperative bank sectors (BVR); therefore, claims of depositors from saving deposits, time deposits and sight deposits are fully covered. In this fragmented framework, the banks themselves fund and administer the deposit insurance funds; the contributions have always been periodical and based on the members' risk, assessed according to the amount of deposits of non-bank institutions. The deposit insurance authorities, moreover, have the power to cancel the membership to the DPS of any participating bank.

Greece: Despite the source of the DPS funding is private, banks and public officials together manage the insurance fund in Greece. The deposit insurance authority cannot take major action to restore a bank's soundness, as for instance imposing a form of temporary administration, nor take legal action against banks director or officials, but it can revoke a bank's participation to the DPS. The participations to the DPS are not only compulsory for domestic banks but also for foreign banks' subsidiaries and branches. Deposits of foreign subsidiaries of domestic banks are, together with interbank deposits, the only form of deposit excluded from the Greek DPS. Even before the Directive 2014/49/EU made these features compulsory, the Greek DPS had *ex-ante* funding, risk-based contributions and no coinsurance. In order to tackle the severe financial crisis that hit Greece, the amount of covered deposits was increased, the Government guaranteed both deposits and banks' debt, the bank's contributions were increased and the reimbursement period was shortened. As the sovereign crisis was particularly severe in Greece, a drastic capital control was imposed in order to avoid deposits flight.

Hungary: The Hungarian DPS funding is provided solely by banks, but the fund is jointly administered by public officers. The contributions to the deposit insurance funds have always been regularly collected and risk based, even before the Directive 2009/14 entered into force. The deposit insurance authority has the legal power to revoke a bank's membership to the national DPS, but cannot directly intervene against banks' officials and directors, nor replace part of the management or impose a form of temporary administration. The participation at the national DPS is compulsory only for domestic banks, but deposits in foreign currency and deposits of both foreign branches or subsidiaries of domestic banks are included in the deposit insurance coverage.

Ireland: In Ireland, the deposit insurance agency is not a stand-alone authority, but it is included within the national Central Bank. Another peculiarity of the Irish DPS is that the funding is entirely provided by banks, but the deposit insurance fund is administered by the public sector alone. The deposit insurance authority, moreover, has the power to heavily intervene in the banks' management, by imposing a form of administration, which temporarily overrides the management, by suspending or replacing part of the management team and by taking legal action against banks' directors or officials. The DPS authority is also allowed to revoke the deposit guarantee for any participating bank. The participation to the national DPS is compulsory for both domestic banks and foreign banks' subsidiaries and branches, whereas the deposits of the foreign branches and subsidiaries of domestic banks are excluded from the insurance coverage, just like interbank deposits. Before respectively Amending Directive 2009/14/EC and Directive 2014/49/EU, the deposits were coinsured and the contributions were *ex-ante* but not risk based. In case the deposit insurance fund cannot cover in full the claimed deposits, the Government would intervene, but the deposit insurance fund is supposed to refund it in subsequent years.

Italy: In Italy, the national DPS is both funded and managed by the private sector alone. The agency authority has very limited powers; it is in charge of managing the payout of the insured portions of the deposits and has access to information collected by the banking supervisor, but it does not have direct intervention power. The national DPS, moreover, is not only used for depositor protection purposes, but can also provide liquidity to banks. Even before respectively Amending Directive 2009/14/EC and Directive 2014/49/EU, the deposits were not coinsured and the contributions were risk based, but the Italian DPS was not prefunded (premia were collected *ex-post*, when needed). Only the banking supervisor can start the depositors' reimbursement process.

Participation in the Italian DPS is compulsory for Italian banks and foreign bank subsidiaries and branches, as well; foreign currency deposits are covered by the Italian DPS, as well as deposits of foreign branches of domestic banks, but interbank deposits and deposits of foreign subsidiaries of domestic banks are not included in the guarantee scheme. The DPS guarantees a maximum coverage of €100,000 per depositor per institution, but before 2014, the coverage limit was the highest in the EU €103,291.38.

Latvia: The deposit insurance agency is not a legally separate authority, but part of the banking supervision agency. The Financial and Capital Market Commission ensures the collection of funds, the compensations' payment and indirectly manages the Deposit Guarantee Fund. By the end of 2010, 79.50% of the total deposit of participating commercial banks was actually covered by the national DPS, one of the largest percentages in the EU28. Even before the 2014/49/EU, the collection of the contributions was *ex-ante* and risk based; in determining the applicable rate, the deposit insurance authority takes into account capital adequacy, liquidity ratio and large exposure ratios of deposit takers as well as the quality of the loan portfolio.

Lithuania: The Lithuanian DPS is funded by banks, but administered by the public sector only. The deposit insurance authority does not have extensive intervention power towards the banks' management; it only has the possibility to have access to information collected by the banking supervision. The Lithuanian DPS includes domestic banks and foreign banks subsidiaries and branches and any typologies of deposits, but the interbank ones. The deposit insurance coverage is per investors per institution, and coinsurance has never been applied. Before Directive Directive 2014/49/EU, the contributions to the deposit insurance schemes were not risk based, but were collected *ex-ante*. A court-declared bankruptcy sentence triggers immediately the claim for payments by the DPS, which in general are fully reimbursed within 30 working days.

Luxemburg: The private sector both funds and manages the DPS in Luxemburg; the evident moral hazard incentive stemming from these characteristics is partially tempered by the intervention power exerted by the insurance agency, which can cancel or revoke a bank's membership to the national DPS and take legal action against banks directors or officials. The Directive 2014/49/EU introduced a deep change, as beforehand the collection of the fund contribution was *ex-post* and did not depend on some assessment of risk. National banks and foreign banks subsidiaries are part of the DPS in Luxemburg, which does not include, though, foreign banks branches. The deposit insurance coverage, moreover, does not include the deposits of the foreign subsidiaries of domestic banks, but covers deposits of the foreign branches of domestic banks. Finally, the deposit insurance coverage is the most generous possible: per depositors per institution without any form of coinsurance, even before the Amending Directive 2009/14/EC banned it.

Malta: The DPS in Malta is a legally separate entity, which is funded by banks but managed by the public sector only. It does not have the authority to revoke a bank's participation to the DPS, but can take direct legal actions against banks' management, replace it or impose temporary external administration, which overrides its power. Before the Directive 2014/49/EU, the Maltese DPS's premia were not risk-based, but their collection has always been *ex-ante*. All deposits from domestic banks, foreign banks' subsidiaries and branches are included in the national DPS, as well as foreign currency deposits and deposits of foreign branches of domestic banks. The only deposits that are not covered by the Maltese DPS are the interbank deposits and the deposits of foreign subsidiaries of domestic banks.

Netherlands: Is one of the rare cases in which the deposit insurance authority is not a legally independent institution, but it is part of the central bank. It is furthermore the only Member State within the EU28 in which the DPS fund is jointly funded by private and public actors, but only public officials administer it; in this way, the possibility of moral hazard by the banking sector's side is virtually nullified. This may explain why the deposit insurance authority does not need the power to directly intervene in the banks' management, cannot take legal actions against the banks directors or officials and does not have the authority to revoke a bank membership to the insurance scheme. Before 2014, the collection of the banks' contributions to the DPS was only *ex-post* and not based on some assessment of the banks' riskiness. Foreign banks branches are excluded from the DPS, as well as deposits of foreign subsidiaries of domestic banks. Whereas, foreign banks subsidiaries' deposits, foreign currency deposits and deposits of foreign branches of domestic banks are covered by the Dutch DPS.

Poland: The Polish DPS is funded by banks only, but the financial resources are jointly managed with public officials; this form of public control is particularly significant, as the Polish DPS also provides liquidity to banks when needed. The deposit insurance agency power is rather weak, it only has on-site examination authority, it cannot directly intervene against the banks' management, nor take legal actions against banks directors or officials and cannot exclude a bank from the DPS. The Polish DPS has always had an *ex-ante* contribution mechanism, but prior to the Directive 2014/49/EU, the single contributions weren't calibrated on the participating banks' riskiness.

Portugal: The Portuguese DPS is funded by the participating banks; although there has been an initial endowment by the national central bank, the fund is managed jointly by the private and public sector. The deposit insurance authority has access to the information collected by the banking supervisor and is in charge of managing the payout of the claimed deposits funds to depositors; only a banking supervisor's statement, though, triggers the depositors' refund process. It has no direct intervention authority. Both Amending Directive 2009/14/EC and Directive 2014/49/EU did not dramatically change the Portuguese DPS, as it has never had coinsurance and the banks' contributions have always been collected *ex-ante* and weighted by some assessment of the contributors' riskiness. Participation to the DPS is compulsory not only for domestic banks, but also for foreign banks' subsidiaries and branches; the deposit insurance coverage includes foreign currency deposits, but interbank deposits and deposits of both foreign branches and subsidiaries of domestic banks are left uncovered. In order to cope with the global financial crisis, the Portuguese DPS was promptly adjusted to adapt to the Amending Directive and the Government guaranteed new issuance of bank debt upon request.

Romania: Only the private sector contributes to the Romanian DPS, which, though, is jointly managed by both private and public officials. The monitoring activity of the deposit insurance authority does not include strong intervention powers, as it cannot exclude a bank from the DPS, nor take legal actions against banks' officials or directors and neither impose a temporary administration. It can, though, decide which kind of resolution option best fits a bank's failure, and it has access to the information collected by the banking supervisors. Both foreign banks' subsidiaries and branches are excluded from the Romanian DPS, which does not cover deposits of the foreign subsidiaries of domestic banks, either. Even before the Amending 2009/14/EC, Romanian DPS excluded any form of coinsurance. Directive Directive 2014/49/EU introduced risk-based contributions but did not change the contributions' collection procedure, which has always been *ex-ante*. The reimbursement process, in the end, is triggered by both a court-declared bank bankruptcy and a banking supervisor's statement.

Slovakia: The source of funding of the DPS in Slovakia is entirely private, but managed by both private and public officials. The intervention authority of the deposit insurance agency is rather limited, it can only have access to the information collected by the banking supervisor and is responsible for the organisation of the payout mechanism of claimed deposits, but it cannot actively intervene towards participating banks' management nor exclude some banks from the DPS. Domestic banks and foreign banks' subsidiaries are required to participate to the DPS, which, though, is not compulsory for foreign banks' branches. Interbank deposits and deposits of the foreign subsidiaries of domestic banks are not covered by the Slovak DPS. There has never been formal coinsurance in Slovakia, and the participating banks' premia collection has always been *ex-ante*, even before Directive 2014/49/EU, which introduced risk-based contribution.

Slovenia: The Slovenian supervisory design is rather centralised: DPS is part of the national central bank, which is also the supervisory authority, and there is no separation of the deposit insurance functions from the other functions of the central bank. The deposit insurance fund, though, is solely used for deposit insurance purposes. The participation in the deposit insurance system is compulsory for domestic banks and foreign banks' subsidiaries, but foreign banks' branches are excluded from the DPS. Apart from domestic deposits and foreign currency deposits, all other typologies of deposits (e.g. interbank deposits and deposits of the foreign branches/subsidiaries of domestic banks) are excluded from the insurance coverage. Before Directive 2014/49/EU was implemented, the Slovenian contributions' collection was *ex-post* and not subject to the banks' risk assessment. From the outburst of the global financial crisis to 31 December 2010, the Slovenian Government guaranteed unlimited coverage for the insured deposits.

Spain: The Spanish deposit protection agency is a legally independent authority; it coordinates the deposit insurance fund, which is not only used for deposit protection purposes, but also for liquidity provision to banks, when needed. The deposit insurance agency has access to the information collected by the banking supervisor and can take legal action against banks' directors and officials, in case of violation of the deposit insurance agency by-laws or regulations. It is also in charge of the claimed deposits' reimbursement process supervision and of the selection of the most suitable failure resolution typology, in case of bank failure. The deposit insurance authority cannot, though, assess the quality of the banks' business and balance sheets and put in place corrective measures, such as raising premia, request improvement in the banks' practices, nor withdraw the insurance coverage of a bank. The deposit insurance authority in Spain does not have intervention authority either, so it cannot, for instance, impose a temporary external administration to a bank or replace managers. Domestic and both foreign banks' subsidiaries and branches are covered by the Spanish DPS, which only exclude interbank deposits and deposits of the foreign subsidiaries of domestic banks from the protection system. The Spanish DPS has never had coinsurance and ex-post contribution system, but before Directive 2014/49/EU, the single contributions were not based on the participating banks' riskiness. After the global financial crisis, in 2009, the Spanish DPS was adapted according to the Amending Directive 2009/14/EC, and a new Fund for the Orderly Restructuring with resolution functions was established.

Sweden[3]: Swedish deposit insurance fund is managed solely by public officers, excluding most possibilities of moral hazard behaviours by the banks' management at their roots. This might be the reason why the deposit insurance authority has limited intervention powers; it cannot withdraw a banks' participation to the DPS, nor take legal actions against banks' management. The contributions to the deposit insurance fund have always been *ex-ante*, but were not based on the participants' riskiness, until Directive 2014/49/EU entered into force. The coverage is per person and is extended to foreign currency deposits, as well.

United Kingdom: The deposit insurance agency is a legally separate entity, whose only purpose is to protect deposits and is both funded and administered by banks only, without any public intervention. The deposit insurance agency powers are particularly narrow, as well: it does not have access to the information collected by the banking supervisors, nor is able to ask for improvements in the banks' management in case of excessive risk-taking. It cannot intervene directly in the banks' management either, nor can replace management or take legal actions against it. It cannot impose a form of administration not even temporary, nor choose the resolution methodology to resolve a bank failure. It has, though, the ultimate power to revoke deposit insurance for a participating bank. Foreign bank branches are excluded from the DPS and so are deposits of the foreign subsidiaries of domestic banks. Deposits of domestic banks' foreign branches, interbank deposits and foreign currency deposits are treated as regular ones, so covered up to the legislative limit.

Just few common trends can be identified among the heterogeneous DPS' designs described in the above overview. In order to be able to somehow compare the DPSs' designs around EU28, the DPSs' characteristics examined have been grouped into three major clusters: the first one comprises the coverage limit and the contributions' characteristics and is the one that has been mostly targeted by the legislative interventions, so it is the most homogeneous across the 28 Member States. The coverage limit has been reasonably the first feature to be homogenised with Directive 94/19/EC, and twenty years later, even the contributions to the DPSs are collected in the same way across Europe (*ex-ante*), and they are all currently anchored to the contributors' riskiness.

There are other characteristics, on the contrary, that are still largely left to the Member States' autonomy. There are a number of different activities that in some jurisdictions the deposit insurance agency can carry out autonomously, such as the possibility to take major actions to bring a bank back to solvency (e.g. to impose a form of temporary administration), the possibility to take legal actions against a bank's management and the possibility to revoke a bank's participation to the DPS; these features have been grouped in the second cluster. Intervention powers, broadly speaking, are particularly relevant in those Member States where the private sector plays an active role in the deposit insurance fund management, because it is an indirect form of supervision on the banks' possible moral hazard incentives (Barth et al. 2004). Only the deposit insurance authority in Ireland, though, has all of the three major intervention powers.

Finally, the funding and management decisions can be grouped together, as their combination significantly influences the possible moral hazard incentives of the participating banks. It is reasonable to expect that the higher the presence of public funds within the deposit insurance funding, the higher the moral hazard incentives on the banks' side, especially if the deposit insurance fund is managed by the banks under a private sector arrangement. On the contrary, the higher the private intervention in the management of the deposit insurance fund, the higher the possible consequent moral hazard incentive for banks' officials. The "fund management" feature is the characteristic that may leave more room to moral hazard, because it defines which actor is in charge to use the funds devoted to the deposits coverage, especially if the contribution is *ex-ante*. In accordance with this interpretation (see Barth et al. 2013), the different possible combinations of public and private intervention in the DPS management and funding leave room to different degrees of moral hazard incentives. Table 8.4 illustrates four simplified combinations of actors that fund and manage the deposit insurance fund, identified with letters D to A, with increasing moral hazard incentives on the banks' side.

Table 8.4 Funding and management design

	Funding actors		Management actors	Room to potential Moral Hazard
A	Government and jointly	&	Banks	↑
B	Banks	&	Banks	
C	Government and jointly	&	Government and jointly	
D	Banks	&	Government and jointly	

The most critical matching is banks' management of governmental or mixed funds (combination A, see Table 8.4), even though from 1994 on the typologies of possible investments shrank significantly. On the extreme opposite situation, when banks are the only source of the DPS funding but they either do not manage their contributions or have the possibility to manage them only in cooperation with public officials (combination D), the moral hazard incentives on the banks' side is minimum. Among the EU28 Member States, there is a pronounced heterogeneity regarding the combination of sources of funding and management of the deposit insurance fund. There is no DPS entirely funded and administered by the public sector, which in a number of cases,[4] though, participates in the fund management, together with banks. In only six cases (Finland, France, Germany, Italy, Luxemburg and UK), banks both fund and administer the DPS; furthermore, in none of these countries, the deposit insurance authority has strong intervention power; only in Luxemburg, it can both take legal action against a banks' management and withdraw a bank's participation to the PDS.

As the characteristics comprised in the first cluster (i.e. the absence of coinsurance, the presence of an *ex-ante* contribution system and of risk-based premia) have been standardised respectively by the Amending Directive 2009/14/EC and by the Directive 2014/49/EU, the analysis of the differences among European DPSs focuses on the management and funding characteristics on one hand and the extension of the intervention power on the other one.

Figure 8.1 presents these two clusters on the vertical and horizontal axis respectively and plots the EU28 Member States.[5] On the vertical

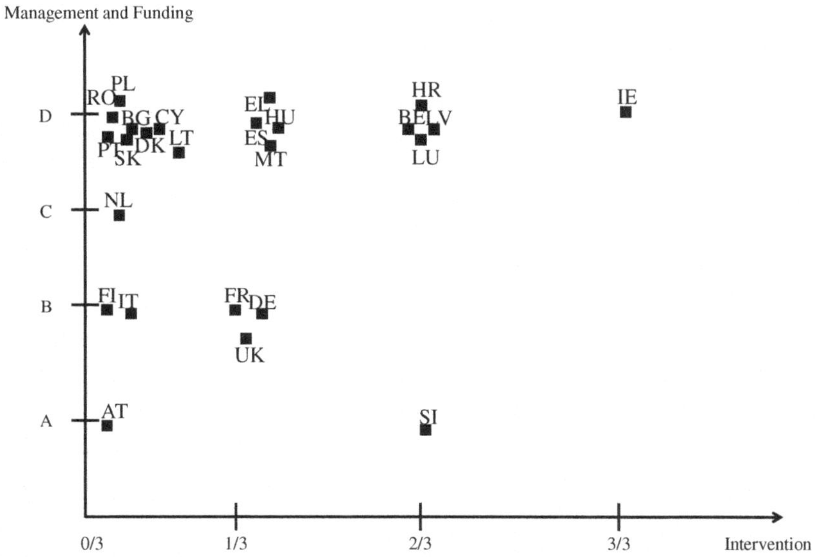

Notes: this graph shows the combination of Intervention and Management & Funding features adopted by the current EU28 Member States

Fig. 8.1 EU28 Member States DPSs' design.

axis, the four combinations of DPS funding and management are ordered from A to D, according to the combinations displayed in Table 8.3; the horizontal axis shows the number of intervention powers delegated to the deposit insurance agency. The strictest DPS should be on the top right corner as this quarter presents, on the vertical axis, the combination of funding and management that leaves least space to the banks' moral hazard and, on the horizontal axis, the deposit insurance authorities with the strongest intervention powers.

The countries are concentrated in the upper left quarter of the graph. In most Member States, the DPS provides the combination of management and funding actors that should most reduce possible imprudent behaviours from the banks' side (private funding, managed by either public officials alone or in a joint effort with private officials). In the vast majority of cases, though, the intervention power left to the deposit insurance authority is particularly limited and the number of countries gradually decreases as the number of intervention powers increases (moving from left to right on the Figure).

The extreme cases are the most surprising ones; the combination that leaves most freedom to banks is in Austria, where the deposit insurance authority has no intervention power, but only supervises the claimed deposits' payout process and the DPS is mix funded but administered by the banks only. In this perspective, moreover, it is quite meaningful to point out that the deposit insurance fund can be used for other purposes than depositors' protection, such as liquidity provision to banks, if needed. On the other extreme, the Irish deposit insurance authority is included within the national Central Bank and has therefore a rather extensive intervention power against the supervised banks, which contribute *ex-ante* to the deposit insurance fund, but do not play any role in the fund management, which is administered by public officials only.

From the qualitative analysis above, it can be concluded that the EU28 Member States seem to prefer to control potential moral hazard incentives by leaving room to public intervention on either the funding or the management of the deposit insurance funds, whereas the insurance agency does not usually have major direct intervention powers, which in most cases are left to the banking supervisor authority.

8.4 Conclusive Remarks

The European legislative framework regulating DPSs has historically left some discretion to the Member States, so that they could adjust their DPSs to the national peculiarities of the banking industry and supervision. In this way, though, the differences among DPSs even within the EU28 became so stark to be perceived as unfitting in the banking union framework. The Directive 94/19/EC and its subsequent modifications have gradually homogenised the DPSs across the EU, by acting firstly on the coverage limit and then on increasingly more specific features, such as the repayment time, the coinsurance and finally on the contributions collection methodology and on risk-based premia, with Directive 2014/49/EU. Despite the remarkable effort spent in the last two decades to harmonise the DPSs around Europe, though, there is still scope for improvement, even because the urge for a unified European Deposit Insurance Scheme (EDIS) is becoming increasingly more pressing. Immediately after the outburst of the global financial crisis, national DGSs in effect proved to be rather vulnerable to large local shocks. Moreover, significant differences among national DGSs can contribute to market fragmentation by affecting the ability and willingness of national banks to expand their businesses cross border.

A strong heterogeneity emerges from the analysis of the single DPSs within the EU28. At least three major groups of features shape each national DPS design: there are characteristics strictly related to the coverage, such as the amount, the risk weighting of the contributions and the collection methodology, which have been homogenised across Europe between 2009 and 2014. A second group of features regards the typology of actors who fund the DPS and manage its financial assets; whereas a third group of features controls for the intervention powers left to the deposit insurance authority. As the first cluster has been legally homogenised, the analysis focuses on the combination of the other two and their possible role in leaving space to potential moral hazard on the banks' side. From a qualitative analysis, the EU28 Member States seem to prefer to control these potential moral hazard incentives by leaving room to public intervention on either the funding or the management of the deposit insurance funds, whereas the insurance agency does not usually have major direct intervention powers.

In order to reduce the deep diversities the national DPSs present, initial incentives towards a unified DPS were included in the Directive 2014/49/EU, as the Legislator opens up the way to the possibility to "merge the DGSs of different Member States or to create separate cross-border schemes on a voluntary basis", as a tangible answer to the *de facto* integration of the European banking industry. Even the possibility for national DPSs to borrow from one another, as an extreme funding source, encourages the creation of networks that do not require formal changes in the national legal frameworks, but still contribute to put in place a unified European DPS. The EDIS would provide a more uniform degree of insurance coverage for all European depositors, ensuring that their level of confidence in a bank's ability to refund their savings would not depend on mere geographical reasons. Furthermore, EDIS would increase the resilience of the banking sector against systemic and national crises within the EU, leading the way towards an increasingly more interconnected Banking Union.

Notes

1. Eligible deposits: deposits repayable by the guarantee scheme under national laws, before the level of coverage are applied.
   Covered deposits: deposits obtained from eligible deposits when applying the level of coverage provided for in your national legislation.
2. Sweden did not participate to the latest World Bank's Bank Regulation and Supervision Survey.
3. Sweden did not take part in the latest Bank Regulation and Supervision survey, so the information provided are taken from the World Bank's Bank Regulation and Supervision survey (2007).
4. Belgium, Bulgaria, Cyprus, Denmark, Estonia, Greece, Hungary, Poland, Portugal, Romania, Slovakia and Spain.
5. Estonia and Sweden are excluded from the graph, because they did not disclose enough information in the World Bank's Bank Regulation and Supervision Surveys, 2012.

References

Acharya, V.V. 2009. A theory of systemic risk and design of prudential bank regulation. *Journal of Banking & Finance* 5 (3): 224–255.

Anginer, D., A. Demirgüc-Kunt, and M. Zhu. 2014. How does deposit insurance affect bank risk? Evidence from the recent crisis. *Journal of Banking and Finance* 48: 312–321.

Angkinand, A., and C. Wihlborg. 2010. Deposit insurance coverage, ownership, and banks' risk-taking in emerging markets. *Journal of International Money and Finance* 29 (2): 252–274.

Arnaboldi, Francesca. 2014. Deposit Guarantee Schemes. In *Deposit Guarantee Schemes: A European Perspective*, 50–85. UK: Palgrave Macmillan.

Barth, J.R., G. Caprio, and R. Levine. 2004. Bank regulation and supervision: What works best? *Journal of Financial intermediation* 13 (2): 205–248.

Barth, J.R., G. Caprio Jr., and R. Levine. 2013. Bank regulation and supervision in 180 countries from 1999 to 2011. *Journal of Financial Economic Policy* 5 (2): 111–219.

Cariboni, Jessica, Elisabeth Joossens, and Adamo Uboldi. 2010. The promptness of european deposit protection schemes to face banking failures. *Journal of Banking Regulation* 11 (3): 191–209.

Carbo-Valverde, S., E.J. Kane, and F. Rodriguez-Fernandez. 2012. Regulatory arbitrage in cross-border banking mergers within the EU. *Journal of Money, Credit and Banking* 44 (8): 1609–1629.

Cordella, Tito, and Eduardo Levy Yeyati. 2002. Financial opening, deposit insurance, and risk in a model of banking competition. *European Economic Review* 46 (3): 471–485.

Demirgüç-Kunt, A., and H. Huizinga. 1999. Market discipline and financial safety net design. World Bank Policy Research Paper 2183.

Demirgüç-Kunt, Asli, and Enrica Detragiache. 2002. Does deposit insurance increase banking system stability? An empirical investigation. *Journal of Monetary Economics* 49: 1373–1406.

Demirgüç-Kunt, Asli, and Edward Kane. 2002. Deposit insurance around the globe: Where does it work? *Journal of Economic Perspectives* 16 (2): 175–195.

Demirgüç-Kunt, A., and H. Huizinga. 2004. Market discipline and deposit insurance. *Journal of Monetary Economics* 51 (2): 375–399.

Demirgüç-Kunt, A., E. Kane, and L. Laeven. 2015. Deposit insurance around the world: A comprehensive analysis and database. *Journal of Financial Stability* 20: 155–183.

Diamond, Douglas W., and Philip H. Dybvig. 1983. Bank runs, deposit insurance, and liquidity. *The Journal of Political Economy*: 401–419.

Directive 2009/14/EC of the European Parliament and of the Council of 11 March 2009 [2009] L68/3.

Directive 2014/49/EU of the European Parliament and of the Council of 16 April 2014 on deposit guarantee schemes [2014] L 173/149.

Duan, J.C., A.F. Moreau, and C.W. Sealey. 1992. Fixed-rate deposit insurance and risk-shifting behavior at commercial banks. *Journal of Banking and Finance* 16: 715–742.

EBA. 2015. Guidelines on methods for calculating contributions to deposit guarantee schemes, EBA/GL/2015/10, 22.09.2015.

Engineer, M.H., P. Schure, and Mark Gillis. 2013. A positive analysis of deposit insurance provision: Regulatory competition among European Union countries. *Journal of Financial Stability* 9 (4): 530–544.

Forssbaeck, J. 2011. Ownership structure, market discipline, and banks' risk-taking incentives under deposit insurance. *Journal of Banking & Finance* 35 (10): 2666–2678.

Gropp, R., and J. Vesala. 2004. Deposit insurance, moral hazard and market monitoring. *Review of Finance* 8: 571–602.

Hovakimiam, A., E.J. Kane, and L. Laeven. 2003. How country and safety-net characteristics affect bank risk-shifting. *Journal of Financial Services Research* 23 (3): 177–204.

IADI. 2013a. Enhanced guidance for effective deposit insurance systems: Deposit insurance coverage, Basel.

IADI. 2013b. Enhanced guidance for effective deposit insurance systems: Mitigating Moral Hazard, Basel.

IADI. 2013c. General guidance on early detection and timely intervention for deposit insurance systems, Basel, 2013.

IADI. 2014. IADI Core principles for effective deposit insurance systems, Basel.

IADI. 2015. Enhanced guidance for effective deposit insurance systems: Ex Ante funding, Basel.

Kane, Edward J. 1995. Three paradigms for the role of capitalization requirements in insured financial institutions. *Journal of Banking & Finance* 19 (3): 431–459.

Laeven, L. 2002. Bank risk and deposit insurance. *World Bank Economic Review* 16: 109–137.

Lambert, C., F. Noth, and U. Schüwer. 2015. How do insured deposits affect bank risk? Evidence from the 2008 Emergency economic stabilization act. *Journal of Financial Intermediation.*

Pennacchi, G. 1987. A Reexamination of the over- (or under-) pricing of deposit insurance. *Journal of Money, Credit and Banking* 19: 340–360.

Pennacchi, G. 2006. Deposit insurance, bank regulation, and financial system risks. *Journal of Monetary Economics* 53: 1–30.

Schich, S. 2008. Financial crisis: Deposit insurance and related financial safety net aspects. *Financial Market trends* 2: 76–121.

Wheelock, D.C., and P.W. Wilson. 1995. Explaining bank failures: Deposit insurance, regulation, and efficiency. *The Review of Economics and Statistics*: 689–700.

9

A Technical Approach to Deposit Guarantee Schemes

Francesca Arnaboldi

9.1 Introduction

Progress towards a common European financial framework has been a constant trend over the past forty years, with ongoing harmonization of national legislation and practices. The financial sector has played a key role in the integration of the European countries. Indeed, financial integration has been enhanced by the introduction of a single currency.

Despite the positive achievements in the integration of European financial markets and economies, the financial crisis confirms that closer coordination of prudential policies and safety nets is required. The European financial system has revealed more fragile than expected. The crisis meant a serious setback for financial integration and the possibility of the break-up of the single currency.

F. Arnaboldi (✉)
University of Milan, Milan, Italy
e-mail: farnaboldi@unimi.it

G. Chesini et al. (eds.), *The Business of Banking*, Palgrave Macmillan Studies in Banking and Financial Institutions, DOI 10.1007/978-3-319-54894-4_9

As regards the European retail banking markets, the financial crisis illustrated once more how banks are susceptible to the risk of bank runs and the need of a coordinated supervision at European level.

Deposit guarantee schemes help preventing such risk, through the reimbursement of a limited amount of deposits to depositors whose bank has failed.

Directive 2014/49/EU set a uniform level of protection for depositors throughout the European Union (EU), thanks to a broadened and clarified scope of coverage, faster repayment periods, improved information and robust funding requirements. However, it did not establish the third pillar of the Banking Union, a European deposit insurance scheme (EDIS). In the first moment, it was decided to delay its creation and to opt instead for a harmonized network of national deposit guarantee schemes (DGSs).[1]

In 2015, progress towards the EDIS accelerated. The Five Presidents' Report (President of the European Commission, in close cooperation with the President of the Euro Summit, the President of the Eurogroup, the President of the European Central Bank and the President of the European Parliament) was published in July 2015 (Juncker et al., 2015). It sets out an ambitious programme of measures to underpin the economic and monetary Union, among which is the European Deposit Insurance Scheme (EDIS). It will be applied alongside the Single Supervisory Mechanism (SSM) and the Single Resolution Mechanism (SRM) and funded by risk-based contributions from banks operating in the Banking Union countries (FITD 2016).

In May 2015, in order to ensure consistent application of Directive 2014/49/EU and to provide incentives to banks to operate under a less risky business model, the European Banking Authority (EBA) issued guidelines to specify methods for calculating the contributions to DGS. In a context where many member states did not have pre-financed DGS, EBA set out principles for technically sound methods for calculating contributions to ensure that costs of deposit insurance are borne primarily by the banking sector (EBA 2015).

The European Commission, in fulfilling a commitment, published in November 2015 a proposal for legislation, which sets out a euro area-wide deposit insurance scheme for bank deposits and further measures to reduce remaining risks in the banking sector in parallel (European Commission 2015a). The legislative proposal proceeds through three successive stages: a reinsurance scheme for participating national DGSs in the first period of 3 years, a co-insurance scheme for participating national DGSs in the second period of 4 years, and full insurance for participating national DGSs in the steady state, which starts in 2024 (European Commission 2015b).

Within this framework, EBA guidelines offer a basis on which to assess progress in the convergence of national practices in calculating contributions to DGSs.

In this chapter, we take advantage of the EBA guidelines and study whether Italian banks would be negatively affected by their implementation, fuelling systemic risk, as opined by some member countries. "Germany, the EU's biggest economy, does not want its depositors to be liable for payouts in the event of bank failures elsewhere. It insists the EU must first take steps to minimise risks before starting talks on shared responsibility. Berlin insisted that any reference to setting up such a deposit scheme be removed at the EU summit in October, and has succeeded in doing so again at the December meeting" (Reuters 2015).

Specifically, this chapter investigates the system of calculating risk-based contributions to DGS currently in use in the Italian banking system and compares this to the system promoted by EBA, using a sample of 172 out of 202 member banks, 85% of the population of the Fondo interbancario di tutela dei depositi (FITD). Using Bankscope data from 2012, when the single supervisory mechanism was established, to 2014, we examine the impact of the EBA system on the classification of Italian banks among risk categories and, subsequently, on the contributions banks have to pay to DGS.

We find that EBA proposal would increase the number of banks in the lower-risk classes, where contribution quota to the DGS would remain unchanged or would decrease.

This chapter contributes to the literature on banking supervision by investigating the third pillar of the Banking Union, that is, deposit guarantee schemes, a matter of which the use of information has been limited in order to prevent such use from affecting the stability of the banking system or depositor confidence (Directive 2014/49/EU art.16 c.5).[2] In particular, the main contribution lies in the comparison of the two methodologies mentioned above and in the prediction of the EBA algorithm's effect on Italian banks contributions. The analysis may have significant policy implications, as it forecasts the future contributions of Italian banks providing an empirical evidence that should reassure about the possible Italian banks' moral hazard.

This investigation shows some caveats: in principle, the FITD uses semi-annual or quarterly data, whereas Bankscope reports annual data. Secondly, for some ratios, it is not possible to match data as described by the FITD documents to data in Bankscope.

However, uncertainty about the real exposure of depositors to bank failures impairs the relationship with clients and with other member states. Therefore, we believe that the FITD, which is the only institution with access to real data, should provide additional information on this relevant topic.

The rest of the chapter is organized as follows. Section 9.2 provides the framework for deposit guarantee schemes in Italy. Section 9.3 analyses the system of calculating risk-based contributions established by the FITD. Section 9.4 applies EBA guidelines to the same sample of domestic banks, using both core and additional ratios and the buckets method. Section 9.5 compares the two systems, and Sect. 9.6 concludes.

9.2 Deposit Guarantee Schemes in Italy

The Fondo interbancario di tutela dei depositi (Interbank Deposit Protection Fund) is a private-law consortium established in 1987 on a voluntary basis, which has since become a mandatory Fund (FITD 2016). Bank participation in a deposit guarantee scheme became mandatory in 1996 with the transposition of the first Directive on Deposit Guarantee Systems, 94/19/EEC, in the Italian legislation. The second DGS was created in Italy in 1997, the Fondo di garanzia dei depositanti del credito cooperativo, which covers mutual banks and replaced the Fondo centrale di garanzia, created in 1978 to guarantee deposits in rural and cooperative banks (Senato 2015). Thus, all Italian banks are members of the FITD, except for mutual banks and branches of non-EU banks authorized in Italy if they already participated in an equivalent scheme in their home country. Italian branches of EU banks also may adhere to FITD, in certain cases, to top-up their home guarantee coverage.

FITD guarantees the deposits in the member banks, which provide the financial resources for FITD to accomplish its mission. The Fund conducts a variety of interventions in favour of member banks when they are under compulsory administrative liquidation, in resolution or in special administration. Pursuant to art. 96-ter of the Legislative Decree 385/1993 (Italian banking Law), the Bank of Italy exercises specific powers of oversight on the deposit guarantee systems.

Today, FITD is regulated by Directive 2014/49/EU and, as a result, it undergoes many changes. These include, among others: (1) the passage from an ex post to an ex ante system of payment of contributions to the scheme; (2) the investment of available financial resources; (3) the reduction to seven working days of the deposit payout time, presently established within 20 working days from the date the compulsory administrative liquidation takes effect, by the end of the year 2023; (4) calculation of banks' risk-based contributions, following EBA guidelines; and (5) use of the Fund's resources for a wide variety of measures, alternative to direct reimbursement (FITD 2016). In this context, the FITD began raising ex ante contributions in December 2015 to avoid an excessive burden in the following financial years given the obligation to reach the target level by the year 2024.

9.3 The FITD's Monitoring System of Bank Riskiness

9.3.1 Balance Sheet Indicators

The Fund has in place a monitoring system to measure and control member banks' riskiness. This system works through balance sheet indicators on four different risk profiles: asset quality, solvency, liquidity and profitability (FITD 2012). The reporting frequency is semi-annual or quarterly, depending on the specific source of data of the Bank of Italy.

Five ratios are computed to measure the four risk profiles: A1, P, L, D1 and D2.

According to FITD (2016), at the end of 2015, member banks were 202. Fourteen banks have been dropped since they do not report data on Bankscope, a Bureau Van Dijk database, and sixteen do not report enough data to compute any ratios over the 2012–2015 sample period. The final sample is, thus, formed by 172 member banks, 85% of the population of member banks to the FITD.[3] The sample period starts in 2012 when it was decided to establish a single supervisory mechanism (SSM) and ends in 2014, because of the paucity if data in 2015.

As previously mentioned, this analysis shows some caveats: in principle, the Fund uses semi-annual or quarterly data, whereas Bankscope reports annual data. Secondly, for some ratios, it is not possible to match data from the Bank of Italy to data in Bankscope. To avoid confusion, the rest of the chapter uses the ratio definitions provided by the Fund (FITD 2012).

The first ratio (A1) measures the capacity of a bank to absorb potential losses without risk of insolvency, and it is given by the ratio of bad debts to supervisory capital (FITD 2012). To compute the asset quality ratio A1, total impaired loans are used. According to Bankscope, total impaired loans are the total value of the loans that have a specific impairment against them. The Fund uses bad loans, that is, loans which will be never repaid, even if this status has not been proved yet in court (Bank of Italy 2016). The computed ratio is, therefore, higher, overestimating the risk of the bank.

P provides a measure of bank's capital: according to the Fund, it is the ratio of supervisory capital (including tier 3) minus total capital requirements to risk-weighted assets. The solvency ratio *P* is not computed since the FITD does not provide clear information on risk-weighted assets, preventing a match to Bankscope data.

The liquidity ratio L measures the structural liquidity of the bank dividing receivables from clients by an aggregate given by the sum of payables from clients, circulating bonds and structured payables from clients and bonds at fair value. The Fund does not specify whether receivables from clients include impairments or not, so both specifications have been computed. Furthermore, the denominator is an aggregate, and it does not have a match in Bankscope; the Fund does not provide a list of the components and of their maturities. Therefore, two components have been used: (1) total deposits, money market and short-term funding which includes total customer deposits, deposits from banks and other deposits and short-term borrowings; (2) trading liabilities, that is, short positions, repos, short-term notes and other liabilities classified at fair value. The computed ratio could under- or overestimate the Fund ratio, which however cannot be estimated.

The fourth risk profile has two ratios: D1 is given by operating expenses to gross income, and it shows whether gross income covers the cost of core banking activity and/or the ability of the bank to meet extraordinary expenses. It does not show critical issues.

D2 measures loan losses on profit before tax. It is computed only if both numerator and denominator are positive; otherwise, it takes the value of zero or four (only if numerator is positive and denominator is negative) (FITD 2012). D2 is computed using total impaired loans and pre-tax profit; once more the estimate is larger than the value provided by the Fund, thus underestimating the true member bank's efficiency.

To better appreciate the pros and cons of the present analysis, the balance sheet ratios measured by the Fund are now compared to the estimated values for years 2012 and 2013 (FITD 2012). Differences can be explained by: (1) the use of proxies, since not all data used by the Fund is publicly available; (2) the frequency of data, semi-annual for the Fund measures, annual in the present estimation. As a consequence, the Fund ratios are the median values of three observations (June and December 2012, June 2013), while the present estimation uses year-end data.

Comparing June 2012 with June 2013, there was a slight worsening in A1 (+18%, from 18.01 to 21.18%), and in D2 (from 37.22 to 50.67%), similar to the change computed for A1 (+21%, from 93 to 119%) and for D2 (from −957 to 1002%), reported in Table 9.1.

Over the same period, there was a slight improvement in the median value of the liquidity ratio (−7.45% points, from 91.73 to 84.18%) and in the profitability ratio D1 (−1.64% points, from 68.17 to 66.53%) (FITD 2012). As for the liquidity ratio, Table 9.1 shows similar trends using both gross and net receivables, but net ratio is preferred since it provides closer estimates (from 92 to 83%, versus from 97 to 88%).

Table 9.1 Balance sheet ratio computed from Bankscope

	2012		2013		2014	
Ratio	# observations	Mean	# observations	Mean	# observations	Mean
A1	149	0.93	148	1.19	148	1.99
D1	165	0.66	164	0.70	161	0.43
D2	151	−9.57	152	10.02	155	29.69
L	167	0.97	164	0.88	162	0.90
Lnet	167	0.92	164	0.83	162	0.81

Source Own computation on Bankscope's data

D1 is the only ratio which is different from the Fund data, and it increases from 66 to 70% (Table 9.1).

9.3.2 Thresholds, Classes and Coefficients

To assess bank's risk, the Fund sets four thresholds per each ratio, which correspond to five classes. FITD assigns a coefficient to each class (Table 9.2).

According to the Fund, the sum of the coefficients of each ratio defines an aggregate indicator (AI) ranging from 0 to 24 (Table 9.3). Since this chapter does not compute P ratio, the aggregate indicator varies from 0 to 20. The aggregate indicator is grouped in clusters, and each cluster corresponds to a statutory position. If the AI is lower than 3.5, the corresponding statutory position for the bank is "low risk", that is the bank is classified as a low-risk bank according to the Fund rules. To avoid distortions due to the fact that AI ranges from 0 to 20 and not from 0 to 24 as stated by the Fund, in this chapter the scale of AI has been changed proportionally.

Figure 9.1 shows the distribution of the sample banks and of the coefficients for each ratio (A1, L, D1 and D2) over the 2012–2014 period. Looking at A1 and D2, 72 and 89.6% of banks, respectively, show the highest coefficient (which equals to eight for A1 and to four for D2) and thus belong to the riskiest class. Conversely, investigating L and D1, 0.72 and 8.32% of banks, respectively, belong to the riskiest class.

Table 9.2 Thresholds, classes and coefficients

	A1		L		D1		D2	
Risk classes	Thresholds (%)	Coefficients	Thresholds (%)	Coeff.	Thresholds	Coeff.	Thresholds (%)	Coeff.
Low risk	<10	0	<90	0	<60 o numerator = 0	0	0–20% o numerator <=0	0
Medium-low	10–20	1	90–100	0.5	60–70	0.5	20–40	0.5
Medium	20–30	2	100–130	1	70–80	1	40–50	1
Medium-high	30–50	4	130–200	2	80–90	2	50–60	2
High risk	>50	8	>200	4	>90 o denominator < 0	4	>60 o denominator < 0	4

Source FITD (2012)

Table 9.3 Statutory position, aggregate indicator and scaled aggregate indicator

Statutory position	Aggregate indicator (*)	Scaled aggregate indicator(**)
Low risk	0–3.5	0–2.9
Medium-low	3.5–6.5	2.9–5.4
Medium	6.5–8	5.4–6.7
Medium-high	8–10.5	6.7–8.8
High risk	10.5–14.5	8.8–12
Expulsion	>14.5	>12

Source FITD (2012)
Note (*) Upper bounds are included
(**) The aggregate indicator has been scaled to take into account that AI ranges from 0 to 20 rather than from 0 to 24

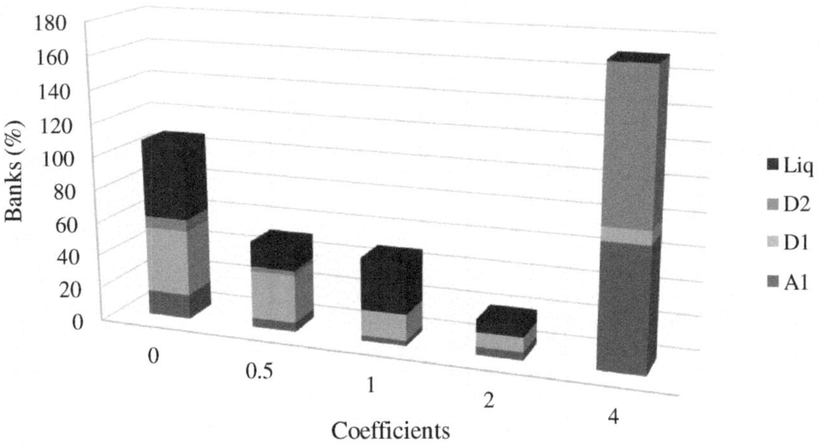

Fig. 9.1 Banks (%) and coefficients *Source* Own computation on Bankscope's data. *Note* As far as ratio A1 is concerned, coefficients are 0, 1, 2, 4 and 8

In fact, 47 and 39% of banks score a coefficient equal to zero, and the lowest risk. Sample banks seem less risky under the liquidity and profitability profiles.

The scaled aggregate indicator is computed summing up the coefficients for each of the four ratios. Then, according to Table 9.3, the statutory position is assigned to each bank of the sample in each year. Table 9.4 investigates the year-to-year statutory position, showing a migration of banks from the highest to the lowest risk position.

Table 9.4 Year-to-year statutory position

Year	2012		2013		2014		2012/2014 change (%)
Statutory position	# banks	%	# banks	%	# banks	%	
Low risk	13	8.9	14	9.46	15	10.2	
Medium-low	4	2.74	6	4.05	9	6.12	40
Medium	10	6.85	10	6.76	5	3.4	
Medium-high	10	6.85	9	6.08	8	5.44	−35
High risk	15	10.27	17	11.49	28	19.05	85
Expulsion	94	64.38	92	62.16	82	55.78	−13
Total	146	100	148	100	147	100	

Source Own computation on Bankscope's data

Over 2012–2014, banks classified in the low and medium-low statutory position increased by 40%; conversely, banks classified in the medium and medium-high risk decreased by 35%.[4] Likewise, banks belonging to the high-risk statutory position increased by 85%, whereas banks classified in the expulsion position decreased by 13%.

As previously mentioned, two caveats apply to the analysis: (1) the statutory position computed in this chapter does not include the P ratio and it is, therefore, incomplete; (2) some proxies have been used to compute the ratios, since actual data are not publicly available.

9.3.3 Contribution Quotas

After calculating the statutory position, the Fund computes the proportional quota of the contribution base which is given by the individual contribution base over the total reimbursable funds. Two correction methods, the regressive mechanism and the weighted average aggregate indicator (WAAI), that may increase or decrease the proportional quota, are then applied (FITD 2012).

The regressive correction method modifies the proportional quota according to the size of the bank: bigger banks get a reduction in the proportional quota, while the smaller ones get an increase.[5]

The second correction method is related to the value of the aggregate indicator, linking contributions to bank riskiness. The WAAI is computed on the last three semi-annual ratios submitted by the bank to the Fund: each semi-annual ratio receives a weight, which is larger the closer in time the ratio is. The weight is four for the closest ratio, two for the middle one and one for the ratio, which refers to the earliest time.

The WAAI is given by the following formula:

$$\text{WAAI} = \sum_{t=1}^{3} \frac{AI_t * \text{weight}_t}{\sum \text{weight}} \tag{9.1}$$

where

t	1, 2 and 3; semi-annual reports
AI	semi-annual aggregate indicator
Weight	1, 2 and 4 if the AI refers to semester 1, 2 or 3, respectively

According to the Fund, when the WAAI is greater than 3.5, the bank's contribution quota shall be increased, proportionally to the WAAI value; when it is greater than zero and less than or equal to 3.5, the bank shall retain its contribution quota unchanged; if the WAAI is equal to zero, the bank shall benefit from a reduction in its contribution quota, linked to the total amount of increases. To account for the change of scale of AI, this chapter uses 2.9 rather than 3.5 as threshold.

9.3.4 The Weighted Average Aggregate Indicator and the Sample Banks

WAAI is computed applying (1) to the sample banks with the goal to determine any changes in the statutory position of banks due to risk. Since Bankscope reports annual data, only two observations are used. The weights are, therefore, equal to one, for the AI of the previous year, and to four for the most recent AI.

The denominator in (1) is equal to seven, given by the sum of the weights, whereas in (2) is equal to five, since the weights are now only two. As a consequence, in this investigation, the WAAI is given by:

$$\mathrm{WAAI}_{\text{computed in } t} = \frac{1 * \mathrm{AI}_{t-1} + 4 * \mathrm{AI}_t}{5} \tag{9.2}$$

Table 9.5 part (a) shows banks with WAAI equal to zero, that would benefit from a reduction in contribution quota. Over 2012–2014 period, five banks would benefit from such reduction. One bank shows a WAAI equal to zero in two years and another one in one single year. Table 9.5 part (b) shows those banks with WAAI greater than zero and less than or equal to 2.9. Those banks would retain their contribution quota unchanged. Once more, the same banks recur over years: six banks belong to the group for 3 years out of three and one bank recurs twice.

When WAAI is greater than 2.9, banks' contribution quota shall be increased. Over 2012–2014, the number of sample banks with WAAI over the threshold remains almost stable (92%); within this group, the average WAAI decreases from 12 to 11.7, the minimum value of WAAI

Table 9.5 Weighted average aggregate indicator

Bank identification number\year	2012	2013	2014	Total
(a) Banks benefitting from a reduction in contribution quota				
1	1	1	1	3
50	1	1	0	2
152	0	0	1	1
155	1	1	1	3
166	1	1	1	3
Total	4	4	4	12
(b) Banks retaining contribution quota unchanged				
8	1	1	1	3
21	1	1	1	3
37	0	0	1	1
42	1	1	1	3
43	1	1	1	3
48	0	0	1	1
55	1	1	1	3
89	1	0	0	1
98	1	0	0	1
161	0	1	1	2
184	1	1	1	3
Total	8	7	9	24

Source Own computation on Bankscope's data

Table 9.6 Changes in statutory position after risk adjustment—all years

SP/RASP	*1*	*2*	*3*	*4*	*5*	*6*	Total
Low risk—1	24	1	0	0	0	0	25
Medium-low—2	0	12	1	0	0	0	13
Medium—3	0	1	13	1	0	0	15
Medium-high—4	0	0	0	13	1	0	14
High risk—5	0	0	0	2	24	18	44
Expulsion—6	0	0	0	0	2	167	169
Total	24	14	14	16	27	185	280
Changes SP—RASP	−1	1	−1	2	−17	16	

Source Own computation on Bankscope's data

remains stable at 4, and the maximum value decreases from 18 to 17 (−6%)[6]. Investigating the adjustment to bank riskiness, less banks would have their contribution quota increased, and the average increase in contribution quota would be lower, thus showing a safer risk profile for the banks under scrutiny.

Applying thresholds in Table 9.3 to the weighted average aggregate indicator, a risk-adjusted statutory position (RASP) can be computed. Table 9.6 investigates the changes in the statutory position when the risk adjustment is applied. Minor changes involve five banks. In particular, one bank moves from the low-risk statutory position (SP equal to one) to medium-low risk-adjusted scaled statutory position (RASP equal to two); one from SP equal to two to three when risk adjustment is applied; medium risk statutory position (SP equal to three) receives this bank but looses one bank which moves to RASP equal to four. The medium-high RASP is now formed by 16 rather than 14 banks. Major change involves the riskiest clusters: 16 banks move from high to expulsion RASP.

9.4 The EBA's Monitoring System of Bank Riskiness

9.4.1 Risk Indicators

This section is based on EBA guidelines on methods for calculating contributions to DGSs (EBA 2015). EBA defines core and additional indicators, as they belong to one of the following risk categories: capital, liquidity and funding, asset quality, business model and management, potential losses for the DGS. This chapter describes only the indicators used in the empirical investigation and refers to EBA (2015) for further details on all risk categories and indicators.

EBA guidelines have been applied to a sample of 171 Italian banks, member of the FITD. From the initial 202 member banks, 14 banks have been dropped because of the lack of data on Bankscope, as we did in the previous analysis on the FITD system. In addition, the year 2015 has been dropped, because only 22 banks out of the remaining 188 (12% of the sample) report data to compute EBA indicators. Seventeen more banks have been excluded because they do not report enough data to compute any EBA indicator over the 2012–2014 sample period. Table 9.7 shows descriptive statistics on core and additional indicators for the final sample of 171 banks.

Table 9.7 Descriptive statistics—EBA core and additional indicators

Indicators	Number of observations	Mean	Standard deviation	Minimum	Maximum
Core					
Leverage ratio	413	0.09	0.07	0.01	0.95
CET1	470	0.19	0.18	0.01	2.98
Capital coverage ratio (%)	472	3.52	3.65	0.11	66.22
Liquidity ratio	494	0.17	0.19	0.00	0.97
NPL ratio	468	0.06	0.05	0.00	0.64
Return on asset (%)	318	0.01	1.25	−7.37	4.65
RWA to total asset	470	0.55	0.19	0.07	1.33
Additional					
Return on equity (%)	318	0.04	17.30	−115.48	49.34
Total asset growth	321	0.08	0.34	−0.89	3.80
Cost income (%)	482	65.78	44.26	9.05	895.25

Source Own computation on Bankscope's data

For the first risk category (capital), EBA proposes two core indicators: leverage ratio, defined as tier 1 capital to total asset ratio, and capital coverage ratio (actual to required CET1 ratio) or common equity tier 1 ratio (common equity tier 1 capital to risk-weighted assets). Capital indicators reflect the level of loss-absorbing capacity of the bank. Higher amounts of capital show that the bank has a better ability to absorb losses internally, thus decreasing its likelihood of failure. Therefore, banks with higher values of capital indicators should contribute less to the DGS (EBA 2015). In the sample, the leverage ratio is on average 9% and CET1 19%. Due to available information, the numerator of CET1 is tier 1 capital and not common equity tier 1 capital. Thus, the computed leverage ratio overestimates the EBA ratio, underestimating the level of risk.[7] Similar considerations can be drawn on the capital coverage ratio, which average is equal to 3.52%.[8]

For the liquidity and funding category, the two core indicators suggested by the authority (liquidity coverage ratio—LCR—and net stable funding ratio—NSFR) cannot be applied until their definition as determined in Regulation (EU) No 575/2013 is fully operational. As a transitional indicator, the liquidity ratio (LR) defined as liquid assets to total assets is computed. It measures the bank's ability to meet its short-term debt obligations as they become due. The higher the ratio, the larger the safety margin to meet obligations and unforeseen liquidity shortfalls. Indeed, low liquidity levels indicate the risk that the institution may be unable to meet its current and future, expected or unexpected, cash-flow obligations and collateral needs. Liquid assets cover 17% of total assets on average. In 6 banks, LR is close to zero indicating possible future liquidity tensions (LR below 0.010 for 1 bank in 2012, for 4 banks in 2013 and for 1 bank in 2014).

The asset quality category shows the extent to which the bank is likely to experience credit losses. Large credit losses may cause financial problems that increase the likelihood of failure, therefore justifying higher contributions to the DGSs. This category includes the non-performing loan (NPL) ratio, given by non-performing loans to total assets. It provides an indication of the type of lending the bank engages in. A high degree of credit losses in the loan portfolio indicates lending to high-risk customers. The NPL ratio is on average 6%. Twenty banks out of 171

(12% of the sample) show a ratio higher than 15% in one or more years (Two banks in 2012, four banks in 2013—of which one already over the threshold in 2012—and 15 banks in 2014). Among those banks, 1 bank has a NPL ratio larger than 50% in 2014 and another one larger than 50% in the same year. These two latter banks have a high degree of credit losses in the loan portfolio, which increases the likelihood of failure.

Business model and management takes into account the risk related to the bank's current business model and strategic plans, and reflects the quality of internal governance and controls. Business model indicators can, for instance, include indicators related to profitability, balance sheet development and exposure concentration. The first core indicator proposed by EBA is risk-weighted assets to total assets ratio, which indicates the kind of risky activities a bank engages in. A higher value indicates higher risk. The second core indicator is return on asset (ROA). A business model which is able to generate high and stable returns indicates lower risk. However, unsustainably high levels of ROA also indicate higher risk (EBA 2015). In the sample, RWA to total assets ratio is 55% on average, but it is larger than 100% for three banks in 2012 and in 2013, raising doubts about the sustainability of the business model. ROA is on average equal to 0.01%.[9] Fifty three banks have a negative value of ROA in 2013 and 54 banks in 2014 (about 32% of the sample). The maximum value of ROA in the sample is 4.65%, and it does not seem unsustainably high.

The last risk category is potential losses for the DGS. EBA (2015) suggests one core indicator (unencumbered assets to covered deposits) which measures the degree of expected recoveries from the bankruptcy estate of the bank, which was resolved or put into normal insolvency proceedings. A bank with a low ratio exposes the DGS to higher expected loss. However, the proposed definition of unencumbered asset does not allow to compute the ratio.[10]

In addition to the core risk indicators, DGSs may include additional risk indicators that are relevant for determining the risk profile of member banks. The additional risk indicators should be classified into the above-listed risk categories. EBA proposes indicators for the asset quality, business model and management and potential losses for the DGS categories. In this chapter, three additional indicators belonging to the business model and management category are applied: (1) excessive balance sheet growth ratio (TAG) that measures the growth rate of the bank's balance sheet. Unsustainably, high growth might indicate higher risk; (2) return on equity (ROE), which measures the ability to generate profits to shareholders from the capital these have invested in the bank. A business model which is able to generate high and stable returns indicates reduced likelihood of failure. However, unsustainably, high levels of ROE indicate higher risk; (3) cost to income ratio (CI) which measures cost efficiency. An unusually high ratio may indicate that the institution's costs are out of control, especially if represented by the fixed costs (i.e. higher risk). A very low ratio may indicate that operating costs are too low for the institution to have the required risk and control functions in place, also indicating higher risk (EBA 2015).

The mean of the sample for total asset growth is 8%. However, 99 banks over 171 (58% of the sample) have a negative asset growth at least in 1 year (72 banks in 2012 and in 2013—of which 45 banks are common to both years); four banks have a TAG ratio larger than 100% (two banks in 2013 and in 2014). Among those four banks, one has a ratio larger than 200% in 2014 and one larger than 300% in 2013. These banks show an unsustainable high growth which indicates higher risk.

On average, ROE is equal to 0.04%, and it is negative for 53 and 54 banks in 2012 and 2013, respectively. EBA (2015) states that unsustainably high levels of profitability ratios also indicate higher risk. The maximum value of ROE in the sample is 49%, and the ratio is larger than 20% for 18 banks (10 banks in 2013 and 11 in 2014). This numbers may suggest some problems of the sustainability of the business model in the long term.

On the efficiency side, the average cost to income ratio is 66%. Nineteen banks have a ratio larger than 100% at least in one year: in particular 7 banks in 2012, 9 in 2013 and 8 in 2014; among them, two banks have a ratio larger than 200%. The unusually high ratio indicates that the bank's costs are out of control. A very low ratio may indicate that operating costs are too low for the bank to have the required risk and control functions in place, also indicating higher risk, but this is not the case for the sample under scrutiny since only seven banks have a CI ratio smaller than 20% (EBA 2015).

Overall, this chapter examines seven over nine core indicators and three over 13 additional indicators, which are enough to perform a significant analysis, in the author's point of view.

9.4.2 Individual Risk Score

As the FITD, also EBA proposes thresholds, classes and weights to compute individual bank risk scores (IRS). Unlike the Fund, however, EBA allows two methods to assign banks to risk classes: the bucket method and the sliding method. The first one uses a fixed number of buckets defined for each risk indicator by setting upper and lower boundaries for each bucket. The number of buckets for each risk indicator should be at least two. The buckets should reflect different levels of risk posed by the member banks (e.g. high, medium, low risk) assessed on the basis of particular indicators (EBA 2015).

Where the calculation method follows the sliding scale approach instead of a fixed number of risk classes, the upper and lower limits are set by the DGS on the basis of regulatory requirements or historical data on the particular indicator. Since the sliding method is based on information available only to the national DGS, this chapter uses the bucket method, which is also closer to the FITD system, thus allowing easier comparison between the two.

9.4.3 Bucket Method

In the bucket method, an individual risk score is assigned to each bucket. The buckets' boundaries should be determined either on a relative or absolute basis. When using the relative basis, the IRSs of banks depend on their relative risk position vis-à-vis other institutions; in this case, institutions are distributed evenly between risk buckets, meaning that institutions with similar risk profiles may end up in different buckets. In the absolute basis, the buckets' boundaries are determined to reflect the riskiness of a specific indicator; in this case, all banks may end up in the same bucket if they all have a similar level of riskiness.

Table 9.8 Buckets, boundaries and individual risk score

Buckets	Boundaries (%)	IRS
1	<2	0
2	=< 2–7 <	50
3	> = 7	100

Source EBA (2015)
Note Risk indicator for which higher values indicate higher risk (NPL ratio)

For each risk indicator, the IRSs assigned to buckets should range from 0 to 100, where zero indicates the lowest risk and 100 the highest risk.

Table 9.8 shows an example of bucket-scoring by type of risk indicator, where higher values of the risk indicator mean higher risk (for example, NPL ratio).

To compute the IRS of the sample banks, buckets and boundaries provided by EBA have been used for LR, NPL ratio, ROA, ROE and total asset growth. EBA does not provide specific examples for the leverage ratio, CET1, RWA/TA and cost to income ratio, thus relative boundaries, which correspond to the 20, 40 and 60th‰ of the sample banks distribution year to year, have been used for those indicators. The percentiles and corresponding IRS have been fixed according to EBA guidelines. Relative boundaries imply an even distribution of banks among risk buckets, and Table 9.9 shows an example of buckets, relative boundaries and individual risk scores.

Table 9.9 Buckets, relative boundaries and individual risk score

Bucket	Boundaries	IRS
1	>60° ‰	0
2	<40°–60° = <	33
3	<20°–40° = <	66
4	=< 20° ‰	100

Source own computation on EBA (2015)
Note Risk indicator for which higher values indicate lower risk (liquidity ratio)

9.4.4 Aggregate Risk Score

EBA (2015) multiplies each IRS by an indicator weight (IW) which should be the same for all banks and calibrated by using supervisory assessment and/or historical data on failures of institutions (EBA 2015).

The sum of weights assigned to all risk indicators is equal to 100%. When assigning weights to particular risk indicators, the minimum weights for the risk categories and core risk indicators, which sum up to 75%, should be preserved.

When only core indicators are computed and NSFR is not yet available, EBA (2015) states that the minimum IW assigned to NSFR is assigned to LR, which belongs to the same risk category. One of the possible allocation of weights suggested by EBA, when both core and additional indicators are computed, allows five additional indicators in four different categories. These indicators can be freely chosen by the DGS.

The aggregate risk score (ARS) is the weighted average of the IRS, according to the following formula:

$$\mathrm{ARS}_i = \sum_{j=1}^{n} \mathrm{IW}_j * \mathrm{IRS}_j \tag{9.3}$$

where: $\sum_{j=1}^{n} \mathrm{IW}_j = 100\%$ and $\mathrm{IRS}_j = \mathrm{IRS}_{x_j}$ when X in $\{A, B, \ldots, M\}$, that is the bucket corresponding to indicator A_j.

Following the guidelines, since NSFR is not computed during the transition period, the IW explained above is applied to core indicators. In addition, as previously mentioned, the ratio of unencumbered assets to covered deposits has not been computed because data on unencumbered assets for the sample banks were not available. Thus, the weight (17%) originally assigned by EBA to this ratio is equally allocated among all other computed indicators.

Consequently, when only core indicators are investigated, the ARS is computed according to:

$$\text{ARS}_{\text{core}} = 0.15 * \text{leverage ratio} + 0.15 * \text{CET 1} + 0.25 * \text{LR} + 0.21 * \text{NPL ratio} + 0.12 * \text{RWA/TA} + 0.12 * \text{ROA} \quad (9.4)$$

When core and additional indicators are considered, weights are applied to each risk category, except for the business model and management. All three additional indicators belong to this category; thus, its weight is given by the sum of the weights of business model and management and of potential losses for the DGS.

$$\text{ARS}_{\text{core + additional}} = 0.115 * \text{leverage ratio} + 0.115 * \text{CET1} + 0.18 * \text{LR} + 0.18 * \text{NPL ratio} + 0.085 * \text{RWA/TA} + 0.085 * \text{ROA} + 0.08 * \text{ROE} + 0.08 * \text{TAG} + 0.08 * \text{CI} \quad (9.5)$$

Descriptive statistics of ARS are computed by applying formula (4) and (5) to the sample banks. Over 2012–2014, the averages of ARScore and ARScore + additional are almost the same, but ARScore + additional standard deviation is lower and the minimum higher than ARScore. This may suggest a lower volatility when additional indicators are taken into consideration.

According to EBA (2015), every ARS has a corresponding aggregate risk weight (ARW), which should be used to calculate the contribution of an individual member bank to the DGS (Table 9.10). When ARW is 75%, the member bank gets a discount on contribution to be paid because it is considered as a low-risk bank. When ARW is 100%, contribution does not change. When ARW is higher than 100% (either 125 or 150%), the member bank is considered as a high-risk bank and has to pay higher contributions.

The average ARS of the sample banks is about 60, which assigns the sample to the ARW of 125%. Overall, banks should pay higher contributions to the national DGS. Of course, ARS is assigned to each member bank year by year: additional information is reported in

Table 9.10 Aggregate risk weight

Risk classes	ARS boundaries	ARW (%)
1	<40	75
2	=< 40–55 <	100
3	=< 55–70<	125
4	> = 70	150

Source EBA (2015)

Table 9.11. Table 9.11 part (a) lists the number of banks in each risk class using only core indicators in the year 2013 and year 2014; part (b) shows the distribution of banks considering both core and additional indicators.

Looking at core indicators [Table 9.11 part (a)], from 2013 to 2014, the number of banks in risk class 1 decreases by 20%, whereas the number of banks in class 2 (ARW = 100%) increases by 45%. Changes in the other two risk classes are negligible. Thus, it seems that the sample banks became more risky in 1-year time, and their contributions to the

Table 9.11 Number of banks, risk classes, ARW_{core} and $ARW_{core+additional}$ (2013 and 2014)

		2013		2014		
Risk classes	ARW_{core} (%)	Number of banks	Percentage	Number of banks	Percentage	Change 2013–2014 (%)
(a)						
1	75	27	20	16	15.53	−20
2	100	27	20	29	28.16	45
3	125	39	28.89	28	27.18	−3
4	150	42	31.11	30	29.13	−4
	Total	135	100	103	100	
(b)						
1	75	18	13.53	13	12.62	−4
2	100	35	26.32	31	30.1	18
3	125	46	34.59	30	29.13	−13
4	150	34	25.56	29	28.16	13
	Total	133	100	103	100	

Source Own computation on Bankscope's data

Fund would not be further discounted. Table 9.11 part (b) confirms this scenario, applying core and additional indicators to sample banks in the year 2013 and year 2014. The number of banks in class 1 diminishes by 4%, and the number of banks in class 2 increases by 18%. The change in the number of banks in class 3 (−13%) is perfectly matched by the change in class 4.

9.5 Comparison Between FITD and EBA Monitoring System of Bank Riskiness

The comparison between the monitoring systems applied by the FITD and proposed by EBA is not straightforward for many motives. First, risk categories are different, for instance the FITD does not consider the potential losses for DGS. Second, within the same category, indicators are computed differently, as, for example, indicator A1 of the FITD and the NPL ratio proposed by EBA, or liquidity ratios, which have different numerator and denominator. Third, the number of indicators is significantly different between the two systems: five indicators for the Italian Fund versus nine core indicators proposed by EBA. Furthermore, EBA suggests to use thirteen additional indicators. Fourth, indicator weights are the same for all ratios except A1 in the case of the FITD, whereas many different scenarios are proposed by EBA, with the only prescription of minimum weights for core indicators. Last but not least, risk classes cannot be easily compared since EBA proposes four classes (75% lowest risk, 100% average risk, 125% risky and 150% most risky), whereas FITD assigns banks to six different classes.

However, notwithstanding all differences, the core of the two systems is the same, since both works on the assessment of member bank's risk and the result of the assessment increase or decrease contributions to be paid to the DGS. Assuming to modify the thresholds in Table 9.4 in order to fit the four risk classes proposed by EBA in Table 9.12, this chapter suggests the match among risk classes reported in Table 9.12.

The match reported in Table 9.12 is based on the level of contributions to be paid to the DGS according to FITD (2012): when WAAI is

Table 9.12 Risk classes (FITD versus EBA)

WAAI	ARW
0	75% lowest risk
0–2.9	100% average risk
2.9–8.8	125% risky
>8.8	150% most risky

Source Own computation on FITD (2012) and EBA (2015)

larger than 3.5, the bank's contribution quota shall be increased as it happens when ARW is greater than 100%; when WAAI is greater than zero and less than or equal to 3.5, the bank shall retain its contribution quota unchanged, as when ARW is equal to 100%; if the WAAI is equal to zero, the bank shall benefit from a reduction in its contribution quota, as it happens when ARW is 75%. The additional threshold (10.5) for WAAI has been identified on the basis of Table 9.3: when WAAI is above 10.5, the member bank is considered at high or expulsion risk. This category is matched with ARW equal to 150%, which means a substantial increase in contribution. Since in this chapter thresholds have been scaled to avoid distortions, the Funds 3.5 and 10.5 are scaled to 2.9 and 8.8.

Table 9.13 summarizes the changes in member banks' classification in 2013 and 2014 when EBA core indicators (panel a) or core and additional indicators (panel b) are applied instead of FITD indicators. When indicators proposed by EBA are applied to Italian banks, the distribution of those banks among risk classes improves.

Table 9.13 panel (a) shows the changes in risk classes when only core indicators are applied. The number of banks belonging to the low-risk class increases by 500% (20 banks) in 2013 and by 367% (11 banks) in 2014. Those banks experience a discount in contribution quota to the Fund. The number of banks in class 2, which retains their contribution quota unchanged, increases by 500% (+20 banks) in 2013 and by 700% (+21 banks) in 2014. Conversely, the number of banks in the highest risk class (class 4) decreases by 59% in 2013 and by 61% in 2014 (−58 and −46 banks, respectively).

When core and additional indicators are applied (Table 9.13 panel b), the number of banks in class 1 would increase by 275% (11 banks) in

Table 9.13 Changes in risk classes

Risk classes	EBA core	2013				*Changes in risk classes from FITD to EBA*	
FITD	0.75	1	1.25	1.5	Total	Number of banks	Percentage (%)
(a)							
1	4	0	0	0	4	20	500
2	3	0	1	0	4	20	500
3	12	7	1	1	21	18	86
4	5	17	37	40	99	−58	−59
Total	24	24	39	41	128		
2014							
	0.75	1	1.25	1.5	Total		
1	3	0	0	0	3	11	367
2	2	1	0	0	3	21	700
3	6	7	0	0	13	14	108
4	3	16	27	29	75	−46	−61
Total	14	24	27	29	94		
(b)							
1	3	1	0	0	4	11	275
2	1	2	1	0	4	28	700
3	8	10	1	1	20	26	130
4	3	19	44	32	98	−65	−66
Total	15	32	46	33	126		
2014							
	0.75	1	1.25	1.5	Total		
1	3	0	0	0	3	8	267
2	2	1	0	0	3	25	833
3	4	9	0	0	13	15	115
4	2	18	28	27	75	−48	−64
Total	11	28	28	27	94		

Source Own computation on Bankscope's data

2013 and by 267% (8 banks) in 2014. In class 2, the number increases by 700% (+28 banks) in 2013 and by 833% (+25 banks) in 2014, whereas the number of banks in class 4 decreases by 66% in 2013 (65 banks) and by 64% in 2014 (48 banks).

9.6 Conclusion

Deposit guarantee schemes are an essential element in the completion of the internal market and an indispensable complement to the system of supervision of banks.

The set-up of a European Deposit Insurance Scheme was mildly welcomed by some member states. They were concerned that sharing the responsibility of backstopping deposits without tackling the remaining risks in banking systems would increase moral hazard. This concern is based on the assumption that EDIS would increase the level of contributions banks of some member states have to pay according to their riskiness.

To test this hypothesis, this chapter analyses monitoring systems of bank riskiness currently applied by the FITD and proposed by EBA on a sample of Italian banks members of the FITD. The conclusion is twofold.

First, the change of indicators, thresholds, weights and risk classes is applied to years 2013 and 2014 and shows that EBA proposal would increase the number of banks in the lower-risk classes, where contribution quota to the DGS would remain unchanged or would decrease. This outcome points out that, on average, sample banks would pay less contributions to the DGS when EBA guidelines are applied. This should reassure member states concerned about Italian banks' moral hazard in the event of the set-up of a common backstop for deposits.

Unfortunately, the results in this chapter are approximate because of the lack of data and information. Since the issue is relevant, the FITD, which is the only one that has the full set of data and information, might consider disclosing the real situation. Uncertainty undermines bank-client relationship and obstacles a trustfully relationship with other member states.

Second, on the effectiveness of EBA implementation of Directive 2014/49/EU goals, this chapter suggests some caution. Carefully analysing the monitoring system proposed by the European regulator, it emerges that EBA proposes many indicators, which composition is not always clear, and allows national DGSs great flexibility in line with the principle of proportionality. The choices of how many and which additional indicators to use, of the weights to assign to each risk category and, within each category, to each indicator, of the bucket or of the sliding method to fix boundaries, and, depending on the chosen method, of boundaries themselves to compute individual risk scores, are just some of the decisions EBA allows national DGSs to take. While it is clear that EBA guidelines will contribute to providing incentives to banks to operate under a less risky business model and to speed up the convergence process, it is not so clear whether such discretionary power allowed to national DGSs on many relevant features would benefit the system. The outcome of the risk assessment can vary strongly, depending on the choices made. This negatively affects the harmonization and comparability of the national schemes, fuelling, once again, concerns among member states about the true riskiness of other member states' banking systems. The goals of Directive 2014/49/EU seem postponed to the near future and rely on the adoption of EDIS.

Notes

1. Further information can be found in "Germany warns on eurozone bank deposit plan" (Financial Times 2015) and in the Deutsche Bundesbank's Monthly Report of December 2015, p. 58–60.
2. D. Lgs. 659/96, art. 2, c. 1, which transposes directive 94/19/CE, states that all information, news or data related to FITD are privileged communications.
3. Six banks out of 172 (3% of the sample) report data to compute only one ratio.
4. The year 2015 is not included in the analysis, since the number of observations is less than 50% compared to the previous years.
5. "This procedure consists of a set of steps made for determining the point of equilibrium quota" which could be only performed by the Fund (FITD 2012, p. 23).
6. Data are available upon request.
7. A higher CET1 indicates a better risk mitigation. Tier 1 capital is given by the sum of common equity tier 1 and of additional tier 1 (BIS 2012).
8. Required tier 1 ratio is 4.5% and 5.5% for the year 2013 and 2014, respectively (BIS 2012).

9. To avoid including one-off events and avoid pro-cyclicality in contributions, an average of 2 years data is used (EBA 2015).
10. EBA defines unencumbered and encumbered asset as the following: "an asset should be treated as encumbered if it has been pledged or it is subject to any form of arrangement to secure, collaterise or credit-enhance any on-balance sheet or off-balance sheet transaction from which it cannot be freely withdrawn (for instance, to be pledged for funding purposes)" (EBA 2015, p. 22).

Appendix

Table A.1 shows the test for equality of means between top- and bottom-performing banks in terms of return on equity (ROE) over 2012–2014. As far as asset quality is concerned, most profitable banks are significantly less risky (A1 equals 50% versus 178%, respectively). Top-performing banks are also less exposed to liquidity risk (L takes the value of 65 versus 97%). Top- and bottom-performing banks do not show any significant difference in means for profitability ratios D1 and D2.

Table A.2 shows the results of the test of the difference in means among banks belonging to the top and bottom quartile in terms of ROE. Top quartile banks have a smaller leverage ratio (66% vs. 96%), a higher liquidity ratio (27% vs. 14%), a higher quality of loan portfolio (NPL ratio equal to 4 and 8%, respectively), lower RWA to total assets

Table A.1 Test for difference in means—ROE

Ratio	Bottom quartile		Top quartile		Difference in means (p-value)
	# observations	Mean	# observations	Mean	
A1	87	1.78	78	0.5	0.0000***
D1	96	0.52	93	0.6	0.3941
D2	87	−16.95	84	−16.43	0.4927
L	96	0.97	94	0.65	0.0000***

Note Top-performing banks belong to the first quartile of yearly distribution, bottom-performing ones to the fourth quartile
Source Own computation on Bankscope's data

Table A.2 Top and bottom quartile—ROE

Indicators	Bottom quartile		Top quartile		Difference in means (p-value)
Core	Number of observations	Mean	Number of observations	Mean	
Leverage ratio	82	0.96	75	0.66	0.0134**
CET1	92	0.19	88	0.22	0.2391
Capital coverage ratio (%)	93	3.8	88	3.78	0.4871
Liquidity ratio	97	0.14	96	0.27	0.0001***
NPL ratio	91	0.08	86	0.04	0.0000***
Return on asset (%)	53	−0.84	55	0.94	0.0000***
RWA to total asset	92	0.59	88	0.43	0.0000***
Additional					
Total asset growth	57	0.1	55	0.12	0.3966
Cost income (%)	92	70.64	95	59.23	0.0021***

Source Own computation on Bankscope's data

(43 vs 59%) and lower CI (59 vs. 71%) than bottom quartile banks. All EBA indicators suggest that top-performing banks in terms of ROE have a lower risk than the worst-performing ones.

References

Bank of Italy. 2016. FAQ—La centrale dei rischi. Available at https://www.bancaditalia.it/servizi-cittadino/servizi/accesso-cr/faq-cr/faq-cr.html#faq8761-9.

BIS. 2012. Basel III. Necessary, but not sufficient, Remarks by W. Byres, Secretary General of the Basel Committee on Banking Superivision to the Financial Stability Institute's 6th Biennial Conference on Risk Management and Supervision, Basel.

Deutsche Bundesbank. 2015. Monthly Report December 2015.

Directive 2014/49/EU of the European Parliament and of the Council of 16 April 2014 on Deposit Guarantee Schemes. *Official Journal of the European Union* L 173/149.

European Commission. 2015a. Proposal for a Regulation of the European Parliament and of the Council amending Regulation (EU) 806/2014 in order to establish a European Deposit Insurance Scheme, Strasbourg, 24.11.2015, COM(2015) 586 final, 2015/0270(COD).

European Commission. 2015b. Factsheet: A stronger banking union, 24 November 2015. Available at: http://ec.europa.eu/finance/general-policy/docs/banking-union/european-deposit-insurance-scheme/151124-factsheets_'en.pdf.

EBA. 2015. Guidelines on Methods for Calculating Contributions to Deposit Guarantee Schemes, EBA/GL/2015/10, 28 May 2015.

Financial Times. 2015. Germany Warns on Eurozone Bank Deposit Plan, 8 December.

FITD. 2012. The FITD's Monitoring System of Bank Riskiness and Risk-Based Contribution, November.

FITD. 2016. Annual Report 2015.

Juncker J-C, Tusk D., Dijsselbloem J., Draghi M., and Schulz M. 2015. Completing Europe's Economic and Monetary Union, July. Available at: http://ec.europa.eu/priorities/sites/beta-political/files/5-presidents-report_en.pdf.

Reuters. 2015. EU Deposit Insurance' Vanishes from EU Leaders' Draft Conclusions, 18 December 2015. Available at: http://uk.reuters.com/article/uk-eurozone-banks-deposits-idUKKBN0U11KP20151218.

Senato. 2015. Dossier del Servizio Studi sull'A.S. n. 1758 "Delega al Governo per il recepimento delle direttive europee e l'attuazione di altri atti dell'Unione europea —Legge di delegazione europea 2014" XVII legislatura, February 2015 n. 197.

Index

G. Chesini et al. (eds.), *The Business of Banking*, Palgrave Macmillan Studies in Banking and Financial Institutions, DOI 10.1007/978-3-319-54894-4

The manufacturer's authorised representative in the EU is Springer Nature Customer Service Centre GmbH, Europaplatz 3, 69115 Heidelberg, Germany. If you have any concerns regarding our products, please contact ProductSafety@springernature.com

Printed and bound by CPI Group (UK) Ltd, Croydon, CR0 4YY

30/09/2026

02225661-0007